英語4技能
リーディング
ハイパートレーニング

長文読解 上級編

問題編

Ｋ 桐原書店

英語4技能 リーディング ハイパートレーニング

長文読解 ⑤ 上級編

問題編

Contents

桐原書店

リーディング問題に取り組むにあたって

1. パッセージ全体のテーマをとらえよう

　タイトルがある文章の場合は，まず最初にタイトルを読み，何について書かれた文章なのかを把握しましょう。次に（タイトルがない文章の場合は最初に）設問に目を通します。それによって，本文のどこに注目して読むべきかがわかります。また，設問はたいてい本文の内容の順に並んでいるので，設問を把握しておくことは文章の流れを理解する手助けにもなるでしょう。選択肢まで先に細かく読む必要はありません。質問やリード文をしっかりと読んで，どのような情報を求めてその文章を読むのかを先に知っておくようにしましょう。

2. 設問に関連する部分を探しながら読もう

　試験には時間制限があるので，一文一文を細かくていねいに読んで，設問に関係しないところの文法や構文で考え込んでしまっては，時間オーバーになってしまいます。1. の作業で，本文で注目すべき場所は見当がつくはずなので，濃淡をつけて読んでいきましょう。

3. 論理マーカーで流れをつかもう

　論理マーカーとは，文と文との論理的関係を示す目印となることばです。たとえば，because（なぜなら）があれば，その前に「結果」が，その後ろに「原因」にあたることが述べられていると予想できます。また，however / but（しかし）なら「逆接」ですが，単にその前後が反対の内容になっているというより，「一般論」however / but「筆者の主張」という順番で，後ろの方に大切なことが述べられているケースもあります。また，for example の前には抽象的なまとめがあり，その後には具体例が続きます。このような論理マーカーを知っておくと，どこに何が書いてあるのかを把握しやすくなります。

Unit (**1**) ⇒本冊 p.10 ~ 19

DATA
● ワード数：272 words
● 目標解答時間：7分

Read each passage and choose the best word or phrase from among the four choices for each blank. Then, on your answer sheet, find the number of the question and mark your answer.

A Classical Music Composer's Peculiar Prank

Johannes Brahms is considered one of the masters of classical music. In fact, he is often said to be on the same level as the other "Three Bs" of the Romantic music period: Beethoven and Bach. He also has a lot in common with other famous composers of classical music: he was born more than 100 years ago, he was a brilliant piano player, and he had a full head of wildly flowing white hair. There was, however, one habit that (1). He had a chair in his apartment that was designed to fall over when a person sat in it. He asked someone to build him this special chair that would either cause his guests to fall forward on their knees or make them fall backward. According to his friends and his servant, he would roar with laughter every time someone got tricked by the chair.

You might be wondering why someone would want to do such a thing. Brahms was a musical genius, but he was not a happy man. (2), he had an unusual and tragic childhood. He grew up in poverty, and he had to start playing music in very low-class bars when he was just 12 years old. According to Brahms, the experience of being in these bars, where people were often drunk and behaving crudely, affected him deeply and made him angry and resentful. Considering this, he probably (3) in his early life. If he had had a decent life, he would have found a better way to entertain himself.

(1) 1 represented his strange personality
2 showed a key to his brilliant ability
3 significantly influenced his life
4 told him how to improve piano skills

(2) 1 On the other hand
2 Consequently
3 In fact
4 Nonetheless

(3) 1 learned how to please people
2 did not have a good role model
3 earned enough money to succeed
4 improved his musical talent

Read each passage and choose the best word or phrase from among the four choices for each blank. Then, on your answer sheet, find the number of the question and mark your answer.

Time to Talk to Your Plants

If you spend any time in flower shops or the gardening section of home improvement stores, you might have come across an unusual piece of advice: "Make sure you talk to your plants." Even Prince Charles of England claims that not only does he talk to his plants, but they respond as well. While this might (1), some evidence suggests that talking to plants is, in fact, good for them. Scientists have been interested in this topic for more than one hundred years, and researchers have come up with at least two possible explanations for the link between speech and plant health.

One explanation is that plants react to vibrations in their surroundings. These vibrations are like signals that are essential for plants to grow. If plants experience no vibrations, such as in a silent room, they might (2). One experiment on MythBusters, a popular American TV show that explores the science behind thought-provoking questions, indicated that plants grew better when they were exposed to the sound of human speech as opposed to being left in silence. However, their sample size was too small to confirm the theory.

The other theory that explains why plants might grow better when people talk to them is that people provide them with carbon dioxide, a gas they require for the production of their food. Humans release carbon dioxide when they exhale as well as when they speak. (3), some experts say that the carbon dioxide produced from speech is too little to make a significant difference.

This debate has not been settled, but it's safe to say that talking to plants may offer them benefits. So, the next time you need to relieve some stress or boast about your latest accomplishment, why not talk to a plant?

(1) 1 benefit the plants

2 cost extra

3 sound like nonsense

4 work better outdoors

(2) 1 grow slower

2 produce a lot of flowers

3 grow faster

4 turn toward the light

(2) ① ② ③ ④

(3) 1 Because of this

2 For example

3 On the other hand

4 Otherwise

(3) ① ② ③ ④

DATA
●ワード数：337 words
●目標解答時間：8分

Read each passage and choose the best word or phrase from among the four choices for each blank. Then, on your answer sheet, find the number of the question and mark your answer.

Aromatherapy: More Than Just a Pretty Smell

In the last decade or so, "essential oils" have (1). There are thousands of oils available to buy, and they have created a huge industry: aromatherapy. Yoga studios use peppermint oil to establish a relaxing atmosphere, hotels use rose oil to make the rooms smell pleasant and inviting, and people use lavender oil in their homes to promote healthy sleep. So what are these oils, and how did this boom start?

Essential oils are made from plants, herbs, fruits, and many other natural substances, such as tree bark and even flowers. These materials are processed in several ways in order to extract concentrated forms of their oils. These processes include steps such as steaming with hot water or pressing with stones. If these sound like old-fashioned techniques, you're right — the use of essential oils actually has a long history. The ancient Egyptians had machines to extract oils from plants, and they used these oils to prepare bodies to be buried. Some Asian cultures used oils both to cure illnesses and to lift their moods. These ancient people were well aware that essential oils have the power to improve health and enhance living spaces, so they probably would not be surprised that today essential oils (2).

Most people today use essential oils with the help of a diffuser, which is a small device that you fill with water and a tiny amount of essential oil. The diffuser then scatters a fine mist up into the air. The key chemicals in the oils are then inhaled or absorbed through the skin.

Some wonder if these oils are as effective as manufacturers would have you believe. (3), there is not enough evidence to give a definite answer. There are a great variety of essential oils in shops, and not all of them are produced with the same standards of quality. It is, therefore, almost impossible to judge if the manufacturers' claims are true or not.

(1) 1 been used to treat serious diseases

2 contributed to cutting-edge research

3 exploded in the marketplace

4 started to become more expensive

(2) 1 are becoming more difficult to find

2 can be found in museums today

3 can be made safe to eat or drink

4 line the shelves at many stores

(3) 1 Therefore

2 Unfortunately

3 Rather

4 On the contrary

DATA
●ワード数：259 words
●目標解答時間：7分

Read each passage and choose the best word or phrase from among the four choices for each blank. Then, on your answer sheet, find the number of the question and mark your answer.

What Is Funny?

From the satirical plays of ancient Greece to the romantic comedies found in modern cinema, humor has always been an integral part of the human experience. The explanation for humor, however, (1). Modern researchers are still working to explain exactly what makes something funny. One of the leading theories about humor was developed by psychologist Peter McGraw. His "Benign Violation Theory" states that for something to be funny, it must contain two specific elements. The first is that it must go against our basic ideas about how people and objects in the world should be. The second is that the action must be benign, meaning harmless.

Consider the following example. Imagine you and your friend are visiting a new city, and you're walking on a dark street late at night. You look over your shoulder, and suddenly you notice a huge figure staring down at you. You and your friend both react in fear and back away from the figure. However, after a moment, you realize it was just a statue. Was this event funny?

McGraw's theory of humor provides a framework through which it can be evaluated. The fact that the statue was in the street in the middle of the night likely went against your idea about (2); after all, streets are homes for stray cats, not statues. Therefore, the event did contain a violation. This event was also benign because, of course, statues are harmless. (3), this event would have indeed been funny according to McGraw's theory.

(1) 1 differs between cultures
    2 has finally been discovered
    3 offers health benefits
    4 remains quite mysterious

(2) 1 how the world should be
    2 what statues are made of
    3 when to travel in a city
    4 where it's safe to walk

(3) 1 After the fact
    2 Besides
    3 Nevertheless
    4 Therefore

(3) ① ② ③ ④

Read each passage and choose the best word or phrase from among the four choices for each blank. Then, on your answer sheet, find the number of the question and mark your answer.

The Stock Market For Beginners: Index Funds

We have all seen pictures of businesspeople going wild on the trading floor, jumping up and down in delight or with their hands covering their faces in disbelief. And we expect tickers of incomprehensible numbers and symbols to scroll along the bottom of the television screen during the business report. But can anyone who doesn't live in a world of balance sheets and IPOs really understand what's going on? The answer is "yes," and by (1), you, too, can make an informed decision about whether to invest your hard-earned cash in the stock market.

Investing is always a risk. When you buy stock in a company, you are essentially buying a piece of that company, and if that company goes bankrupt, your piece is gone. On the other hand, if the company's value goes up, then the value of your piece goes up as well. This is why smart investors always give the same advice: Diversify, diversify, diversify. Instead of putting all of your invested money into one or two companies, you should buy stock in a variety of companies in different industries. (2), if one of them starts to lose their value, you don't have to watch all of your money sink down with it.

So which companies should you look for? Thankfully, you don't have to spend hours upon hours looking for candidates yourself. Many trading brokers offer something called index funds. These funds are the collections of the stocks of companies in one of the major stock market indexes, like the Dow Jones or the S&P 500. An index fund is not likely to (3), but it is a solid investment that offers stable growth. In fact, index funds frequently perform better than professionals who claim that they can beat the market.

(1) 1 purchasing a few stocks
    2 making sure to save money
    3 starting your own company
    4 understanding the basics

(2) 1 Despite this
    2 For example
    3 Moreover
    4 That way

(2) ① ② ③ ④

(3) 1 be popular with professionals
    2 yield a vast fortune
    3 have a wide variety of stocks
    4 make any money

(3) ① ② ③ ④

Read each passage and choose the best answer from among the four choices for each question. Then, on your answer sheet, find the number of the question and mark your answer.

The American Gothic Painting

The famous *American Gothic* painting provides a glimpse into life in the 20th-century rural American Midwest. On display at the Art Institute of Chicago, it features a bald farmer and his blonde daughter with stern expressions on their faces. This couple represents the conservative, traditional values that characterized rural life at the time. Behind the farmer and his daughter sit a red barn and a simple white house with a distinct style of window. The image is striking, and it quickly became popular both in its original form and through its imitation in many different contexts.

American Gothic was painted by Grant Wood in 1930. Before its exhibition at the Art Institute of Chicago, which brought him widespread fame and respect, Wood lived a humble life. He was born in rural Iowa, and his father died when he was ten years old. He was an artist from a very young age, starting his career as an apprentice in a metal shop and going on to art school in Minneapolis after his high school graduation. He traveled to Europe to study various styles of painting, Impressionism in particular, before moving back to Iowa. Back home, he felt a renewed love for Midwestern life and started to create images of his surroundings, which soon resulted in the painting of *American Gothic.*

The small white house behind the farmer and his daughter is a real house in the small town of Eldon, Iowa. When Grant Wood saw this house, he decided to paint it and to include in his painting the kind of people that he thought would live in it. Grant Wood used real people as models for the painted couple. The farmer was modeled by Wood's dentist, and the daughter by Wood's younger sister, Nan. The clothes worn by the painted couple represent typical clothing from 18th-century America. Wood's painting style, while inspired by his American surroundings, was influenced by Renaissance art that he had studied during his trips to Europe.

Today, *American Gothic* remains one of the most well-known paintings of the 20th-century rural American Midwest. The white house featured in the painting is still located in Eldon, Iowa. Next door is a small museum commemorating the *American Gothic* painting and the life of Grant Wood. The museum has a small room where visitors can watch a documentary about Grant Wood, and it also has a large exhibit featuring many of the *American Gothic* imitations that have been created over the years. The museum gift shop sells copies of the *American Gothic* painting along with several other products. The museum also has a set of costumes that match the clothing of the *American Gothic* farmer and his daughter. People can put them on and take their own pictures outside in front of the same small house. The museum is free to the public.

(1) What was one thing that made the *American Gothic* painting special?
    1 It offered a unique way of looking at the 20th-century American architecture.
    2 It had a strong image that shows the traditional values of the 20th-century rural Midwest.
    3 It showed the unfriendly relationship between farmers and neighbors in the rural Midwest.
    4 It was painted in a style more conservative than other paintings of its time.

(1) ① ② ③ ④

(2) According to the passage, which of the following statements about Grant Wood is true?
    1 He always dreamed of moving away from home when he was a child.
    2 He became famous when he established his own art institute.
    3 He studied Impressionism before traveling to another country.
    4 He started working with metal before graduating from high school.

(2) ① ② ③ ④

(3) What is one characteristic of the *American Gothic* painting?

1 The building as well as the people painted in the picture had a real model.

2 The people in the picture wear clothes that were in fashion when the picture was painted.

3 He painted the picture when he was inspired by American and European surroundings.

4 The local farmer and his daughter agreed to be the models of the picture.

(4) Visitors in Eldon, Iowa can

1 look at pictures that were inspired by the *American Gothic* painting.

2 view a documentary about the design of the house in the *American Gothic* painting.

3 try painting their own imitation of the *American Gothic* painting at the museum.

4 watch a documentary of the models in the *American Gothic* painting.

DATA
●ワード数：490 words
●目標解答時間：14 分

Read each passage and choose the best answer from among the four choices for each question. Then, on your answer sheet, find the number of the question and mark your answer.

The Weird and Wonderful Platypus

There are few creatures whose appearance seems as absurd as the platypus. Native to Australia and often found around rivers and lakes, the animal resembles a beaver wearing a duck mask. However, it is not directly related to either animal. Rather, it is a member of a rare group of mammals called the "monotremes." Along with the platypus, the only other animal alive today that belongs to this category is the echidna, an animal covered in spines* that is also native to Australia as well as New Guinea. Although monotremes are probably more than 110 million years old, the platypus is thought to have lived in its current form for around 100,000 years. Fossils show that thousands of years ago, the platypus had other living relatives that were larger in size.

The modern platypus is small, about 40 to 50 cm in length, and covered in short, dark brown fur. It is a mammal with mismatched features: its duck-like mouth, or bill, and webbed* feet look more like they belong to a bird than to a furry creature. However, the platypus bill is softer and more leathery than a duck's, and the webbing between its toes can be pulled back to help it walk on land. Its tail looks like a beaver's, but it is thicker and covered in short fur. When the first dead platypus was sent from Australia to England in the late 18th century, British naturalist George Shaw assumed it was a joke or a hoax*, put together from parts of different animals. Shaw believed that such a strange-looking creature could not possibly be real.

The behavior and abilities of the platypus are as unique as its appearance. Its bill is covered in specialized sensors that can detect food even in dark, muddy water. It is a carnivore, which means it eats flesh. The diet of the platypus consists mostly of small animals such as shellfish, worms, and insects. However, the platypus has no teeth for chewing. Instead, it fills its cheeks with small stones that it uses to help grind up its food. Even though female platypuses lay eggs like a bird or a reptile*, they also produce milk to feed their young. The platypus loves sleeping — it spends half of its day doing so and spends the other half looking for food. The male platypus is also venomous*, which is an extremely rare trait for a mammal. It has a sharp stinger on each back leg that can deliver its painful venom.

While the platypus' unusual nature had scientists confused for many years, it has also helped make the animal popular among the general public throughout the world. Loveable platypus characters have been used in cartoons, in advertising, and as mascots. There is a platypus character on an animated TV show in America, and popular mascots based on the unusual animal have been created for organizations in Australia and Japan.

*spine: a long and sharp body part like a needle on some animals
*webbed: having thin skin in between the "toes" or "fingers"
*hoax: something to fool people, to deceive them
*reptile: an animal such as a snake, lizard, alligator or turtle
*venomous: having a poison in the body that is used to attack enemies

(1) What best characterizes the platypus described in the first paragraph?
   1 It is a kind of mammal that is related to the beaver.
   2 It once had relatives, almost all of which died out a long time ago.
   3 It has kept the same physical characteristics for 110 million years.
   4 It has an ancestor that was much smaller than today's platypus.

(1) ① ② ③ ④

(2) What is true of the platypus described in the second paragraph?
   1 It resembles a bird, rather than a mammal that it actually is.
   2 It has a duck-like mouth that a lot of mammals in Australia have.
   3 It has webbing between its toes that are pulled back to swim in the water.
   4 It has webbed feet that are best suited for walking on land.

(2) ① ② ③ ④

(3) The platypus has the ability to

    1   deliver venom through all of its legs to attack other animals.

    2   eat the flesh of small animals by using sharp teeth.

    3   see better in the dark, which is helpful to search for food.

    4   use stones to make the food in its mouth easier to eat.

(4) According to the passage, the unusual appearance of the platypus

    1   was criticized by some scientists when it was used in advertising.

    2   made it popular partly because scientists were confused by it.

    3   was exaggerated in several cartoon programs that are shown worldwide.

    4   made it a model for mascots that are popular all over the world.

DATA
●ワード数：502 words
●目標解答時間：14 分

Read each passage and choose the best answer from among the four choices for each question. Then, on your answer sheet, find the number of the question and mark your answer.

The Mysterious Dancing Fever of 1518

In the northeast of France lies the city of Strasbourg, known for its rich history spanning 2,000 years. Behind Strasbourg's elegant halls and charming homes, however, lies a mystery that has baffled* both scientists and historians for centuries. It starts with a woman known simply as "Frau Troffea." One day in July 1518, Frau Troffea walked out into the streets of Strasbourg and began to dance. There was no music playing, and soon her fervent* dancing caught the attention of people around her. Their amusement at this odd display by the local woman soon turned to horror when she continued dancing into the night — and only stopped six days later.

But the dancing did not end with Frau Troffea. During the days that she had been dancing, 34 more people came down to dance in the streets of Strasbourg. Within a month, approximately 400 people had joined in this dancing fever. No one knew why it began, and no one knew how to stop them. The dancers themselves did not seem to enjoy what had taken over their bodies; they cried and begged for help while they danced. The city provided extra dance halls and musicians to encourage its citizens to dance away the fever, but for some the experience proved fatal: citizens of the city continued to dance until they died from strokes, heart attacks, or exhaustion. During one month, it was recorded that about 15 people died every day. And then, just as suddenly as it began, the dancing came to an end.

While these accounts seem strange, there is no doubt that the dancing fever of 1518 actually occurred. Many documents were produced at the time of the fever; historians have access to notes from physicians and the texts of religious speeches given at the Strasbourg cathedral, as well as local and regional records that describe the event in great detail. Indeed, this dancing fever was recorded several more times in medieval Europe. Similar circumstances might have led to the sudden and persistent dancing, such as stressful events stemming from failing crops, natural disasters, or an outbreak of disease, combined with beliefs in the power of curses. Attempts at curing the dancers with more music usually only worsened the situation, as music invited more people to join in the dancing.

Some researchers believe that the dancing fever of 1518 was a form of mass hysteria, resulting from the high levels of stress experienced by the people of Strasbourg and further worsened by their religious beliefs. Indeed, the inhabitants of Strasbourg had prior belief and fear of spirits that could explain this dancing curse. Other modern theories about the phenomenon point to the ingestion* of ergot, a toxic fungus that can cause hallucinations*. But even with all the research conducted on the topic, no final explanation for the dancing fever in Strasbourg has yet been found. The cause of the sudden dancing — and its sudden disappearance — is a mystery that may never be solved.

*baffle: make you (confused and) completely unable to solve a problem
*fervent: full of passion and energy
*ingestion: eating something
*hallucination: a strange vision you have in your mind

(1) How did the residents of Strasbourg react when Frau Troffea began to dance in public?

1 They were amused by her fervent dancing and played music to help her dance more.

2 They were annoyed by her dancing and tried to avoid looking or walking by her.

3 They were delighted to see her enthusiastic dancing and stayed to watch her for six days.

4 They were entertained by her strange dancing at first but it eventually scared them.

(2) What happened to the citizens after they began dancing?

1 The number of people dancing increased further because they enjoyed it a lot.

2 They were unable to control their bodies in the way they wanted to.

3 No one asked for help to stop dancing because they were too busy dancing.

4 The dancing fever ended because most people died from diseases or exhaustion.

(3) What was a similarity shared by the various dancing fevers?

1 They occurred after stressful events such as when natural disasters took place in medieval Europe.

2 People affected by the dancing fevers said they had been visited by spirits that terrorized them.

3 Most of the dancers in medieval Europe believed they were cured through the power of religious speeches.

4 Each town experienced an outbreak of disease after the dancing fevers came to an end.

(4) What is one possibility that caused the dancing fever?

1 Mental exhaustion caused mainly by a belief in spirits was common among people in Strasbourg.

2 High levels of stress as the result of the deaths of many citizens caused people to become agitated.

3 There was a belief that the only way to escape a deadly curse was to gather together and dance.

4 People in Strasbourg experienced hallucinations that had been caused by mushrooms frequently sold at markets.

Read each passage and choose the best answer from among the four choices for each question. Then, on your answer sheet, find the number of the question and mark your answer.

The History of Locks

Since the Industrial Revolution enabled the spread of manufactured goods throughout the world, the average person has more material possessions than ever before. People owning these items naturally desire to keep them safe from theft. Locks have consequently become a basic necessity of modern life. People lock their homes and their cars, their offices and their stores, their personal diaries, and more. There are also digital locks for phones, computers, and bank accounts. While the concept of a physical lock is ancient, most people do not understand how these devices work. Furthermore, because sophisticated locks have become so cheap and common, they are often taken for granted.

The oldest known locks were created thousands of years ago in the ancient Assyrian city of Nineveh, which eventually became part of Iraq. These locks were made of wood and required a key to lift a series of pins to release the fastener. The "warded lock," found in ancient China and Rome, was a popular lock that can still be seen today. The inside of the lock has many differently shaped "teeth," and the shape of the key must match them in order to turn without being blocked. The "combination lock" is another design that has been around for many centuries. This type of lock requires people to input a specific code by turning a dial, and today it is commonly found on gym and school lockers.

By the late 9th century, people had managed to create locks made entirely out of metal. From then on, metal locks and keys were used almost exclusively. During the Industrial Revolution, locking devices were manufactured at greater volumes and with increasingly more complicated designs. The "tumbler lock" was one such design, and several variations of it were developed. A man named Joseph Bramah developed a similar lock that he claimed no one could pick. Indeed, it was so secure that it took 67 years before an American locksmith proved him wrong. Inventors also came up with other new features during the Industrial Revolution, such as markers indicating whether someone had attempted to open the lock with an incorrect key.

Since ancient times, one of the biggest issues in lock design has been the key itself. Keys can be lost, and they can be inconvenient to carry or hold on to. Wealthy Romans often wore their keys as rings on their fingers to keep them safe and easily within easy reach at all times. Later, keyrings were often used to fasten keys to belts and clothing. Today, however, locks are undergoing a digital revolution. Some locks can be opened with a key card that fits right into your wallet. When one of these key cards is put near a lock, it sends a digital signature that is compared against a signature stored in a database. If the signature matches, a motor causes a lock's bolt to slide out of place, allowing a door to be opened. And if a key card is lost, like at a hotel, a new card can be issued quickly.

(1) According to the passage, the physical lock
   1 has not always been made of metal throughout history.
   2 is getting replaced by digital locks these days because they are harder to pick.
   3 is so complicated to use that it is not convenient to use it in daily life.
   4 was designed during the Industrial Revolution, when people desired to keep their items safe.

(2) One characteristic of the "combination lock" is
   1 it was mostly used by people in the upper class.
   2 people used it only for a short period of time.
   3 it was invented to be used for lockers in a gym or a school.
   4 users do not rely on keys to operate it.

(3) During the Industrial Revolution,

    1 a lock was invented that no one has been able to open ever since.

    2 the number of cases of theft increased as the picking technique improved.

    3 more varieties of locks were developed and they were harder to pick.

    4 wooden locks were still more popular than metal ones among ordinary people.

(4) Because of the digital revolution,

    1 keys have become more secure because they use a database.

    2 fewer people lose their keys because many people carry keyrings.

    3 keys do not need to physically touch the locks to open them.

    4 even if people lose a key card, they can issue a new key card by themselves.

(4) ① ② ③ ④

Read each passage and choose the best answer from among the four choices for each question. Then, on your answer sheet, find the number of the question and mark your answer.

Secrets of the Sherpas

The Sherpa people live in the Himalaya Mountains in Nepal. Ever since the Sherpa Tenzing Norgay and Sir Edmund Hillary of England made the first successful climb to the top of Mt. Everest, Sherpas have been known for their amazing stamina and ability to survive at high altitudes. Most climbers have trouble breathing at high altitudes due to the lack of oxygen in the air, and in serious cases they can suffer from swelling of the brain or fluid in the lungs, both of which can be deadly. While Sherpas are not immune to these dangers, they experience them less frequently. It was once believed that Sherpas must have more red blood cells because those are the cells that carry oxygen. It was discovered, however, that the opposite is true. Since it appeared that Sherpa's blood had less ability to carry oxygen, it did not seem to make sense that they were able to perform so well at high altitudes. This was highly puzzling to researchers.

To solve the mystery, researcher Andrew Murray of the University of Cambridge studied a group of non-Sherpas and a group of Sherpas who all lived at low altitudes. He took them up to 5,300 meters, an altitude where many people start to feel sick, and studied how their bodies reacted to the high altitude. All human cells contain mitochondria, and these are responsible for producing energy. Murray found that although the amounts of mitochondria were similar, the Sherpa's mitochondria were able to convert much more oxygen into energy than the mitochondria of non-Sherpas. Murray says, "This shows that it's not how much oxygen you've got; it's what you do with it that counts." In total, Sherpas' mitochondria produced over 30 percent more energy.

The Sherpas in the experiment had been living in a city at a much lower altitude than other Sherpas, and they were eating exactly the same foods as the non-Sherpas. This was done to make the two groups as similar as possible. Also, before the experiment began, the same tests were conducted on the Sherpas while they were still living at a low altitude. The researchers discovered that the Sherpas' cells were able to get just as much oxygen from the air at a low altitude as they were at a high altitude. This suggests that the differences are genetic rather than being acquired during an individual's lifetime.

Every year in the UK, one out of every five people admitted to the intensive care unit of a hospital dies, and one of the main reasons is hypoxia, or a lack of oxygen in the body's organs. In patients suffering from diseases that cause hypoxia, including lung illnesses, heart attacks, and cancer, the body tries to compensate by producing more red blood cells. However, this causes the blood to become thicker and can cause it to flow less well. Since this does not happen to the same degree in Sherpas' bodies, scientists hope that learning about the mechanisms that make their cells more efficient could help to improve the chances of survival for patients in ICUs.

(1) What did researchers have a hard time understanding about the Sherpas?

    1 Despite a higher rate of swelling of the brain and fluid in the lungs, they were able to perform well at high altitudes.

    2 Although they had great stamina at high altitudes, they tended to become ill when they were at lower altitudes.

    3 Despite complaining that they had trouble breathing, most Sherpas seemed to be getting as much oxygen as other climbers.

    4 Although they have fewer red blood cells, they suffer less from high altitudes than other climbers do.

(2) What did Andrew Murray discover about the Sherpa's cells?

1 They contain much larger and more active mitochondria than the cells of non-Sherpas.

2 The mitochondria in them were a lot more efficient at producing energy from oxygen.

3 The size of the mitochondria in the Sherpa climbers' cells increased greatly when they were at an altitude of 5,300 meters.

4 The Sherpas' mitochondria functioned better than other people's during intensive exercise.

(3) Because the Sherpas in the experiment lived at a low altitude,

1 their ability to perform well at high altitudes suggests that they are born with it.

2 their cells were not able to get as much oxygen as the cells of Sherpas who live at a high altitudes.

3 researchers believe that the lifestyle of the Sherpa is responsible for their ability to perform well at high altitude.

4 their genetic advantage over non-Sherpas may have been weakened due to their less active lifestyles.

(4) Scientists hope to help patients in intensive care units by

1 finding out why Sherpas can use red blood cells more efficienthy than non-Sherpas do.

2 comparing the way that Sherpas' cells react when they suffer from lung illnesses, heart attacks, and cancer.

3 finding out the reasons that Sherpas' blood becomes thicker when they are at high altitudes.

4 using Sherpas' blood to make sure that they have enough oxygen flowing through their bodies.

Read each passage and choose the best answer from among the four choices for each question. Then, on your answer sheet, find the number of the question and mark your answer.

The Speed of Time

People often say that time "flies" when they are enjoying themselves, but it "drags" when they are bored. On vacation, for example, it can feel like hardly any time has gone by between the time you first arrive at the destination and the time you have to leave. But at less interesting moments, like during a boring class at school, time seems to move at a slow pace. A bored student might feel like every minute lasts an hour while staring at the clock, hoping the second hand will move faster. For years, researchers have tried to find the scientific reason behind this difference in time perception by studying the brain. And after what may have felt like an eternity, scientists may have achieved a breakthrough.

In 2016, a team of researchers in Portugal put together a study using mice to help understand the way time is experienced by the mind. Scientists often use rodents* to analyze brain functions because they share a similar brain structure with humans. In their experiment, the scientists first taught the mice how to judge the amount of time that had passed between two sounds. The mice then had to indicate with their noses whether a sound was longer or shorter than 1.5 seconds. When they gave the correct answer, they were given a reward. While the mice provided their responses, the scientists observed dopamine neurons* in a specific area of the brain which is known for its role in processing time.

The results of the initial experiment were promising. The researchers observed that when the mice underestimated the amount of time that had passed, there was greater neural activity in that specific area. In other words, time seemed to fly by when the brain was stimulated. In order to provide more support for this finding, the scientists attempted to show a causal link* between neural stimulation and time assessment. By using a technique called "optogenetics," researchers directly manipulated brain neurons using light and found that with increased stimulation, the mice underestimated the amount of time that passed by, whereas they overestimated the passing of time when there was no stimulation. The researchers concluded that the mice's judgment of time could be radically altered through the direct manipulation of brain neurons or external stimulations that trigger similar activity in the neurons.

The researchers admit that a limitation of the study is their inability to know the actual feelings of the animals. They could only interpret the mice's behavior to make conclusions about how the mice perceived time. Still, the results have exciting implications: the findings point to a deeper understanding of how the human brain processes time experiences. It explains, for example, why time would seem to pass more quickly when there are plenty of activities to stimulate the mind, whereas time crawls by slowly when a person is bored in class without mental stimulation. In other words, it could all be related to the neurons in our brain. So, to make time go faster in a boring class, find an activity that stimulates your neurons — it just might trick your mind into perceiving time as moving faster.

*rodent: a small animal like a rat or mouse
*neuron: brain cell
*causal link: something that makes another thing happen

(1) According to the passage, scientists

　1　have conducted research to find out why time perception differs from person to person.

　2　made a breakthrough about time perception by observing people on vacation.

　3　have completely understood the mechanism behind the perception of time.

　4　confirmed that when people stare at a clock, they feel that time passes more quickly.

(1) ① ② ③ ④

(2) In the experiment on time perception, the mice

　1　demonstrated that they would work harder to get more rewards.

　2　were not trained properly, which caused the scientists to reach a wrong conclusion.

　3　got a dopamine boost when they received a reward from the scientists.

　4　received a reward if they indicated the correct length of a sound.

(2) ① ② ③ ④

(3) According to the passage, the results of the experiment

　1　proved that most of the mice underestimated how much time was passing by.

　2　showed that time appeared to fly by when the scientists used optogenetics.

　3　were promising because they showed that neural activity is related to perception of time.

　4　led to the discovery that brain neurons were triggered even when there was no stimulation.

(3) ① ② ③ ④

(4) What is one conclusion that can be made based on the passage?

　1　People feel time passes more quickly when their neurons are stimulated.

　2　Keeping yourself busy has no effect on stimulating neurons in your brain.

　3　The amount of your activities has nothing to do with the perception of time.

　4　Watching the clock frequently would help to create more mental stimulation.

(4) ① ② ③ ④

Read each passage and choose the best answer from among the four choices for each question. Then, on your answer sheet, find the number of the question and mark your answer.

The Cassini Space Probe

The Cassini space probe captured the world's imagination for nearly twenty years with breathtaking images of the planet Saturn and its surrounding satellite system. NASA hails its mission as one of tremendous historical importance. The unprecedented data it gathered over the years, the flawless execution of various sub-missions, and the fascination with our solar system that it was able to inspire in the general public are some of the many reasons it was considered such a success. On September 15, 2017, the Cassini mission came to an end, concluding nearly two decades of space exploration and revolutionizing how humans comprehend the vastness of space.

NASA launched the Cassini space probe on October 15, 1997, sending it on a six-year, 1.2-billion-kilometer journey through the solar system towards Saturn. The probe fixed itself in orbit at its final destination on July 1, 2004, and it immediately began transmitting data from the distant planet and its expansive moon system back to Earth. Only a single year into its mission, Cassini accomplished its greatest feat by successfully landing the Huygens lander on Saturn's largest moon, Titan. The parachute drop remains mankind's only successful landing beyond our solar system's asteroid belt, and Huygens holds the record as the most distant man-made object residing on a foreign celestial body. Credit is also given to Cassini for discovering new moons never before observed by NASA and even uncovering the potential for alien life on Saturn's moon Enceladus.

Originally, NASA intended to conclude Cassini's mission after just four years, but extensions granted to the program in 2008 and 2010 allowed it to continue well into the age of social media. NASA wisely incorporated the Internet and up-and-coming social media websites such as Twitter into Cassini's mission to make its images readily available to the general public. Every day people were granted easy access to knowledge and photographs, and Cassini's scientific mission quickly gained millions of followers. The broad and popular support that the probe enjoyed granted NASA the ability to continue its mission for an additional ten years beyond what it had intended.

Unfortunately, due to the machine's age and funding issues back on Earth, NASA announced plans in 2014 for Cassini to be deliberately destroyed by crashing it into Saturn. Cassini did not have enough fuel to escape from Saturn's orbit, and the planet's surface was deemed to be the safest place for the probe to retire. NASA did not want to biologically contaminate any of Saturn's moons' surfaces and destroy the potential for life. After 22 months of dipping Cassini into Saturn's ring system and examining the planet from a closer viewpoint than any other object in history, the time for Cassini's retirement finally arrived. NASA hosted a "Grand Finale" celebration on its website, enabling the millions of fans the probe had attracted over the years to witness its final moments. Many in both NASA and the general public called the final mission "bittersweet," stating that while they were sad that Cassini was no longer orbiting Saturn, they felt grateful knowing that they witnessed such an important moment in scientific history and expanded their knowledge about worlds beyond our own.

(1) The Cassini mission
1 helped provide people with a new understanding of the size of the universe.
2 is sometimes criticized for not being able to fulfill its primary purpose.
3 continues to send important data back to Earth through one of its satellites.
4 traveled farther than any other space probe ever launched from Earth.

(2) The Huygens lander is important because it

1 found the first moon beyond the asteroid belt.

2 identified a nearby planet that is potentially capable of supporting life.

3 sent back information about Saturn and several of its moons.

4 was the first spacecraft that successfully used a parachute to land.

(3) How was NASA able to extend Cassini's mission for so long?

1 NASA's budget grew because the probe was able to sell so much valuable data.

2 People valued the technologies that came about due to the mission.

3 A lot of people were willing to fund the Cassini mission via the Internet.

4 Public support for the mission grew because of a strong social media campaign.

(3) ① ② ③ ④

(4) Why did Cassini crash on Saturn's surface?

1 An accident happened to the probe because it became too old.

2 NASA did not want to risk dropping foreign matter on any of Saturn's moons.

3 NASA wanted to collect data about chemicals on the planet's surface.

4 The general public decided that Saturn would be an appropriate resting place.

(4) ① ② ③ ④

Read each passage and choose the best answer from among the four choices for each question. Then, on your answer sheet, find the number of the question and mark your answer.

Will Permaculture Save the World?

Buying a home is not as easy as merely signing a contract, and for those who choose to build their homes from scratch there are questions of location, materials, and even what kind of heating and cooling system to install. As concerns for the environment mount, however, a concept has emerged that attempts to address many of these significant challenges: permaculture. Permaculture is a combination of the words "permanent" and "culture," and it is a system of thinking about a home in a way that is sustainable for the people in it and the rest of the environment. While it doesn't go as far as helping new homeowners resolve questions about property taxes and local school systems, it does contribute to their health and wellbeing.

According to a report written by Kara Greenblott and Kristof Nordin in 2012, the three basic goals of permaculture are to care for the Earth, to care for people, and to use resources fairly. Those goals are both ambitious and vague, so it's not surprising that permaculture refers to a wide range of areas. These areas include organic farming, "green" energy like solar panels, waste reduction, and integrative landscaping. These concepts are not just for people with money to spend, however. On the contrary, those living in poverty can use some principles of permaculture to live both cheaply and sustainably, providing their own food, managing their own waste, and reducing their carbon footprint.

So what would a home built on the principles of permaculture actually look and feel like? Picture this: as you enter the driveway, you smell the fragrance of flowers. Those flowers aren't just there to produce a pleasant perfume, though; they attract bees, which pollinate other plants and also produce delicious honey for the owners. The house itself is sturdy, built from thick, recycled wood salvaged from a nearby house that was being rebuilt. Under the gutters in the corners of the house, there are large barrels, which collect rainwater that will be used to nourish the fruit trees in case of a drought. The inside of the house is bright, thanks to the large windows in the kitchen, wherein you see a wall of live herbs and salad greens that grow year-round. When you enter the backyard, you spot a wooden enclosure that is surrounded by large flies and mosquitos. You look inside and see compost: rich, black dirt full of crushed up eggshells, chicken bones, and orange peels that help sustain the garden.

The world of permaculture is not without its challenges. In fact, using the principles of permaculture can require far more planning, research, and, in some cases, even money. So-called "green technologies," for instance, are without a doubt better for the environment, but can cost more than standard technologies, especially considering the initial investment. For example, buying an electric car might not be an option for someone who only has a few thousand dollars to spend. However, the idea behind permaculture is not to be perfect; it's about trying to be thoughtful about every detail of your home's future and considering how every decision will affect your family, your community, and even the Earth itself.

(1) Permaculture is gaining popularity because it

    1 uses new technologies to help people construct houses without spending so much money.

    2 can help people build houses using only materials that are good for the environment.

    3 allows people to pay fewer property taxes after they buy a new home.

    4 helps to improve both people's health and the health of the environment.

(2) In order to take advantage of permaculture, people

   1 can try to build a garden to grow their own organic fruit and vegetables.

   2 must follow a clearly defined set of rules when building a new home.

   3 need their communities to work together to invest in green technologies.

   4 should come up with three ways they can help improve the environment.

(3) Which of the following is NOT an example of permaculture?

   1 Building a home with wood that might have been thrown away.

   2 Taking advantage of natural lighting to grow food inside a home.

   3 Throwing all of the garbage into the garden to nourish plants.

   4 Collecting rainwater for use when there is a lack of rain.

(3) ① ② ③ ④

(4) How can permaculture present a challenge?

   1 Making use of some permaculture technologies is only possible for people with enough money.

   2 Electric cars are good for the environment but are produced using unsustainable methods.

   3 It is extremely difficult for people to find stores selling older permaculture products.

   4 The laws in some regions prevent people from applying the newest permaculture technologies.

(4) ① ② ③ ④

Read each passage and choose the best answer from among the four choices for each question. Then, on your answer sheet, find the number of the question and mark your answer.

The Historical Ups and Downs of Roller Coasters

The roller coaster is one of the most popular amusement park rides ever invented. Some eager thrill-seekers even travel all over the world seeking the adrenaline rush provided by the tallest and fastest coasters. While thousands of people in the U.S. alone are injured each year and some of them are seriously injured, roller coasters remain a remarkably safe and exciting ride for children and adults alike. In fact, millions of people ride them each year without any incidents, and thanks to new computerized controls, they are safer than ever before. But while the modern idea of a "roller coaster" is familiar to many, this ride has changed significantly during the course of its 400-year-long history.

The structures that we recognize today as "roller coasters" began as ice slides in Russia. During the 17th century, residents of St. Petersburg would climb to the top of special structures and slide down wooden ramps that were covered with thick sheets of ice. Over time, these slides became popular among European upper-class people and were recreated outside of Russia. By the 18th century, both the Russians and the French had engineered a ride that was similar to the original ice slides that did not require any ice. The new ride, called a "coaster," used wheeled carriages attached to tracks — similar to train tracks — that guided riders up and over a series of small hills. It could be ridden at any time of the year. Soon, people began to build bigger coasters that incorporated loops and higher platforms from which to release the carriages. Public demand for roller coasters continued to grow throughout the years, and coaster designs continued to improve.

One major improvement came with a change in material. Most companies built coasters primarily out of wood until, in 1959, Disney built the first steel roller coaster at Disneyland Park in California. The use of steel had many benefits for roller coaster designers. Because steel is not as rigid as wood, it can be bent easily to form loops, curves, and so on. Using steel, modern roller coasters are able to take riders on many more twists and turns through the air than wooden coasters. The carriages can hang beneath the steel track instead of simply sitting on top of it, allowing riders to coast with no "floor" to block their view of the ground. Steel also offers a smoother ride for passengers than wood. Thrill-seeking people welcomed this additional excitement, and most of the newest coasters today continue to be made from steel.

Today there are incredible roller coasters in amusement parks all over the world, and there is strong international competition to build the longest, fastest, and tallest coasters. According to the Guinness World Records group, the tallest roller coaster is currently the 139-meter Kingda Ka coaster located at an amusement park in the U.S. A few years ago, a different American amusement park announced plans to build an even taller coaster, but was met with resistance from the local government. The proposed roller coaster designs violated local laws regarding height limits for structures in that neighborhood. A controversy occurred, but in the end, the amusement park won the legal battle. The world's new tallest roller coaster, the Skyscraper, is expected to begin exciting thrillseekers in 2021.

(1) Which of the following statements is true regarding roller coasters?

1 Thanks to modern technology, the number of roller-coaster-related accidents has decreased.

2 Children are more likely to get injured while riding on roller coasters than adults.

3 The taller a roller coaster is, the more likely people are to be involved in an accident.

4 Millions of people get injured from roller coaster accidents around the world each year.

(1) ① ② ③ ④

(2) Ice slides fell out of favor because

1 people could ride a coaster with wheeled carriages throughout the year.

2 they were so slippery and dangerous that many people did not want to ride them.

3 they took a lot of time to build and were too expensive to maintain.

4 the new roller coasters had wheeled carriages that made them safer.

(3) Which of the following is a benefit of using steel to build roller coasters?

1 It is much cheaper to build steel roller coasters than wooden ones.

2 It is so smooth that coasters can run much faster.

3 It can be made into more types of shapes than with wood.

4 It enables coasters to go higher and provide a better view.

(4) Why was there controversy over the construction of the Skyscraper?

1 The local government changed the laws regarding height limits for buildings.

2 Local people insisted that the tall structure spoiled the town's scenery.

3 The Guinness World Records group did not make an official measurement.

4 The roller coaster was too high and the local government was against it.

Read each passage and choose the best answer from among the four choices for each question. Then, on your answer sheet, find the number of the question and mark your answer.

The Equal Rights Amendment

While America has long been known as a world leader in feminism and women's rights, surprisingly, there is no guarantee of equality for women in the United States Constitution. During the 1960s, feminist leaders helped to create support for adding a new section to the Constitution. The Equal Rights Amendment (ERA) would give women "Equality of rights under the law." Making amendments to the Constitution is a complicated process, however. Both the national government, known as Congress, and a three-quarter majority of the 50 states must approve any change. Incidents like nationwide women's protests, a flood of media articles, and overwhelming support in opinion polls convinced the nation's lawmakers to approve the ERA in 1972. Although a seven-year time limit was set for 38 of the 50 states to pass the ERA, 30 had already done so by 1973, convincing nearly everyone that it would succeed. When the deadline came in 1979, however, only 35 states had passed it, and although the deadline was extended, the amendment died.

One woman, a lawyer named Phyllis Schlafly, is widely thought to have been responsible for defeating the ERA. Schlafly created a large group of volunteers composed mainly of churchgoing Christians who helped to convince large numbers of citizens and politicians that the ERA would not have the effect people expected. The group focused on earlier laws intended to protect women, such as those forcing men to provide financial support to their ex-wives in the event of a divorce, or allowing women to avoid required service in the military. Schlafly argued that the ERA would likely kill these laws because they would mean that men and women were not being treated "equally." This shocked people who had previously supported the ERA as a symbolic confirmation of women's equality and convinced politicians in many states to stop supporting it.

Many women feel that the ERA should have become part of the Constitution, pointing to continuing problems like the fact that women's average salaries are still lower than men's. They argue that although today there are various laws that protect women's rights, if voters change their minds about a law that protects women's rights, it can easily be removed from the law books. Having the ERA in the Constitution, however, would make this extremely unlikely to happen.

Despite the ERA's defeat, many of its supporters' goals have been achieved in other ways, such as laws passed by Congress and actions taken by the Supreme Court. Laws such as Title IX forced universities to offer more educational opportunities to women, for example. The ERA is reintroduced into Congress every year, but it generally attracts little attention. Perhaps the saddest legacy of the ERA is the break-up of a once unified feminist movement. Today, there is tremendous disagreement about whether to advance the rights of women through the ERA or through other methods and this has prevented them from working together to achieve other goals that would improve women's status in society.

(1) In 1973, the Equal Rights Amendment

1 had become a part of the Constitution, but in the next few years, several states forced the amendment to be removed.

2 seemed certain to become part of the Constitution because it had been passed by Congress and a large number of state governments.

3 had won overwhelming public support because the rights of women were not protected by law.

4 had failed to be approved by Congress, but had a hope of success if three-quarters of the state government supported it.

(2) What did Phyllis Schlafly believe about the ERA?

1 It could lead to an increase in the number of women who would decide to get divorces from their husbands.

2 It would make it much more difficult for Christian women to practice their religion freely.

3 It would not be as financially effective as the earlier laws that provided money for divorced women.

4 It could make it more difficult for women who wanted a chance to serve in the American military.

(2) ① ② ③ ④

(3) What is one reason that supporters of the ERA are unhappy about its defeat?

1 They think that it will cause voters to stop supporting laws designed to protect the rights of women.

2 They think that it will make it difficult to make important changes to the Constitution in the future.

3 They think that without the ERA it will be easy for women to lose their legal protections.

4 They think that laws protecting women's rights have been greatly weakened since it was defeated.

(3) ① ② ③ ④

(4) What is one long-term effect of the attempt to get the ERA into the Constitution?

1 It has made it more difficult for Congress to pass other laws that would protect the rights of women.

2 Disagreement came about among feminists about the best way to increase women's rights.

3 The Supreme Court has become less likely to make decisions that favor the rights of women.

4 It has given women so many protections that some people are complaining that things have gone too far.

(4) ① ② ③ ④

桐原書店

978-4-342-20584-2

英語4技能
リーディング
ハイパートレーニング

東進ハイスクール講師 **安河内哲也**

ハーバード大学
教育学大学院修士 **アンドリュー・ロビンス** [監修]

長文読解 **5** 上級編

桐原書店

　本書は4技能のうち，リーディング力を高めることを主目的としています。**さらに，音声を活用してリーディングを学ぶことにより，同時にリスニングの力を伸ばすこと**を狙います。

　リーディングとリスニングを融合して学習することには多くの利点があります。耳と口と目をフル活用して英語を学ぶことで，相互に助け合いそれぞれの技能を支え合うのです。たとえば，音声を耳で聞いて，口を動かしながら読むことによって，英語をそのまま左から右へと理解する最高の読解訓練ができます。また，学習が終了し，理解できるようになった英文を耳で聞くことにより，語彙，表現，内容を保持するための復習が容易にできるわけです。

　このように，リーディングをリスニングと組み合わせて学ぶことにより，学習効果は増幅します。4技能の英語をマスターするためには，4技能を別々に学ぶのではなく，極力融合して学ぶことが大切なのです。

　本書で訓練するリーディングの内容や語彙は，スピーキングやライティングのネタとしても使えるでしょう。このように，内容を4技能で使い回しすることにより，将来も役に立つスピード感のある英語力を，皆さんが身につけることを願います。

安河内 哲也

本書の内容と使い方

問題（別冊）

CEFR のレベルに準拠して作成された問題です。設問は，どのような試験にでも応用できる力を身につけるために，語句空所補充と内容一致選択を中心としたオーソドックスなものとしています。

解答と解説

各設問に対して，該当部分などを示し，解答の根拠をわかりやすく説明しています。解説を読み，どう考えれば正解に至ることができるのかを理解してください。また，語句は長文の中で学んで覚えていくのが最良の勉強方法です。本書には単語集としての機能も持たせてあります。

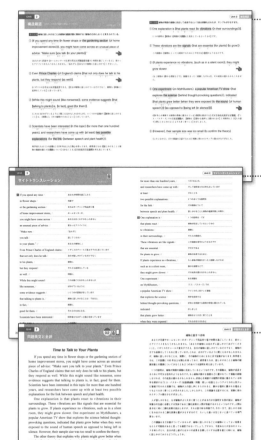

構造確認

各文章の構造を，記号や SVOC を付し，確認できるようにしました。あくまでも読み違えたときの確認のためのものであり，自分でこのような作業をすることを求めるものではありません。

サイトトランスレーション

英文をチャンクごとに分け，英語と日本語を左右に分けて編集することにより，英文を前からすばやく読むためのさまざまな練習を可能としました。後置修飾部分も「後から説明」と考えながら，前からすばやく英文を処理する練習をしてください。最終的には，日本語を見ずに英語が理解できることを目指しましょう。

問題英文と全訳

和訳は英文を読む目的ではありませんが，読み違えがないかどうかの確認には便利です。その用途を意識し，本書ではできるだけ構造に忠実な和訳を心がけています。

本書に準拠した音声と練習用動画に関して

　本書の英文を使って，チャンクリピーティング，オーバーラッピング，シャドウイング，リスニングなどの練習ができるダウンロード音声と動画が準備されています。皆さんは，これらの音声や動画の画面を使って以下のような基礎訓練をし，読解力と聴解力を向上させてください。

【チャンクリピーティング】

　チャンクごとに分けて読まれる英語の後に続けて，本や画面の文字を見ながら，英文を音読しましょう。また，このようにして，文字を見ながら英文の意味が理解できるようになったら，次は本や画面の文字を見ないで，音だけでリピートしながら意味を理解する訓練をしてみましょう。

3

【オーバーラッピング】

テキストや画面の文字を見ながら，ネイティブスピーカーと一緒に音読してみましょう。その際，音だけに集中しすぎず，英文の意味を理解しようと努めましょう。

【シャドウイング】

ネイティブスピーカーの音声から一拍遅れながら，耳だけでネイティブスピーカーの音声を真似てみましょう。非常に難しい訓練なので，できなくても心配する必要はまったくありませんが，一つの目標として挑戦してみてください。

【リスニング】

本や画面の文字を見ずに，英語だけを聞いて意味が理解できるか確認してみてください。100％理解できたら，その英文をマスターしたと言えるでしょう。その後も復習として，ラジオを聞く感覚で，文章を耳で聞いて，内容，語彙，表現を忘れないようにしましょう。

本書の英文に関して

本シリーズの英文は，アンドリュー・ロビンス氏の監修のもと，作成されています。本書では，ロビンス氏が，日米のネイティブスピーカーのアイテムライターをチーム化し，英語学習者が力を伸ばすのにふさわしいレベルの多くの英文をプロデュースしました。本書の英文は，CEFR（ヨーロッパ言語共通参照枠）という国際的言語教育の枠組みに準拠して作成されています。

この目的を達成するために，ロビンス氏は，語彙レベルや構造レベルを色分けし，直感的なフィードバックを与えるソフトウェアを開発しました。このソフトウェアでは，一般に公表されている CEFR-J※ の語彙リストや，CEFR との準拠を公表している4技能試験で出題頻度の高い語彙を色別表示することができます。このことにより，アイテムライターは，使用している語彙が当該の CEFR レベルにマッチするものなのかをつねに確認しながらライティング作業を進めることができるようになりました。

しかしながら，このような機械によるアルゴリズム分析には大きな限界があります。それは，機械の判断では，文脈からの意味判定が非常に難しいということです。たとえば，free という形容詞が「自由な」という意味で使用された場合，CEFR-J では A1 のレベルですが，「ない」という意味で使用されている場合は，より高いレベルに分類されると考えられます。

また，内容の選択に関しても，機械分析には限界があります。特定の予備知識を持っていなければ理解できないような素材は，基礎から学んでいる学生の学習素材として適しているとは言えません。そこで本書では，内容選択においても各種4技能試験に準拠し，一般的，基礎的な常識を備えていれば読めるものを選択しています。

このように，本書の英文は，機械分析と熟練した編著者，アイテムライターを組み合わせ，CEFR レベルの準拠と等価を行い，ロビンス氏の監修のもとで作成されました。

※ CEFR-J：実質上の国際標準となっている CEFR を，日本のような環境に適合させるために開発された枠組み。レベル別の語彙リストが一般に公表されている。

もくじ

　構造確認のページは，誤読が生じた場合にその原因を確認するためのものです。ただし，5文型や句や節の分類には何通りもの解釈があり，本書ではその一つを示しているにすぎません。これらの記号を使えなければならないということを意味しているわけではないので，このページを詳細に学習する必要はありません。あくまでも，誤読しないための参考資料として，適宜使用するにとどめてください。

使用されている記号一覧

主文 [主節] の構造：S ＝主語　V ＝動詞　O ＝目的語　C ＝補語

主文 [主節] 以外の構造：S'＝主語　V'＝動詞　O'＝目的語　C'＝補語

[　　] ➡ 名詞の働きをするもの（名詞，名詞句，名詞節）

〈　　〉➡ 形容詞の働きをするもの（形容詞，形容詞句，形容詞節）

(　　) ➡ 副詞の働きをするもの（副詞，副詞句，副詞節）

＿＿〈　　〉➡ 形容詞の働きをするものが，後ろから名詞を修飾

名詞の働きをするもの

● **動名詞**

I like [watching baseball games].

私は [野球を見ること] が好きだ。

● **不定詞の名詞的用法**

[To see] is [to believe].

[見ること] は [信じること] である。

● **疑問詞＋不定詞**

I don't know [what to do next].

私は [次に何をすべきか] わからない。

● **that 節「S が V するということ」**

I think [that he is right].

私は [彼は正しい] と思う。

● **if 節「S が V するかどうか」**

I don't know [if Cathy will come].

私は [キャシーが来るかどうか] わからない。

● **疑問詞節**

Do you know [where he lives]?

あなたは [彼がどこに住んでいるか] 知っていますか。

● **関係代名詞の what 節**

[What he said] is true.

[彼が言ったこと] は本当だ。

● **前置詞＋名詞**

Look at the girl ⟨in a white dress⟩.

⟨白い服を着た⟩女の子を見てごらん。

● **過去分詞**

The ambulance carried a child ⟨hit by a truck⟩.

救急車は⟨トラックにはねられた⟩子供を運んだ。

● **不定詞の形容詞的用法**

I have many friends ⟨to help me⟩.

私は⟨私を助けてくれる⟩たくさんの友人がいる。

● **関係代名詞節**

He is the boy ⟨who broke the window⟩.

彼が⟨窓を壊した⟩少年だ。

● **現在分詞**

Look at the building ⟨standing on that hill⟩.

⟨あの丘の上に建っている⟩建物を見なさい。

● **関係副詞節**

Wien is the city ⟨where I want to live⟩.

ウィーンは⟨私が住みたい⟩町だ。

※名詞に接続する同格節［句］は本来，名詞の働きをするものですが，本書では英文を理解しやすくするために，あえて ⟨ ⟩ 記号にしてあります。

● **同格の that 節**

There is some hope ⟨that he will recover⟩.

⟨彼が回復するという⟩いくぶんの希望がある。

● **カンマによる同格補足**

We visited Beijing, ⟨the capital of China⟩.

私たちは⟨中国の首都である⟩北京を訪れた。

● **前置詞＋名詞**

The sun rises (in the east).

太陽は（東から）昇る。

● **従属接続詞＋ＳＶ**

I went to bed early (because I was tired).

（私は疲れていたので）早く寝た。

● **分詞構文（Ving）**

(Hearing the news), she turned pale.

（そのニュースを聞いて），彼女は青ざめた。

● **不定詞の副詞的用法**

I was very glad (to hear the news).

私は（その知らせを聞いて）とてもうれしい。

● **受動分詞構文（Vpp）**

(Seen from the sky), the islands look really beautiful.

（空から見ると），島々は本当に美しく見える。

サイトトランスレーションについて ——センスグループの分け方——

　スラッシュなどで英文を区切るセンスグループの分け方には，明確なきまりがある わけではありませんが，基本的には2〜5語ほどの「意味のかたまり」でリズムよく 分けていきます。大切なのは，「切る」という作業が目標になってしまわないことです。 皆さんの目標は「読んでわかる」ことであり，切り方ばかりに集中するあまり，読むの が遅くなってしまっては本末転倒です。最初はおおざっぱに切り分けてどんどん読んで いき，徐々に文法を意識した適切な切り方を覚えていきましょう。ここでは，センスグ ループを切り分ける際の5つの大切なルールを学習します。例文を音読しながら，2〜 5語のリズムを体得してください。

SVOC の要素で切る

　S, V, O, C は文の最も基本的な要素なので，これらはセンスグループを切り分け る際にも非常に重要なヒントとなります。1つの要素が4語や5語のような大きなも のになる場合は，それを1つのセンスグループとするとよいでしょう。

He told me / **a very interesting story.**
S　V　O　　　　　　　O
彼は私に語った / とても興味深い話を

Mr.Thompson found / **an incredibly cheap restaurant.**
S　　　　V　　　　　　　O
トンプソン氏は見つけた / とんでもなく安いレストランを

文頭の副詞句の後ろで区切る

　文頭に副詞句や副詞節が置かれる場合は，それらの副詞句や副詞節と主語の間では必 ず切って読み進みましょう。文頭で副詞句の働きをするものとしては，前置詞句や分詞 構文などが考えられます。

In case of emergency, / **you should stay calm.**
　　　前置詞句　　　　　　　S　　　V　　C
緊急事態には　　　　　　 / 平静を保つべきだ。

Seeing my face, / **she kindly smiled.**
　分詞構文　　　　　　S　　　V
私の顔を見て / 彼女は優しく微笑んだ。

　主語の直後に長い修飾部分が続く場合は，その主語と述語動詞を切り分けて読むことが重要です。通常一拍おいて読まれ，少々強い切れ目となります。

The boy / singing a song / under the tree / is my brother.
　主語　　　　　　　＋分詞　　　　　　　　＋副詞句　　　　　　　述部
少年は　　/ 歌を歌っている　/ 木の下で　　　　/ 私の弟だ。

The products / that they produced / had many defects.
　主語　　　　　　　＋関係代名詞節　　　　　　　述部
製品は　　　/ 彼らが生産した　　　/ 多くの欠陥があった。

前置詞や接続詞の前で切る

　前置詞や接続詞は直後に続く要素と結びついてかたまりを作るため，多くの場合その直前で切って読みます。前置詞とその目的語の間で切ることはまずありません。

He stayed　　 / in the house / during the afternoon.
S　　　V　　　　　　　前置詞句　　　　　　　前置詞句
彼はとどまった / 家の中に　　　/ 午後の間は

I like him,　　 / although everybody hates him.
　主節　　　　　　　　接続詞＋ SV（副詞節）
私は彼が好きだ / 皆は彼を嫌っているけれども

カンマやセミコロンなどがある箇所で切る

　，（カンマ）は日本語の読点と似ていて，やはり一拍おいて読む箇所を示しています。当然カンマのある箇所では切って読んでいきます。―（ダッシュ）や；（セミコロン）などのマークの箇所でも切って読んでいきます。

He was born / in Beijing,　　　 / the capital of China.
　主文　　　　　前置詞＋名詞＋カンマ　　　　同格説明
彼は生まれた / 北京で　　　　　　/ 中国の首都の

I took the medicine; / otherwise / I would have died.
SVO ＋セミコロン　　　　副詞　　　S　　　　V
私は薬を飲んだ　　　　　/ さもなければ / 私は死んでいただろう。

⇒別冊 p.4 〜 5

解答と解説

解答

(1) ①　　(2) ③　　(3) ②

解説

(1) 第 1 段落の空所の後には,「人が座ると倒れる椅子」についての記述がある。このような椅子に客を座らせて楽しんでいたということは彼の奇妙な性格を表していると言える。そのことから考えて,正解は 1。

選択肢の和訳

○ 1 彼の奇妙な性格を表した

× 2 彼の素晴らしい能力への鍵を示した

× 3 彼の人生に大きな影響を与えた

× 4 ピアノの技術を向上させる方法を彼に教えた

(2) この空所の前の,第 2 段落の第 2 文に,ブラームスが幸せな人でなかったという記述があり,空所の後で,現実にどんな不幸があったかについて説明している。したがって,正解は 3。このように, in fact は前出の内容をさらに詳しく述べる場合に用いられる。

選択肢の和訳

× 1 一方で

× 2 その結果

○ 3 実際に

× 4 それにもかかわらず

(3) この空所を含む文の 1 つ前の文までが,ブラームスの悲惨な子供時代の説明であり,空所の後で,彼はまともな生活を送れなかったために,よい楽しみ方を見つけられなかったということが述べられている。よって,1 は誤り。3・4 は文脈に合わない。正解は 2。

選択肢の和訳

× 1 人を喜ばせる方法を学んだ

○ 2 よい手本となる人がいなかった

× 3 成功するのに十分なお金を稼いだ

× 4 彼の音楽的才能を向上させた

語句

〈タイトル〉

☐ composer	(名) 作曲家
☐ peculiar	(形) 奇妙な
☐ prank	(名) 悪ふざけ，いたずら

〈第1段落〉

☐ Romantic music period	ロマン派音楽時代
☐ a full head of wildly flowing white hair	無造作に伸びた白髪
☐ be designed to do	～するよう設計されている
☐ fall over	倒れる
☐ fall forward on one's knees	前へひざまずく，ひざをつく

☐ fall backward	後ろに倒れる
☐ roar with laughter	大笑いする
☐ get tricked by ～	～にだまされる，一杯食わされる

〈第2段落〉

☐ tragic	(形) 悲惨な
☐ low-class bar	低級な酒場
☐ behave crudely	粗野に振る舞う
☐ resentful	(形) 怒りっぽい
☐ role model	(模範となる) 役割モデル，手本
☐ decent	(形) まともな，きちんとした

11

構造確認 ※誤読した部分の確認に使用してください。

⇒別冊 p.4 ～ 5

第 1 段落 クラシック音楽の巨匠ブラームスは風変わりで，人を特別な椅子で陥れて笑う性癖があった。

① Johannes Brahms is considered one 〈of the masters 〈of classical music〉〉.
    S   V   C

ヨハネス・ブラームスは《《クラシック音楽の》巨匠の》1 人と見なされています。

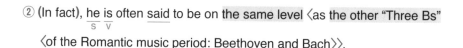

② (In fact), he is often said to be on the same level 〈as the other "Three Bs"
         S V

〈of the Romantic music period: Beethoven and Bach〉〉.

(実のところ)，彼はしばしば《《ロマン派音楽時代の，ベートーベンやバッハといった》ほかの「三大
B」と》同じ水準であると言われます。

③ He also has a lot 〈in common〉 (with other famous composers 〈of classical
  S①   V① O①

music〉): he was born (more than 100 years ago), he was a brilliant piano
        S② V②   S③ V③   C③

player, and he had a full head 〈of wildly flowing white hair〉.
           S④ V④   O④

彼にはまた (《クラシック音楽の》ほかの有名な作曲家との)〈共通点が〉たくさんあります，彼は (今
から 100 年以上前に) 生まれ，優れたピアノ奏者で，そして〈無造作に伸びた白髪で〉ふさふさした頭
をしていました。

④ There was, (however), one habit 〈that represented his strange personality〉.
     V   S   V'

(しかしながら)，〈彼のその風変わりな性格を示す〉1 つの性癖がありました。

⑤ He had a chair (in his apartment) 〈that was designed to fall over (when a
  S V   O   V'

person sat (in it))〉.

彼は (自分のアパートに)〈(人が (それに) 座ると) 倒れてしまうように作られた〉椅子を持っていまし
た。

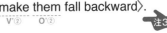

⑥ He asked someone to build him this special chair 〈that would either cause
　　S　 V　　　　O
his guests to fall forward (on their knees) or make them fall backward〉.
　　O'①　　　　　　　　　　　　　V'②　　O'②　　　　　注3

彼は〈来客が前に倒れて（膝をついて）しまうか，後ろに倒れてしまうであろう〉この特別な椅子を作るよう人に依頼したのです。

⑦ (According to his friends and his servant), he would roar with laughter
　　　　　　　　　　　　　　　　　　　S　　　V
(every time someone got tricked (by the chair)).　　
　　　　　　S'　　　V'　　　　　　　　　　　　注4

（彼の友人たちや使用人によると），彼は（誰かが（その椅子で）一杯食わされるたびに）大笑いしていたそうです。

第2段落　悲惨な子供時代を過ごし，手本となる人がいなかったことが，彼の性格に影響したのだろう。

① You might be wondering [why someone would want to do such a thing].
　　S　　　V　　　　　　O　　S'　　　V'　　　　　O'

あなたは［人がなぜそんなことをしたいと思うのか］不思議に思うかもしれません。

② Brahms was a musical genius, but he was not a happy man.
　　S①　V①　　C①　　　　　　S②　V②　　C②

ブラームスは音楽の天才でしたが，幸せな人ではありませんでした。

③ (In fact), he had an unusual and tragic childhood.
　　　　　　S　V　　　　　O

（実際），彼は普通ではない悲惨な子供時代を送りました。

④ He grew up (in poverty), and he had to start playing music (in very low-class
　　S①　V①　　　　　　　S②　　　V②　　　　O②
bars) (when he was just 12 years old).
　　　　　　S'　V'　　　C'

彼は（貧困の中で）育ち，（まだ12歳だった時に）（非常に低級な酒場で）音楽を演奏し始めなければなりませんでした。

13

⑤ (According to Brahms), <u>the experience</u> ⟨of [being in these bars, ⟨where
S

people were often <u>drunk</u> and <u>behaving</u> crudely⟩]⟩, <u>affected</u> <u>him</u> deeply and
S'   V'   V①   O①

<u>made</u> <u>him</u> <u>angry and resentful</u>.
V② O②   C②

👉注5

（ブラームスによると），⟨[⟨人々がしばしば酔って粗野に振る舞う⟩，これらの酒場にいた] という⟩経験が，彼に大きく影響し，彼を短気で怒りっぽくしました。

⑥ (Considering this), <u>he</u> (probably) <u>did not have</u> <u>a good role model</u> (in his early
S   V   O

life).

👉注6

（このことを考えると），彼には（おそらく）（幼い頃に）よい手本となる人がいなかったのでしょう。

⑦ (If <u>he</u> <u>had had</u> <u>a decent life</u>), <u>he</u> <u>would have found</u> <u>a better way</u> ⟨to entertain
S'   V'   O'   S   V   O

himself⟩.

👉注7

（もし彼がまともな生活を送っていたら），⟨楽しむのに⟩もっとよい方法を見つけていたことでしょう。

注1　consider O C は「O が C であると見なす」という意味だが，受動態になると O be considered C という形となり，「O は C であると見なされる」という意味を表すことができる。

注2　コロン（：）は，その前にあるブラームスとほかの作曲家との共通点を具体的に示すために用いられている。A, B and C という形で，3つの文で共通点が示されている。

注3　either A or B は「A か B かいずれか」という意味だが，A, B の部分にはさまざまな品詞を並べることができる。この文では，cause と make という動詞が並べられている。

注4　according to ～は「～によれば」という意味で，情報源を示す場合に用いられる。

注5　この文の主語は the experience で，of から crudely までの部分が主語の修飾部分。述語動詞は affected で，主語と離れているため注意。

注6　Considering ～は分詞構文の慣用表現で，「～を考えれば」という意味。

注7　If S' had V'pp, S would have Vpp は，過去の事実に反することを仮定する場合に使う形。「もしも S' が V' していたならば，S は V していただろう」という意味。

サイトトランスレーション

⇒別冊 p.4 ～ 5

1 Johannes Brahms is considered /	ヨハネス・ブラームスは見なされています
one of the masters /	巨匠の 1 人と
of classical music. //	クラシック音楽の。
In fact, /	実際に，
he is often said /	彼はしばしば言われます
to be on the same level /	同じレベルにあると
as the other "Three Bs" /	ほかの「三大 B」と
of the Romantic music period: /	ロマン派音楽時代の，
Beethoven and Bach. //	ベートーベンやバッハ（といった）。
He also has a lot in common /	彼にはまた共通点がたくさんあります
with other famous composers /	ほかの有名な作曲家との
of classical music: /	クラシック音楽の，
he was born /	彼は生まれました
more than 100 years ago, /	100 年以上前に，
he was a brilliant piano player, /	彼は優れたピアノ奏者でした，
and he had /	そして彼は持っていました
a full head of wildly flowing white hair. //	無造作に伸びた白髪でふさふさした頭を。
There was, however, one habit /	しかしながら，1 つの性癖がありました
that represented his strange personality. //	彼の風変わりな性格を示す。
He had a chair /	彼は椅子を持っていました
in his apartment /	自分のアパートに
that was designed to fall over /	倒れてしまうように作られた

15

when a person sat in it. //	人がそれに座ると。
He asked /	彼は依頼しました
someone to build him /	誰かに彼のために作るように
this special chair /	この特別な椅子を
that would either cause his guests to fall forward on their knees /	来客を前に転ばせ膝をつかせるか
or make them fall backward. //	または彼らを後ろに倒れさせる。
According to his friends and his servant, /	彼の友人たちや使用人によると,
he would roar with laughter /	彼は大笑いしていたそうです
every time someone got tricked /	誰かがだまされるたびに
by the chair. //	その椅子によって。
2 You might be wondering /	あなたは不思議に思うかもしれません
why someone would want to do such a thing. //	人がなぜそんなことをしたいと思うのか。
Brahms was a musical genius, /	ブラームスは音楽の天才でした,
but he was not a happy man. //	しかし彼は幸せな人ではありませんでした。
In fact, /	実際,
he had /	彼は持ちました
an unusual and tragic childhood. //	普通ではない悲惨な子供時代を。
He grew up /	彼は育ちました
in poverty, /	貧困の中で,
and he had to start /	そして彼は始めなければなりませんでした
playing music /	音楽を演奏することを
in very low-class bars /	非常に低級な酒場で
when he was just 12 years old. //	彼がたった12歳だった時に。

According to Brahms, /	ブラームスによると,
the experience /	その経験が
of being in these bars, /	これらの酒場にいたという,
where people were often drunk /	人々がしばしば酔う
and behaving crudely, /	そして粗野に振る舞う,
affected him deeply /	彼に大きく影響しました
and made him angry and resentful. //	そして彼を短気で怒りっぽくしました。
Considering this, /	このことを考えると,
he probably did not have /	彼はおそらく持ちませんでした
a good role model /	よい手本を
in his early life. //	幼い頃に。
If he had had a decent life, /	もし彼がまともな生活を送れていたら,
he would have found /	彼は見つけていたでしょう
a better way to entertain himself. //	楽しむためのもっとよい方法を。

17

⇒別冊 p.4 ～ 5

A Classical Music Composer's Peculiar Prank

Johannes Brahms is considered one of the masters of classical music. In fact, he is often said to be on the same level as the other "Three Bs" of the Romantic music period: Beethoven and Bach. He also has a lot in common with other famous composers of classical music: he was born more than 100 years ago, he was a brilliant piano player, and he had a full head of wildly flowing white hair. There was, however, one habit that represented his strange personality. He had a chair in his apartment that was designed to fall over when a person sat in it. He asked someone to build him this special chair that would either cause his guests to fall forward on their knees or make them fall backward. According to his friends and his servant, he would roar with laughter every time someone got tricked by the chair.

You might be wondering why someone would want to do such a thing. Brahms was a musical genius, but he was not a happy man. In fact, he had an unusual and tragic childhood. He grew up in poverty, and he had to start playing music in very low-class bars when he was just 12 years old. According to Brahms, the experience of being in these bars, where people were often drunk and behaving crudely, affected him deeply and made him angry and resentful. Considering this, he probably did not have a good role model in his early life. If he had had a decent life, he would have found a better way to entertain himself.

あるクラシック音楽の作曲家による奇妙ないたずら

　ヨハネス・ブラームスは，クラシック音楽の巨匠の1人と見なされています。実のところ，彼はしばしば，ロマン派音楽時代のほかの「三大B」，すなわちベートーベンやバッハに匹敵すると言われます。彼にはまた，ほかの有名なクラシック音楽の作曲家との共通点がたくさんあります。例えば，彼は今から100年以上前に生まれ，優れたピアノ奏者で，そしてその頭は無造作に伸びた白髪でふさふさしていました。しかしながら，彼にはその風変わりな性格を示す1つの性癖がありました。彼は自分のアパートに，人が座ると倒れてしまうように作られた椅子を持っていました。彼は誰かに依頼して，来客が前に倒れて膝をついてしまうか，後ろに倒れてしまうようなこの特別な椅子を作ったのです。彼の友人たちや使用人によると，彼は誰かがこの椅子で一杯食わされるたびに大笑いしていたそうです。

　あなたは，人がなぜそんなことをしたいと思うのか不思議に思うかもしれません。ブラームスは音楽の天才でしたが，幸せな人ではありませんでした。実際，彼は普通ではない悲惨な子供時代を送りました。彼は貧困の中で育ち，まだ12歳だった時に非常に低級な酒場で音楽を演奏し始めなければなりませんでした。ブラームスによると，客たちが酔っぱらって粗野に振る舞うことの多い酒場にいた経験が彼に大きく影響し，彼を短気で怒りっぽくしたということです。このことを考えると，おそらく彼には幼い頃によい手本となる人がいなかったのでしょう。もし彼がまともな生活を送れていたら，もっとよい楽しみ方を見つけていたことでしょう。

⇒別冊 p.6 ～ 7

解答と解説

解答

(1) ③　　(2) ①　　(3) ③

解説

(1) 空所を含む文の前を見てみると，2つ前の文にも同様に「植物に話しかける」ことについての記述がある。その記述の前に you might have come across an unusual piece of advice (変わったアドバイスをもらうかもしれません) とあることから，空所部分も似たような文脈で考える。正解は3。

選択肢の和訳

× 1 植物に利益をもたらす
× 2 追加料金がかかる
○ 3 ばかげているように聞こえる
× 4 屋外での作業が改善される

(2) 空所は，植物が静かなところで振動を経験しなかった場合どうなるかについての内容が入る。空所の後の文を見ると，テレビ番組で行われた実験についての記述があり，その結果が indicated that plants grew better when they were exposed to the sound of human speech as opposed to being left in silence (植物が人の話し声にさらされると，静かな場所に置かれる場合よりもより大きく育つことが示されました) であることから考えると，正解は1。

選択肢の和訳

○ 1 成長が遅くなる
× 2 多くの花を咲かせる
× 3 成長が早くなる
× 4 光の方へ向かう

(3) 第3段落の内容を確認すると，空所の前では，人が話す時の二酸化炭素の放出が植物が大きく育つ理由だとする説があることが述べられている。そして，空所の後では，その説を否定する専門家の意見についての記述がある。それらの内容をつなぐ言葉として最も適当な3が正解。このように，on the other hand は対称的な内容を前後に置いて用いられる。

選択肢の和訳

× 1 このため
× 2 例えば
○ 3 一方で
× 4 さもなければ

語句

〈第 1 段落〉

☐ home improvement store	日曜大工店，ホームセンター
☐ come across ～	～に出くわす
☐ make sure ～	確実に［忘れずに］～する
☐ claim that ～	～と主張する
☐ respond	(動) 返事をする
☐ nonsense	(名) ばかげたこと
☐ come up with ～	～を思いつく，考え出す
☐ link	(名) 関連

〈第 2 段落〉

☐ react	(動) ～に反応する
☐ vibration	(名) 振動
☐ surroundings	(名) 周囲の環境

☐ explore	(動) ～を探究する
☐ thought-provoking	(形) いろいろ考えさせられる，思考力を刺激されるような
☐ be exposed to ～	～にさらされる
☐ as opposed to ～	～とは対照的に

〈第 3 段落〉

☐ release	(動) ～を放出する
☐ exhale	(動) 息を吐く
☐ significant	(形) 有意(義)な，顕著な

〈第 4 段落〉

☐ settle	(動) ～を終わらせる，確定させる
☐ it is safe to say that ...	…と言ってもよい

構造確認 ※誤読した部分の確認に使用してください。

⇒別冊 p.6 ～ 7

第 1 段落 植物に話しかけることは植物の健康状態に関係する（植物のためによい）と考えられている。

① (If you spend any time (in flower shops or the gardening section ⟨of home
improvement stores⟩)), you might have come across an unusual piece of
advice: "Make sure [you talk (to your plants)]."

 注1

（あなたが（花屋や⟨ホームセンターの⟩ガーデニング用品売り場で）時間を過ごしていると），変わったアドバイスをもらうかもしれません，「忘れずに [(あなたの植物に) 話しかけて] ください」と。

② Even Prince Charles ⟨of England⟩ claims [that not only does he talk to his
plants, but they respond (as well)].

注2

⟨イギリスの⟩チャールズ皇太子でさえ，[自分が植物に話しかけているだけでなく，植物も（同様に）返事をしている] と言っています。

③ (While this might sound (like nonsense)), some evidence suggests [that
[talking to plants] is, (in fact), good (for them)].

（これは（ばかげているように）聞こえるかもしれませんが），いくつかの証拠が [[植物に話しかけること] は，（実際に），（その植物のために）よい] と示しています。

④ Scientists have been interested (in this topic) (for more than one hundred
years), and researchers have come up with (at least) two possible
explanations ⟨for the link ⟨between speech and plant health⟩⟩.

科学者たちは（この話題に）（100 年以上も）関心を持っており，研究者たちは ⟨⟨話しかけることと植物の健康状態との⟩関係について⟩（少なくとも）2 つのありうる説明を考え出しています。

第2段落 植物が周囲の振動に反応して成長するという説は実験もされたが，サンプルが少なすぎた。

① One explanation is [that plants react (to vibrations ⟨in their surroundings⟩)].
　　　　S　　　　　 V　 C　 　　S'　　 V'

1つの説明は［植物が（⟨周囲の⟩振動に）反応しているというもの］です。

② These vibrations are like signals ⟨that are essential (for plants) (to grow)⟩.
　　　　S　　　　 V　 C　　　　　　 V'　　 C'

この振動は⟨（植物にとって）（成長するために）不可欠な⟩信号のようなものです。

③ (If plants experience no vibrations, (such as in a silent room)), they might
　　 S'　　 V'　　　 O'　　　　　　　　　　　　　 S　 V
grow slower.　　　　　　　　　　　　　　　　　　　　　　注3

（もし植物が（静かな部屋などで），振動をまったく経験しなければ），その成長は遅れるかもしれません。

④ One experiment ⟨on MythBusters⟩, a popular American TV show ⟨that
　　　 S
explores the science ⟨behind thought-provoking questions⟩⟩, indicated
　 V'①　　　 O'①　　　　　　　　　　　　　　　　　　　 V
[that plants grew better (when they were exposed (to the sound ⟨of human
　 O　 S'②　 V'②
speech⟩)) (as opposed to [being left (in silence)])].　　　　注4

⟨⟨好奇心を刺激する疑問の背後に隠されている⟩科学を探求する⟩アメリカの人気テレビ番組，⟨『ミス・バスターズ』での⟩ある実験が，［植物は（［（静かな場所に）置かれるの］と対照的に）（（⟨人の話す⟩声に）さらされると）より大きく育つこと］を示しました。

⑤ (However), their sample size was too small (to confirm the theory).
　　　　　　　 S　　　　 V　 C

（しかしながら），（その推論を立証するには）実験に使われたサンプル数は少なすぎました。

第3段落 人が話す時に出す二酸化炭素で植物が育つという説は，少量すぎて大差ないとも言われる。

① The other theory 〈that explains [why plants might grow better (when people
　　S　　　　　　　　　　　　　　　　　　　　　V'①
talk to them)]〉 is [that people provide them (with carbon dioxide, a gas 〈they
　　　　　　　　　V　C　　S'②　　　V'②　　O'②
require (for the production 〈of their food〉)〉)].

注5

〈[(人々が話しかけると) なぜ植物がより大きく育つことがあるのか] を説明する〉別の説は [〈〈植物が
〈〈栄養分の〉 生産に) 必要とする〉気体，二酸化炭素を) 人が供給するというもの] です。

② Humans release carbon dioxide (when they exhale) (as well as when they
　　S　　V　　　O　　　　　　　　S'①　V'①　　　　　　　　　S'②
speak).
V'②

人間は (話す時と同様に) (息を吐く時) 二酸化炭素を放出します。

③ (On the other hand), some experts say [that the carbon dioxide 〈produced
　　　　　　　　　　　　S　　　　V　　O　　　　　　　　　　S'
(from speech)〉 is too little (to make a significant difference)].
　　　　　　　　V'　　C'

(その一方で)，[〈(話しかけることから) 生み出される〉二酸化炭素は量が少なすぎるので (たいした
違いは生じない)] と述べている専門家もいます。

第4段落 議論は決着していないが，よい効果をもたらす可能性があるので，植物に話しかけてみよう。

① This debate has not been settled, but it's safe [to say [that [talking (to
　　S①　　　　　V①　　　　　　　　S②V②　C②　　　　　　　　　　S'
plants)] may offer them benefits]].
　　　　　V'　　O'　　O'

この議論はまだ決着がついていませんが，[[(植物に) 話しかけること] は植物にとってよい効果をも
たらす可能性がある] と言っても] 過言ではないでしょう。

② So, (the next time you need to relieve some stress or boast (about your
　　　　　　　　　S'　　V'①　　　　　　O'①　　　　　　V'②
latest accomplishment)), why not talk (to a plant)?
　　　　　　　　　　　　　　　　V

注7

ですから，(今度あなたが自分のストレスを和らげたり (自分が成し遂げたばかりの成果を) 自慢した
りする必要を感じた時には)，(植物に) 話しかけてみたらどうでしょうか。

注1 might have Vpp は「V したことがあるかもしれない」という意味で，過去のことを推測する
　　場合に使う表現。

注2 not only ... but ... は「…するばかりではなく，…する」という意味。not only の直後には，
　　疑問文のような倒置形が続く。

注3 such as や like は「～のように」という意味の表現。これらの表現の直後には，名詞だけでな
　　く，この文のように前置詞句などが続くこともある。

注4 as opposed to ～は「～とは反対に」という意味で，対比するものを挙げる場合に使う表現。

注5 carbon dioxide の直後のカンマは，これを直後の a gas ... に同格的に言い換えるはたらきを
　　している。このように，人名や専門的な用語をカンマを使って言い換えることがある。

注6 on the other hand は「その一方で」という意味で，前に書かれていることと対比される内容
　　を直後に述べる場合に使われる。

注7 the next time S V は「次に S が V する時」という意味の副詞節のはたらきをする。

サイトトランスレーション

⇒別冊 p.6 〜 7

1 If you spend any time /	あなたが時間を過ごしたら
in flower shops /	花屋で
or the gardening section /	またはガーデニング用品売り場
of home improvement stores, /	ホームセンターの,
you might have come across /	あなたは出くわすかもしれません
an unusual piece of advice: /	変わったアドバイスに,
"Make sure /	「忘れずに
you talk /	話してください
to your plants." //	あなたの植物に。」
Even Prince Charles of England claims /	イギリスのチャールズ皇太子でさえ言っています
that not only does he talk /	自分が話しかけているだけでなく
to his plants, /	植物に,
but they respond /	それらも返事をしている
as well. //	同様に。
While this might sound /	これは聞こえるかもしれませんが
like nonsense, /	ばかげているように,
some evidence suggests /	いくつかの証拠が示しています
that talking to plants is, /	植物に話しかけることは…であると,
in fact, /	実際に,
good for them. //	それらのためになる。
Scientists have been interested /	科学者たちはずっと関心を持っています
in this topic /	この話題に

for more than one hundred years, /	100 年以上も,
and researchers have come up with /	そして研究者たちは考え出しています
at least /	少なくとも
two possible explanations /	2 つのありうる説明を
for the link /	その関係について
between speech and plant health. //	話しかけることと植物の健康状態との間の。
2 One explanation is /	1 つの説明は…です
that plants react /	植物が反応しているというもの
to vibrations /	振動に
in their surroundings. //	それらの周囲の。
These vibrations are like signals /	この振動は信号のようなものです
that are essential /	不可欠である
for plants to grow. //	植物が成長するために。
If plants experience no vibrations, /	もし植物が振動をまったく経験しなければ,
such as in a silent room, /	静かな部屋などで,
they might grow slower. //	その成長は遅れるかもしれません。
One experiment /	ある実験は
on MythBusters, /	『ミス・バスターズ』での,
a popular American TV show /	アメリカの人気テレビ番組
that explores the science /	科学を探求する
behind thought-provoking questions, /	好奇心を刺激する疑問の背後に隠れている,
indicated /	示しました
that plants grew better /	植物がより大きく育つことを
when they were exposed /	それらがさらされると

27

to the sound of human speech /	人の話し声に
as opposed to being left in silence. //	静かな場所に置かれるのと対照的に。
However, /	しかしながら,
their sample size was too small /	そのサンプル数が少なすぎました
to confirm the theory. //	その推論を立証するには。
3 The other theory /	別の説は
that explains why plants might grow better /	なぜ植物がより大きく育つことがあるのかを説明する
when people talk to them /	人々がそれらに話しかけると
is that people provide them /	人々がそれらに供給するというものです
with carbon dioxide, /	二酸化炭素を,
a gas /	気体
they require /	それらが必要とする
for the production /	生産のために
of their food. //	栄養分の。
Humans release /	人間は放出します
carbon dioxide /	二酸化炭素を
when they exhale /	息を吐く時に
as well as /	同様に
when they speak. //	話す時。
On the other hand, /	その一方で,
some experts say /	何人かの専門家たちは言っています
that the carbon dioxide produced /	二酸化炭素は生み出された
from speech /	話しかけることから

is too little to make /	少なすぎるので生じない
a significant difference. //	大きな違いを。
4 This debate has not been settled, /	この議論はまだ決着がついていません,
but it's safe to say /	しかしそれは言っても過言ではありません
that talking to plants /	植物に話しかけることは
may offer them benefits. //	それらによい効果をもたらす可能性がある。
So, /	ですから,
the next time /	次回
you need to relieve some stress /	あなたがストレスを和らげる必要がある
or boast about your latest accomplishment, /	またはあなたの最近の成果を自慢する,
why not talk /	話しかけてみてはどうでしょうか
to a plant? //	植物に。

Time to Talk to Your Plants

If you spend any time in flower shops or the gardening section of home improvement stores, you might have come across an unusual piece of advice: "Make sure you talk to your plants." Even Prince Charles of England claims that not only does he talk to his plants, but they respond as well. While this might sound like nonsense, some evidence suggests that talking to plants is, in fact, good for them. Scientists have been interested in this topic for more than one hundred years, and researchers have come up with at least two possible explanations for the link between speech and plant health.

One explanation is that plants react to vibrations in their surroundings. These vibrations are like signals that are essential for plants to grow. If plants experience no vibrations, such as in a silent room, they might grow slower. One experiment on MythBusters, a popular American TV show that explores the science behind thought-provoking questions, indicated that plants grew better when they were exposed to the sound of human speech as opposed to being left in silence. However, their sample size was too small to confirm the theory.

The other theory that explains why plants might grow better when people talk to them is that people provide them with carbon dioxide, a gas they require for the production of their food. Humans release carbon dioxide when they exhale as well as when they speak. On the other hand, some experts say that the carbon dioxide produced from speech is too little to make a significant difference.

This debate has not been settled, but it's safe to say that talking to plants may offer them benefits. So, the next time you need to relieve some stress or boast about your latest accomplishment, why not talk to a plant?

植物と話すべき時

　あなたが花屋やホームセンターのガーデニング用品売り場で時間を過ごしていると，変わったアドバイスをもらうかもしれません，「あなたの植物には忘れずに話しかけてあげてください」と。イギリスのチャールズ皇太子でさえ，自分が植物に話しかけているだけでなく，植物の方でも返事をしてくれると言っています。これは，ばかげているように聞こえるかもしれませんが，植物に話しかけることは，実際に，その植物のためになると示す証拠があります。科学者たちは，この話題に100年以上も関心を持っており，研究者たちは，話しかけることと植物の健康状態との関係について少なくとも2つのありうる説明を考え出しています。

　1つの説明は，植物が周囲の振動に反応しているというものです。その振動は，植物が成長するために不可欠な信号のようなものです。もし植物が静かな部屋などに置かれていて振動を経験しなければ，その成長は遅れるかもしれません。好奇心を刺激する疑問の背後に隠されている科学を探求する『ミス・バスターズ（伝説撲滅隊／邦題：怪しい伝説）』というアメリカの人気テレビ番組で行われた実験では，植物が人の話し声にさらされると，静かな場所に置かれる場合よりもより大きく育つことが示されました。しかしながら，この推論を立証するには，実験に使われたサンプル数は少なすぎました。

　人が話しかけると，なぜ植物がより大きく育つことがあるのかを説明する別の説は，植物が栄養分の生産に必要とする気体である二酸化炭素を人間が供給するからというものです。人間は息を吐く時に二酸化炭素を放出しますが，それは話す時も同様です。その一方で，話しかける時に生み出される二酸化炭素は量が少なすぎるので，たいした違いは生じないと述べている専門家もいます。

　この議論はまだ決着がついていませんが，植物に話しかけることは植物にとってよい効果をもたらす可能性があると言っても過言ではないでしょう。ですから，今度あなたが自分のストレスを和らげたり，自分が成し遂げたばかりの成果を自慢したりする必要を感じた時には，植物に話しかけてみたらどうでしょうか。

解答と解説

解答

(1) ③　　(2) ④　　(3) ②

解説

(1) 空所を含む文の後に，There are thousands of oils available to buy, and they have created a huge industry: aromatherapy. (数千種類のオイルが購入でき，それがアロマセラピーという巨大産業を生み出しています。)と続くので，その文脈に最も合う 3 が正解。

選択肢の和訳

× 1 深刻な病気の治療に使用されている

× 2 最先端の研究に貢献した

○ 3 市場で爆発的に普及している

× 4 より高価になり始めた

(2) 空所を含む文の前半に，These ancient people were well aware that essential oils have the power to improve health and enhance living spaces(このような昔の人たちは，エッセンシャルオイルには健康を増進させ，生活空間を改善させる力があることをよく知っていた)とある。であれば，今日のエッセンシャルオイルの普及にも驚かないと考えられる。正解は 4。

選択肢の和訳

× 1 見つけるのが難しくなっている

× 2 今日，博物館で見つけることができる

× 3 安全に食べたり飲んだりできる

○ 4 多くのお店で棚に並んでいる

(3) 空所の前には，消費者の疑念が述べられている。それをサポートする形で，空所の後には，質のバラつきについての記述がある。マイナスの内容を述べる前置きとなる 2 が正解。1 の Therefore は，直前の内容が理由となるわけではないので使えない。

選択肢の和訳

× 1 それゆえに

○ 2 残念なことに

× 3 むしろ

× 4 それどころか

語句

〈タイトル〉

☐ aromatherapy　（名）アロマセラピー，芳香療法

☐ more than just ～　単に～にとどまらない

〈第 1 段落〉

☐ essential oil　エッセンシャルオイル，精油

☐ explode in the marketplace　市場で急激に拡大する，爆発的に増える

☐ establish　（動）～を作る

☐ relaxing atmosphere　リラックスさせる雰囲気

☐ inviting　（形）誘惑するような，心地よい

〈第 2 段落〉

☐ natural substance　自然［天然］物質

☐ tree bark　樹皮

☐ process　（動）～を処理する

☐ extract　（動）～を抽出する

☐ concentrated　（形）高濃度の

☐ steam　（動）蒸す

☐ press　（動）圧搾する

☐ bury　（動）～を埋葬する

☐ lift someone's mood　～の気分を高める

☐ be well aware　十分に意識している，よく知っている

☐ enhance　（動）～を向上させる，さらによくする

☐ line　（動）～を埋めつくす，～に並べる

〈第 3 段落〉

☐ diffuser　（名）ディフューザー，拡散器

☐ scatter　（動）～を撒き散らす

☐ fine mist　細かい霧

構造確認 ※誤読した部分の確認に使用してください。

⇒別冊 p.8 ～ 9

第1段落 過去約10年でエッセンシャルオイルは急激に普及しアロマセラピーという巨大産業を生んだ。

① (In the last decade or so), "essential oils" have exploded (in the
　　　　　　　　　　　　　　　　　　　　S　　　　　　　V
marketplace).

(過去10年ほどの間に)，「エッセンシャルオイル」は (市場の中で) 爆発的に普及しています。

② There are thousands of oils ⟨available to buy⟩, and they have created a
　　　　V①　　　　S①　　　　　　　　　　　　　　　　　　　S②　　　V②
huge industry: aromatherapy.
　　　　　O②

⟨購入可能な⟩ 数千種類のオイルがあり，それがアロマセラピーという巨大産業を生み出しています。

③ Yoga studios use peppermint oil (to establish a relaxing atmosphere), hotels
　　S①　　　V①　　O①　　　　　　　　　　　　　　　　　　　　　　　　S②
use rose oil (to make the rooms smell pleasant and inviting), and people
V②　O②　　　　　　　　　　　　　　　　　　　　　　　　　　　　　S③
use lavender oil (in their homes) (to promote healthy sleep).
V③　　O③

ヨガ教室はペパーミントオイルを使って (リラックスできる雰囲気を作り出し)，ホテルはローズオイ
ルを使って (客室を心地よく魅惑的な香りにし)，人々は (自宅で) ラベンダーオイルを使って (健康的
な眠りの助けにしています)。

④ So what are these oils, and how did this boom start?
　　　C①　V①　　S①　　　　　　　V②　　　S②

では，こうしたオイルはどのようなもので，このブームはどのようにして始まったのでしょうか。

第2段落 エッセンシャルオイルはさまざまな天然物質から作られていてその利用には長い歴史がある。

① Essential oils are made (from plants, herbs, fruits, and many other natural
　　　S　　　　V
substances, ⟨such as tree bark and even flowers⟩).

エッセンシャルオイルは (植物やハーブ，果物，そして⟨樹皮やさらには花といった⟩，そのほかのい
ろいろな天然物質から) 作られています。

② These materials are processed (in several ways) (in order to extract
    S   V

concentrated forms ⟨of their oils⟩).

こうした材料は (⟨それらのオイルの⟩高濃度抽出のために) (いくつかの方法で) 処理されます。

③ These processes include steps ⟨such as [steaming (with hot water)] or
    S   V   O

[pressing (with stones)]⟩.

これらの処理方法には⟨[(熱湯で) 蒸す] または [(石で) 押しつぶす] などの⟩手段が含まれています。

④ (If these sound (like old-fashioned techniques)), you're right—the use ⟨of
    S'   V'   S① V① C①   S②

essential oils⟩ (actually) has a long history.
                      V②   O②

(これらが (旧式の技術のように) 聞こえるとしたら), そのとおりです——⟨エッセンシャルオイル
の⟩利用には (実は) 長い歴史があるのです。

⑤ The ancient Egyptians had machines ⟨to extract oils (from plants)⟩, and
        S①   V①   O①

they used these oils (to prepare bodies to be buried).
 S② V②   O②

古代エジプト人は⟨(植物から) オイルを絞り出す⟩装置を持っていて, こうしたオイルを (埋葬する前
の遺体を処理するのに) 使っていました。

⑥ Some Asian cultures used oils (both to cure illnesses and to lift their
      S   V   O

moods).

アジアの文化圏の中には (病気を治療したり気分を高揚させたりするために) オイルを使っていたとこ
ろもあります。

⑦ These ancient people were well aware [that essential oils have the power
   S①   V①   O①   S'①   V'①   O'①

〈to improve health and enhance living spaces〉], so they (probably)
                                             S②

would not be surprised [that (today) essential oils line the shelves (at many
  V②   O②   S'②   V'②   O'②

stores)].

こうした昔の人たちは [エッセンシャルオイルには〈健康を増進させ，生活空間を改善させる〉力があること] をよく知っていたので，彼らは (おそらく) [(今日) エッセンシャルオイルが (多くの店の) 棚にずらりと並んでいること] に驚かないでしょう。

第3段落 化学物質はディフューザーが空中拡散する細かい霧によって呼吸または皮膚から吸収される。

① Most people (today) use essential oils (with the help of a diffuser, 〈which is
    S   V   O   V'

a small device 〈that you fill (with water and a tiny amount of essential oil)〉).
   C'

(現在) 大半の人はエッセンシャルオイルを使うのに (ディフューザーの助けを借りていて，〈これは〈(水とごく少量のエッセンシャルオイルを) 入れる〉小型の装置です〉)。

② The diffuser (then) scatters a fine mist (up into the air).
    S   V   O

(そうすると) ディフューザーは細かい霧を (空中に) 拡散します。

③ The key chemicals 〈in the oils〉 are (then) inhaled or absorbed (through the
          S   V

skin).

(そうすると)〈オイル中の〉主要な化学物質が呼吸で吸い込まれたり (皮膚から) 吸収されたりします。

第4段落 エッセンシャルオイルの製造業者が主張する効果が事実かを判断するのはほぼ不可能である。

① Some wonder [if these oils are as effective as manufacturers would have
  S   V   O   S'   V'   C'

you believe].
                                        ➡注4

[このようなオイルに製造業者があなたに信じ込ませようとしているほどの効果があるのか] 疑問に思う人もいます。

② (Unfortunately), there is not enough evidence ⟨to give a definite answer⟩.
                 V   S

(残念ながら)，⟨はっきりした答えを出すのに⟩十分な証拠はありません。

③ There are a great variety of essential oils (in shops), and not all of them are
     V①   S①   S②

produced (with the same standards ⟨of quality⟩).   注5
 V②

(お店には) 多種多様なエッセンシャルオイルがあり，そのすべてが (同じ ⟨品質の⟩ 基準で) 生産され
ているわけではありません。

④ It is, (therefore), almost impossible [to judge [if the manufacturers' claims
 S V   C   S'

are true or not]].
 V'   C'

(したがって)，[[製造業者の主張が事実かどうか] を判断するの] は，ほぼ不可能です。

注1 explode は「爆発する」という意味だが，比喩的に爆発的な増加や波及を表す場合によく用い
     られる。

注2 A, B, and C は，「A と B と C」というように同種の要素を並べる場合に用いられるが，ここ
     では3つの文が並べられている。

注3 both A and B は「A と B の両方」という意味だが，A と B の部分には，名詞だけでなく，さ
     まざまな要素を並べることができる。ここでは，副詞的用法の不定詞が並べられている。

注4 if は「かどうか」という意味で用いられることもあり，wonder if S V で「S が V するかどう
     か疑問に思う」という意味になる。

注5 not all of them は部分否定の表現。「それらのすべてが…というわけではない」という意味。

サイトトランスレーション

1 In the last decade or so, /	過去 10 年ほどの間に,
"essential oils" have exploded /	「エッセンシャルオイル」は爆発的に普及しています
in the marketplace. //	市場の中で。
There are thousands of oils /	数千種類のオイルがあります
available to buy, /	購入することの可能な,
and they have created /	そしてそれらが生み出しています
a huge industry: /	巨大産業を,
aromatherapy. //	アロマセラピー（という）。
Yoga studios use /	ヨガ教室は使います
peppermint oil /	ペパーミントオイルを
to establish a relaxing atmosphere, /	リラックスできる雰囲気を作り出すために,
hotels use /	ホテルは使います
rose oil /	ローズオイルを
to make the rooms smell pleasant and inviting, /	部屋を楽しく魅惑的な香りにするために,
and people use /	そして人々は使います
lavender oil /	ラベンダーオイルを
in their homes /	自宅で
to promote healthy sleep. //	健康的な眠りを助けるために。
So /	では
what are these oils, /	こうしたオイルはどのようなものでしょうか,
and how did this boom start? //	そしてこのブームはどのように始まったのでしょうか。

2 Essential oils are made /	エッセンシャルオイルは作られています
from plants, herbs, fruits, /	植物，ハーブ，果物から，
and many other natural substances, /	そしてそのほかのいろいろな天然物質，
such as tree bark and even flowers. //	樹皮やさらには花など（の）。
These materials are processed /	こうした材料は処理されます
in several ways /	いくつかの方法で
in order to extract /	抽出するために
concentrated forms /	高濃度の形態を
of their oils. //	それらのオイルの。
These processes include /	これらの処理方法は含んでいます
steps /	手段を
such as steaming with hot water /	熱湯で蒸すなどの
or pressing with stones. //	あるいは石で押しつぶす。
If these sound like old-fashioned techniques, /	これらが旧式の技術のように聞こえるとしたら，
you're right /	そのとおりです
— the use of essential oils /	―エッセンシャルオイルの利用は
actually has a long history. //	実は長い歴史があるのです。
The ancient Egyptians had machines /	古代エジプト人は装置を持っていました
to extract oils /	オイルを絞り出す
from plants, /	植物から，
and they used /	そして彼らは使っていました
these oils /	これらのオイルを
to prepare bodies /	遺体を準備するために

to be buried. //	埋葬される。
Some Asian cultures used /	アジアの文化圏の中には使っていたところもあります
oils /	オイルを
both to cure illnesses /	病気を治療するためにも
and to lift their moods. //	そして気分を高揚させたりするために。
These ancient people were well aware /	このような昔の人たちはよく知っていました
that essential oils have the power /	エッセンシャルオイルには力があることを
to improve health /	健康を増進するため
and enhance living spaces, /	そして生活空間を改善させる,
so they probably would not be surprised /	だから彼らはおそらく驚くことはないでしょう
that today /	今日…であることを
essential oils line /	エッセンシャルオイルが並んでいる
the shelves /	棚に
at many stores. //	多くのお店の。
3 Most people today use /	現在,大半の人は使います
essential oils /	エッセンシャルオイルを
with the help of a diffuser, /	ディフューザーの助けを借りて,
which is a small device /	それは小型の装置です
that you fill /	入れる
with water /	水を
and a tiny amount of essential oil. //	そしてごく少量のエッセンシャルオイルを。
The diffuser then scatters /	そうするとディフューザーは拡散します
a fine mist up into the air. //	細かい霧を空中に。

The key chemicals in the oils /	オイルの中の主要な化学物質が
are then inhaled /	そうすると呼吸で吸い込まれます
or absorbed through the skin. //	あるいは皮膚から吸収されます。
4 Some wonder /	疑問に思う人もいます
if these oils are as effective /	このようなオイルに効果があるのかどうか
as manufacturers would have you believe. //	製造業者があなたに信じさせようとしているほどの。
Unfortunately, /	残念ながら,
there is not enough evidence /	十分な証拠はありません
to give a definite answer. //	はっきりした答えを出すのに。
There are a great variety of essential oils /	多種多様なエッセンシャルオイルがあります
in shops, /	お店には,
and not all of them are produced /	そしてそれらのすべてが生産されているわけではありません
with the same standards of quality. //	同じ品質基準で。
It is, therefore, almost impossible /	それは, したがって, ほぼ不可能です
to judge /	判断するのは
if the manufacturers' claims are true or not. //	製造業者の主張が事実かどうかを。

Aromatherapy: More Than Just a Pretty Smell

In the last decade or so, "essential oils" have exploded in the marketplace. There are thousands of oils available to buy, and they have created a huge industry: aromatherapy. Yoga studios use peppermint oil to establish a relaxing atmosphere, hotels use rose oil to make the rooms smell pleasant and inviting, and people use lavender oil in their homes to promote healthy sleep. So what are these oils, and how did this boom start?

Essential oils are made from plants, herbs, fruits, and many other natural substances, such as tree bark and even flowers. These materials are processed in several ways in order to extract concentrated forms of their oils. These processes include steps such as steaming with hot water or pressing with stones. If these sound like old-fashioned techniques, you're right — the use of essential oils actually has a long history. The ancient Egyptians had machines to extract oils from plants, and they used these oils to prepare bodies to be buried. Some Asian cultures used oils both to cure illnesses and to lift their moods. These ancient people were well aware that essential oils have the power to improve health and enhance living spaces, so they probably would not be surprised that today essential oils line the shelves at many stores.

Most people today use essential oils with the help of a diffuser, which is a small device that you fill with water and a tiny amount of essential oil. The diffuser then scatters a fine mist up into the air. The key chemicals in the oils are then inhaled or absorbed through the skin.

Some wonder if these oils are as effective as manufacturers would have you believe. Unfortunately, there is not enough evidence to give a definite answer. There are a great variety of essential oils in shops, and not all of them are produced with the same standards of quality. It is, therefore, almost impossible to judge if the manufacturers' claims are true or not.

アロマセラピー：単によい香り以上の効果

　過去10年ほどの間に，「エッセンシャルオイル」は市場の中で爆発的に普及しています。数千種類のオイルが購入でき，それがアロマセラピーという巨大産業を生み出しています。ヨガ教室はペパーミントオイルを使ってリラックスできる雰囲気を作り出し，ホテルはローズオイルを使って客室を心地よく魅惑的な香りにし，人々は自宅でラベンダーオイルを使って健康的な眠りの助けにしています。では，こうしたオイルはどのようなもので，今のブームはどのように始まったのでしょうか。

　エッセンシャルオイルは植物やハーブ，果物，そして樹皮やさらには花など，そのほかのいろいろな天然物質から作られています。こうした材料は，それに含まれるオイルを高濃度で抽出するために，いくつかの方法で処理されます。その処理方法には，熱湯で蒸したり，石で押しつぶしたりするなどの手段が含まれています。これが旧式の技術のように聞こえるとしたら，そのとおりです――エッセンシャルオイルの利用には，実は長い歴史があるのです。古代エジプト人は植物からオイルを絞り出す装置を持っていて，そのオイルを埋葬する前の遺体の処理に使っていました。アジアの文化圏の中には，病気を治療したり，気分を高揚させたりするためにオイルを使っていたところもあります。そのような昔の人たちは，エッセンシャルオイルには健康を増進させ，生活空間を改善させる力があることをよく知っていたので，今日，エッセンシャルオイルが多くの店の棚にずらりと並んでいることに，おそらく驚くことはないでしょう。

　現在，大半の人はエッセンシャルオイルを使うのにディフューザーの助けを借りていますが，これは，水とごく少量のエッセンシャルオイルを入れて使う小型の装置です。そうするとディフューザーは，細かい霧を空中に拡散します。そうすると，オイルに含まれる主要な化学物質が呼吸で吸い込まれたり，皮膚から吸収されたりします。

　このようなオイルに，製造業者があなたに信じ込ませようとしているほどの効果があるのか疑問に思う人もいます。残念ながら，はっきりした答えを出すのに十分な証拠はありません。店頭には多種多様なエッセンシャルオイルがあり，そのすべてが同じ品質基準で生産されているわけではありません。したがって，製造業者の主張が事実かどうかを判断するのは，ほぼ不可能です。

⇒別冊 p.10 ～ 11

解答と解説

解答

(1) ④　　(2) ①　　(3) ④

解説

(1) 空所の後の文を見ると，研究者たちが今でもユーモアについて解明しようとしている（つまり，いまだに解明されていない）ことがわかる。よって，正解は 4。

選択肢の和訳

× 1 文化によって異なる　　　　　　× 2 ついに発見された

× 3 健康上の利益を提供している　　○ 4 かなり謎のままである

(2) 空所の後にセミコロンがあり，after all, streets are homes for stray cats, not statues.（というのは，通りというものは野良猫が住むところであり，彫像があるべき場所ではない。）という文が続いている。この内容と文脈的に合う 1 が正解。

選択肢の和訳

○ 1 世界はどうあるべきか　　× 2 彫像は何でできているか

× 3 都市を旅行すべき時　　　× 4 歩いても安全な場所

(3) 空所の前を見ると，彫像の例について，それが「世の中がどうあるべきか」に反するものであること，そして悪意のない出来事であるということが述べられている。それらはマグロウの説にあるユーモアの 2 つの要素と一致する。正解は 4。

選択肢の和訳

× 1 事後に　　　　　　　　× 2 さらに

× 3 それにもかかわらず　　○ 4 したがって

語句

〈第 1 段落〉

□ satirical	（形）風刺の
□ romantic comedy	ラブ・コメディ
□ integral	（形）不可欠な
□ develop a theory	理論を構築する
□ benign	（形）無害な
□ violation	（名）違反，侵害
□ state that ...	…と述べる
□ specific	（形）明確な，特定の
□ harmless	（形）悪意のない，無害の

〈第 2 段落〉

□ look over one's shoulder	肩越しに見る，後ろを振り返る
□ figure	（名）姿，人影
□ stare down at ～	～をじっと見おろす
□ back away from ～	～から後ずさりをする

〈第 3 段落〉

□ framework	（名）枠組み，構造
□ evaluate	（動）～を評価する
□ stray cat	野良猫

構造確認 ※誤読した部分の確認に使用してください。

⇒別冊 p.10 ～ 11

第 1 段落 ユーモアは人が生きていく上で欠かせない要素だが，説明するとなると未だ謎に満ちている。

① **(From** the satirical plays ⟨of ancient Greece⟩**) (to** the romantic comedies

⟨found (in modern cinema)⟩**),** humor has always been an integral part ⟨of
　　　　　　　　　　　　　　　　　　　S　　　V　　　　　　　　　　C

the human experience⟩.

(⟨古代ギリシアの⟩風刺劇から) (⟨⟨(現代の映画で) 見られる⟩ラブ・コメディまで)，ユーモアはいつ
でも⟨人が生きていく上で⟩欠かせない要素です。

② The explanation ⟨for humor⟩, (however), remains quite mysterious.
　　　　S　　　　　　　　　　　　　　　　　　V　　　　C

(しかし)，⟨ユーモアの⟩解釈は，かなり謎に満ちたままです。

③ Modern researchers are still working (to explain exactly [what makes
　　　　S　　　　　　　V　　　　　　　　　　　　　　　　S'　　　V'

something funny]).
　　　O'　　　C'

現代の研究者たちは，今でもまだ，(実際に [何が物事をおかしくするのか] 解明し) ようとしていま
す。

④ One ⟨of the leading theories ⟨about humor⟩⟩ was developed (by
　　　S　　　　　　　　　　　　　　　　　　　　　V

psychologist Peter McGraw).

⟨⟨ユーモアに関する⟩有力な説の⟩1 つは (心理学者のピーター・マグロウによって) 練り上げられま
した。

⑤ His "Benign Violation Theory" states [that (for something to be funny), it
　　　　S　　　　　　　　　　　　V　　O　　　　　　　　　　　　　　　S'

must contain two specific elements].
　　V'　　　　　　　　O'

彼の「無害な逸脱理論」は [(あることがおかしい状態であるためには)，2 つの明確な要素を含む必要
がある] と明言しています。

⑥ The first is [that it must go (against our basic ideas ⟨about [how people and objects ⟨in the world⟩ should be]⟩)].

　　S　　V　C　S'　　V'

第一に [それが (⟨[⟨世の中の⟩ 人や物がどうあるべきか] についての⟩ 私たちの基本的な考えの逆を) 行くものである必要があるの] です。

⑦ The second is [that the action must be benign, meaning harmless].

　　S　　　V　C　　S'　　　　　V'　　　　C'

第二に [その行為は無害，つまり悪意がないものでなければならないということ] です。

第2段落 暗い通りで人が見おろしていると思い怯えた直後それが彫像と気づいた出来事はおかしいか。

① Consider the following example.

　　V　　　　　O

次の例を考えてみてください。

② Imagine [you and your friend are visiting a new city, and you're walking (on a dark street) (late at night)].

　V　　O　　S'①　　　　　V'①　　　　O'①　　　　　　S'②　　V'②

[あなたと友人が，初めて訪れた町にいて，(夜遅く) (暗い通りを) 歩いている] と想像してみましょう。

③ You look (over your shoulder), and (suddenly) you notice a huge figure staring down (at you).

　S①　V①　　　　　　　　　　　　　　S②　V②　　O②

あなたたちが (後ろを振り返って) 見ると，(突然) とても大きな人間が (あなたたちを) 見おろしているのに気づきます。

④ You and your friend both react (in fear) and back away (from the figure).

　　　S　　　　　　V①　　　　　　V②

あなたも友人も (恐怖で) 反応し (その人物から) 後ずさりします。

⑤ (However), (after a moment), you realize [it was just a statue].

　　　　　　　　　　　　　　S　V　O'S' V'　　C'

(しかし)，(その後すぐに)，あなたたちは [それが単なる彫像だった] と気づきます。

⑥ Was this event funny?
　　 V 　　　 S 　　 C

この出来事はおかしかったでしょうか。

第3段落 マグロウの理論では，世の中の基本的な考え方から逸脱し，かつ無害なこの出来事はおかしい。

① McGraw's theory 〈of humor〉 provides a framework 〈through which it
　　　　 S 　　　　　　　　　　　　　 V 　　　 O 　　　　　　　　　　　 S'

can be evaluated〉.
　　 V'

〈ユーモアについての〉マグロウの理論は〈それを判断するための〉枠組みを提供してくれます。

② The fact 〈that the statue was (in the street (in the middle of the night))〉 likely
　 S① 　　　 S'① 　　　　　　 V'①

went (against your idea 〈about [how the world should be]〉); (after all),
 V'① 　　　　　　　　　　　　　　　　　　 S'② 　　　　　 V'②

streets are homes 〈for stray cats, not statues〉.
 S② 　 V'② 　 C②

〈その影像が（（真夜中の）通りに）あったという〉事実はおそらく（〈[世の中がどうあるべきか] につい
ての〉あなたの考え方に反して）いたでしょう，（いずれにしても），通り（というもの）は〈影像では
なく，野良猫の〉住むところです。

③ (Therefore), the event did contain a violation.
　　　　　　　　　　 S 　　 V 　　　 O

（したがって），この出来事には明らかに１つの逸脱が含まれていたのです。

④ This event was also benign (because, (of course), statues are harmless).
　　 S 　　 V 　　　 C 　　　　　　　　　　　　　 S' 　 V' 　 C'

また，この出来事は無害です，（なぜなら，（当然ながら），影像というものは悪意がないものから
です）。

⑤ (Therefore), this event would have indeed been funny (according to
　　　　　　　　　 S 　　 V 　　　　　　　　　　 C

McGraw's theory).

（したがって），（マグロウの理論によれば）この出来事は確かにおかしかったはずです。

注1　however（しかしながら）という副詞は，一般論の後で，重要トピックを紹介する場合に使われることがある。ここでは，この前文の第1文が一般論で，文章全体のトピックはこの第2文。

注2　不定詞の直前に意味上の主語を置く場合には，for という前置詞を用いる。

注3　この文の The first と次の文の The second はセットで用いられている。両方とも leading theory が直後に略されていると考えるとよい。

注4　notice ～ Ving は「～がV しているのに気づく」という意味。notice のような知覚動詞の直後には，このように名詞＋分詞の形を続けることがある。

注5　the fact that S V は「S がV するという事実」という意味。この that は同格のはたらきをし，the fact に続く that 節が the fact の内容説明となっている。

注6　however（しかしながら）が逆接で前後の文の意味をつなぐのに対して，therefore（それゆえに）は順接で前後の文の意味をつなぐ。

サイトトランスレーション

⇒別冊 p.10 ~ 11

1 From the satirical plays /	風刺劇から
of ancient Greece /	古代ギリシアの
to the romantic comedies /	ラブ・コメディまで
found in modern cinema, /	現代の映画で見られる,
humor has always been an integral part /	ユーモアはつねに不可欠な要素になっています
of the human experience. //	人間の経験の。
The explanation for humor, /	ユーモアについての解釈は,
however, /	しかし,
remains quite mysterious. //	かなり謎に満ちたままです。
Modern researchers are still working /	現代の研究者たちは今でもまだしようとしています
to explain /	解明を
exactly /	実際に
what makes something funny. //	何が物事をおかしくするのか。
One of the leading theories /	有力な説の1つは
about humor /	ユーモアに関する
was developed /	練り上げられました
by psychologist Peter McGraw. //	心理学者のピーター・マグロウによって。
His "Benign Violation Theory" states /	彼の「無害な逸脱理論」は述べています
that for something to be funny, /	あることがおかしいためには,
it must contain two specific elements. //	2つの明確な要素が含まれている必要があります。
The first is /	第一に…です
that it must go against our basic ideas /	それが基本的な考えに逆らうものでなくてはならない

about how people and objects in the world should be. //	世の中の人や物がどうあるべきかについて。
The second is /	第二に…です
that the action must be benign, /	その行為は無害でなければならない,
meaning harmless. //	つまり悪意がないもの。
2 Consider the following example. //	次の例を考えてみてください。
Imagine /	想像してみましょう
you and your friend are visiting /	あなたと友人は訪れています
a new city, /	新しい（初めての）町を,
and you're walking /	そしてあなたたちは歩いています
on a dark street /	暗い通りを
late at night. //	夜遅く。
You look over your shoulder, /	あなたたちは後ろを振り向きます,
and suddenly /	そして突然
you notice /	あなたは気づきます
a huge figure /	とても大きな人間が
staring down at you. //	あなたたちを見おろしている。
You and your friend both react /	あなたも友人も反応します
in fear /	恐怖で
and back away /	そして後ずさりします
from the figure. //	その人物から。
However, /	しかし,
after a moment, /	その後すぐに,
you realize /	あなたたちは気づきます

it was just a statue. //	それが単なる彫像だったと。
Was this event funny? //	この出来事はおかしかったでしょうか。
3 McGraw's theory of humor provides /	マグロウのユーモアの理論は提供します
a framework /	枠組みを
through which it can be evaluated. //	それが評価される。
The fact /	事実は
that the statue was in the street /	その彫像が通りにあったという
in the middle of the night /	真夜中の
likely went against your idea /	おそらくあなたの考え方に反していたでしょう
about how the world should be; /	世界がどうあるべきかについての,
after all, /	いずれにしても,
streets are homes /	通りは住むところです
for stray cats, /	野良猫たちが,
not statues. //	彫像ではなく。
Therefore, /	したがって,
the event did contain /	この出来事は明らかに含んでいました
a violation. //	1つの逸脱を。
This event was also benign /	また, この出来事は無害でした
because, /	なぜなら,
of course, /	もちろん,
statues are harmless. //	彫像は悪意のないものです。
Therefore, /	したがって,
this event would have indeed been funny /	この出来事は確かにおかしかったでしょう
according to McGraw's theory. //	マグロウの理論によれば。

What Is Funny?

From the satirical plays of ancient Greece to the romantic comedies found in modern cinema, humor has always been an integral part of the human experience. The explanation for humor, however, remains quite mysterious. Modern researchers are still working to explain exactly what makes something funny. One of the leading theories about humor was developed by psychologist Peter McGraw. His "Benign Violation Theory" states that for something to be funny, it must contain two specific elements. The first is that it must go against our basic ideas about how people and objects in the world should be. The second is that the action must be benign, meaning harmless.

Consider the following example. Imagine you and your friend are visiting a new city, and you're walking on a dark street late at night. You look over your shoulder, and suddenly you notice a huge figure staring down at you. You and your friend both react in fear and back away from the figure. However, after a moment, you realize it was just a statue. Was this event funny?

McGraw's theory of humor provides a framework through which it can be evaluated. The fact that the statue was in the street in the middle of the night likely went against your idea about how the world should be; after all, streets are homes for stray cats, not statues. Therefore, the event did contain a violation. This event was also benign because, of course, statues are harmless. Therefore, this event would have indeed been funny according to McGraw's theory.

何がおかしいのか

　古代ギリシアの風刺劇から現代の映画で見かけるラブ・コメディまで，ユーモアはいつでも人が生きていく上で欠かせない要素です。しかし，ユーモアを解釈するとなると，かなり謎に満ちたままです。現代の研究者たちは，今でもまだ，実際に何が物事をおかしくするのか解明しようとしています。ユーモアに関する有力な説の1つは，心理学者のピーター・マグロウによって練り上げられました。彼の「無害な逸脱理論」の主張によると，あることがおかしいためには，2つの明確な要素が含まれている必要があります。第一に，それが世の中の人や物がどうあるべきかについての私たちの基本的な考えに逆らうものである必要があります。第二に，その行為は無害，つまり悪意がないものでなければならないということです。

　次の例を考えてみてください。あなたと友人が，初めて訪れた町にいて，夜遅く暗い通りを歩いていると想像してみましょう。あなたたちが後ろを振り向くと，突然，とても大きな人間が自分たちを見おろしているのに気づきます。あなたも友人も恐怖のあまり，その人物から後ずさりします。しかし，その後すぐに，あなたたちはそれが単なる彫像だったと気づきます。この出来事はおかしいでしょうか。

　マグロウのユーモアの理論は，それを判断するための枠組みを提供してくれます。その彫像が真夜中の通りに立っていたという事実はおそらく，世の中がどうあるべきかについての，あなたの考え方に反するでしょう。いずれにしても，通りというものは野良猫が住むところであり，彫像があるべき場所ではありません。したがって，この出来事には明らかに1つの逸脱が含まれていたのです。また，この出来事は無害です。なぜなら，当然ながら，彫像というものは悪意がないものだからです。したがって，マグロウの理論によれば，この出来事は確かにおかしかったはずです。

⇒別冊 p.12 ～ 13

解答と解説

解答

(1) ④　　(2) ④　　(3) ②

解説

(1) 2（節約）・3（会社設立）に関する記述は本文中にない。1 は「いくつかの株を購入することによって，お金を株式市場に投資すべきかどうか判断を下せる」という不自然な文になってしまう。正解は 4 で，株式の基本を説明している第 2 段落以降の内容ときれいにつながる。

選択肢の和訳

× 1 いくつかの株を購入する
× 2 確実にお金を節約する
× 3 自分の会社を始める
○ 4 基本を理解する

(2) 空所の前に「資金を投資するなら，さまざまな企業の株式を購入すべき」という記述があり，空所の後には「その中の 1 つが値を下げ始めたとしても，すべての資産の価値が落ち込むことにはならない」とある。この 2 つの文をつなぐ言葉として最も適当な 4 が正解。

選択肢の和訳

× 1 これにもかかわらず
× 2 例えば
× 3 そのうえ
○ 4 そうすることで

(3) 空所の後の but 以下の内容「安定した成長」と逆の意味を持つ 2 が正解。1（専門家がインデックス・ファンドを利用するか否か）に関する記述は本文中にないため，not likely to に続けて「可能性が低い」かどうかは判断できない。3・4 を入れると本文の内容と矛盾してしまう。

選択肢の和訳

× 1 専門家に人気がある
○ 2 莫大な財産をもたらす
× 3 多種多様な株式を持っている
× 4 お金を稼ぐ

語句

〈タイトル〉

□ stock market	株式市場
□ index fund	インデックス・ファンド

〈第 1 段落〉

□ go wild	熱狂する
□ trading floor	証券取引所の立会場
□ jump up and down	（上下に）飛び跳ねる
□ in delight	歓喜して
□ in disbelief	信じられないという様子で
□ ticker	（名）ティッカー，テロップ（証券取引の情報を遠隔地へ伝えて自動的に印字する機械，またはその機械によって印字された値段や数量などの情報）

□ incomprehensible	（形）不可解な
□ make an informed decision	情報に基づく決定を行う
□ hard-earned	苦労して稼いだ

〈第 2 段落〉

□ essentially	（副）本質的に
□ diversify	（動）（投資）を分散する
□ invested money	投資する金額，出資金

〈第 3 段落〉

□ trading broker	取引仲介業者，証券会社

構造確認 ※誤読した部分の確認に使用してください。

⇒別冊 p.12 ～ 13

第1段落 株式市場の基本を理解すれば自分のお金を投資すべきか十分な情報に基づいた判断を下せる。

① We have all seen pictures ⟨of businesspeople ⟨going wild (on the trading
  S   V   O
floor), jumping (up and down) (in delight) or (with their hands covering their

faces (in disbelief))⟩⟩.   ➡注1

私たちは誰でも⟨((証券取引所の) 立会場において) 大騒ぎしたり，(喜びで) (上下に) 跳んだり，((信
じられないと) 顔を手で覆ったりしている)⟩社員たちの⟩映像を見たことがあります。

② And we expect tickers ⟨of incomprehensible numbers and symbols⟩ to
      S   V   O
scroll (along the bottom ⟨of the television screen⟩) (during the business

report).

また (ビジネス関連のニュース中には) (⟨テレビ画面の⟩下部に) ⟨意味不明な数字や記号の⟩ティッカー
(テロップ) が次々に表示されていくものだと思っています。

③ But can anyone ⟨who doesn't live (in a world ⟨of balance sheets and
      V   S   V①
IPOs⟩)⟩ really understand [what's going on]?
                           O S'② V'②
しかし⟨(⟨バランスシートや IPO の⟩世界に) 生きていない (詳しくない)⟩人は実際に [何が起こって
いるのか] 理解できるでしょうか。

④ The answer is "yes" , and (by [understanding the basics]), you, too,
   S①   V① C①   S②
can make an informed decision ⟨about [whether to invest your hard-earned
    V②   O②
cash (in the stock market)]⟩.   ➡注2

答えは「できる」であり，([基本を理解すること] で)，あなたも，⟨[苦労して稼いだお金を (株式市場
に) 投資するかどうか] について⟩十分な情報に基づいた判断を下すことができます。

第2段落 資金すべてを少数の企業に投資せずに，さまざまな企業の株式を購入して分散すべきである。

① Investing is always a risk.
     S   V   C

投資とはつねにリスクが伴う行為です。

② (When you buy stock ⟨in a company⟩), you are (essentially) buying a piece
       S'① V'① O'①   S① V①   O①

⟨of that company⟩, and (if that company goes bankrupt), your piece is
                                 S'②   V'②   C'②   S②   V②

gone.
C②

(⟨ある会社の⟩株を買う時)，あなたは(本質的に)⟨その会社の⟩一部を買っているのであって，(その会社が倒産するようなことがあれば)，あなたの持ち分はなくなってしまいます。

③ (On the other hand), (if the company's value goes up), (then) the value ⟨of
                                S'   V'   S

your piece⟩ goes up (as well).
          V

(その一方で)，(会社の価値が上がると)，(その時は)⟨あなたの持ち分の⟩価値も(同様に)上がります。

④ This is why smart investors always give the same advice: Diversify,
     S   V C   S'   V'   O'

diversify, diversify.

注4

こういうわけで抜け目ない投資家はつねに同じようなアドバイスをします，(すなわち)分散，分散，そして分散(ということです)。

⑤ (Instead of putting all ⟨of your invested money⟩ (into one or two

companies)), you should buy stock ⟨in a variety of companies ⟨in different
             S   V   O

industries⟩⟩.

(⟨投資する資金の⟩すべてを(1つか2つの企業に)投資するのではなく)，⟨⟨異なる産業分野の⟩さまざまな企業の⟩株式を購入すべきなのです。

⑥ (That way), (if one ⟨of them⟩ starts to lose their value), you don't have to

                S'   V'   O'   S   V

watch all ⟨of your money⟩ sink down (with it). 注5

       O   C

(そうすることで)，(⟨そのうちの⟩1つが値を下げ始めたとしても)，(それで)⟨あなたの資産の⟩すべて (の価値) が落ち込むのを見なくてもよいのです。

第3段落 インデックス・ファンドは莫大な財産は産み出さないが，安定した成長をもたらす投資である。

① So which companies should you look for?

         O   V   S

それでは，どの企業を選ぶべきなのでしょうか。

② (Thankfully), you don't have to spend hours upon hours (looking for

              S   V   O

candidates yourself).

(ありがたいことに)，(自分で候補を探すのに) 何時間も費やす必要はありません。

③ Many trading brokers offer something ⟨called index funds⟩.

         S   V   O

多くの証券会社は⟨インデックス・ファンドと呼ばれる⟩ものを提供しています。

④ These funds are the collections ⟨of the stocks ⟨of companies ⟨in one ⟨of the

    S   V   C

major stock market indexes, ⟨like the Dow Jones or the S&P 500⟩⟩⟩⟩⟩. 注6

これらのファンドは⟨⟨⟨⟨⟨ダウ=ジョーンズやS＆P 500などの⟩，**主要な株式市場指数の⟩**いずれかにある⟩企業の⟩株式を⟩集めたものです。

⑤ An index fund is not likely to yield a vast fortune, but it is a solid

    S①   V①   O①   S②V②   C②

investment ⟨that offers stable growth⟩.

              V'   O'

インデックス・ファンドはそれほど莫大な財産を産み出しませんが，⟨安定した成長をもたらす⟩堅実な投資です。

⑥ (In fact), index funds (frequently) perform better (than professionals 〈who

　　　　　　　S　　　　　　　　　　　V

claim [that they can beat the market]〉).

　V'　　　　　O'

(実際), インデックス・ファンドは (〈[市場で優位に立つことができる] と主張する〉専門家よりも)
よりよい運用実績を残すことが (よく) あります。

注1　with 名詞＋分詞 は「〜を…の状態にしている」という意味で, 付属するものの状態を表すことができる。

注2　whether to V は「V するかどうか」という意味の名詞句を作ることができる。

注3　on the other hand は「その一方で」という意味で, 前に書かれていることと対比される内容を直後に述べる場合に使われる。

注4　this is why ... は「そういうわけで…」という意味で, 直前までの内容の結果を直後に示す場合に用いられる。

注5　that way は「そのようにして」という意味で, 直前に示された様態や方法によって, 直後のことが起こるような場合に用いられる。

注6　like という前置詞は, 直前の名詞の具体例を直後に示す場合に用いられる。この文では, the Dow Jones や the S&P 500 が, the major stock market indexes の例となっている。

サイトトランスレーション

⇒別冊 p.12 ～ 13

1 We have all seen /	私たちは誰でも見たことがあります
pictures /	光景を
of businesspeople /	社員たちの
going wild /	大騒ぎしている
on the trading floor, /	立会場で,
jumping up and down /	上下に飛び跳ねて
in delight /	喜びで
or with their hands covering their faces /	あるいは手で顔を覆っている
in disbelief. //	信じられないといった様子で。
And we expect /	そして私たちは思っています
tickers /	ティッカー（テロップ）が
of incomprehensible numbers and symbols /	意味不明な数字や記号の
to scroll /	次々に表示されていく
along the bottom of the television screen /	テレビ画面の下部に
during the business report. //	ビジネス関連のニュース中には。
But /	しかし
can anyone who doesn't live in a world /	世界に生きていない人はできるでしょうか
of balance sheets /	バランスシートの
and IPOs /	そして IPO
really understand /	実際に理解することが
what's going on? //	何が起こっているのか。

The answer is "yes," /	その答えは「できる」です,
and by understanding the basics, /	そして基本を理解することで,
you, too, can make /	あなたは, また, することができます
an informed decision /	十分な情報に基づいた判断を
about whether to invest /	投資すべきかどうかについて
your hard-earned cash /	あなたの苦労して稼いだお金を
in the stock market. //	株式市場に。
② Investing is always a risk. //	投資はつねにリスクがあります。
When you buy stock /	あなたが株を買う時
in a company, /	ある会社の,
you are essentially buying /	あなたは本質的に買っています
a piece of that company, /	その会社の一部を,
and if that company goes bankrupt, /	そしてその会社がもし倒産すれば,
your piece is gone. //	あなたの一部はなくなってしまいます。
On the other hand, /	その一方で,
if the company's value goes up, /	もしその会社の価値が上がれば,
then the value /	その時その価値は
of your piece /	あなたの一部の
goes up /	上がります
as well. //	同様に。
This is why /	こういうわけで
smart investors always give /	抜け目ない投資家はつねに与えます
the same advice: /	同じようなアドバイスを,
Diversify, diversify, diversify. //	分散, 分散, 分散（せよと）。

Instead of putting all of your invested money /	投資する資金のすべてを投資するのではなく
into one or two companies, /	1つか2つの企業に,
you should buy stock /	あなたは株式を購入すべきです
in a variety of companies /	さまざまな企業の
in different industries. //	異なる産業分野の。
That way, /	そうすることで,
if one of them /	もしそれらのうちの1つが（…としても）
starts to lose their value, /	価値を失い始める,
you don't have to watch /	あなたは見る必要はありません
all of your money /	あなたの資産のすべてが
sink down with it. //	それとともに落ち込むのを。
3 So /	それでは
which companies /	どの企業を
should you look for? //	あなたは探すべきでしょうか。
Thankfully, /	ありがたいことに,
you don't have to spend /	あなたは費やす必要はありません
hours upon hours /	何時間も
looking for candidates yourself. //	自分で候補を探すのに。
Many trading brokers offer /	多くの証券会社は提供しています
something called index funds. //	インデックス・ファンドと呼ばれるものを。
These funds are the collections /	これらのファンドはコレクション（集めたもの）です
of the stocks /	株式の
of companies /	企業の

in one of the major stock market indexes, /	主要な株式市場指数のいずれかにある,
like the Dow Jones /	ダウ＝ジョーンズなどの
or the S&P 500. //	あるいは S & P 500。
An index fund is not likely to yield /	インデックス・ファンドはそれほど産み出しません
a vast fortune, /	莫大な財産を,
but it is a solid investment /	しかし堅実な投資です
that offers stable growth. //	安定した成長をもたらす。
In fact, /	実際,
index funds frequently perform better /	インデックス・ファンドはよりよい利益を生むことがよくあります
than professionals /	専門家よりも
who claim /	主張する
that they can beat the market. //	市場で勝てると。

The Stock Market For Beginners: Index Funds

We have all seen pictures of businesspeople going wild on the trading floor, jumping up and down in delight or with their hands covering their faces in disbelief. And we expect tickers of incomprehensible numbers and symbols to scroll along the bottom of the television screen during the business report. But can anyone who doesn't live in a world of balance sheets and IPOs really understand what's going on? The answer is "yes," and by understanding the basics, you, too, can make an informed decision about whether to invest your hard-earned cash in the stock market.

Investing is always a risk. When you buy stock in a company, you are essentially buying a piece of that company, and if that company goes bankrupt, your piece is gone. On the other hand, if the company's value goes up, then the value of your piece goes up as well. This is why smart investors always give the same advice: Diversify, diversify, diversify. Instead of putting all of your invested money into one or two companies, you should buy stock in a variety of companies in different industries. That way, if one of them starts to lose their value, you don't have to watch all of your money sink down with it.

So which companies should you look for? Thankfully, you don't have to spend hours upon hours looking for candidates yourself. Many trading brokers offer something called index funds. These funds are the collections of the stocks of companies in one of the major stock market indexes, like the Dow Jones or the S&P 500. An index fund is not likely to yield a vast fortune, but it is a solid investment that offers stable growth. In fact, index funds frequently perform better than professionals who claim that they can beat the market.

初心者のための株式市場：インデックス・ファンド

　私たちは誰でも（証券取引所の）立会場で社員たちが喜びのあまり飛び跳ねて大騒ぎしたり，信じられないといった様子で顔を手で覆ったりしている光景を見たことがあります。また，ビジネス関連のニュース中には，テレビ画面の下部に意味不明な数字や記号のティッカー（テロップ）が次々に表示されていくものだと思っています。しかし，バランスシートやIPO（新規株式公開）の世界に詳しくない人は，何が起こっているのか実際に理解できるでしょうか。答えは「できる」であり，基本を理解すれば，あなたも苦労して稼いだお金を株式市場に投資すべきかどうかについて，十分な情報に基づいた判断を下すことができます。

　投資とは，つねにリスクが伴う行為です。ある会社の株を買う時，あなたは本質的にその会社の一部を買っているのであって，その会社が倒産するようなことがあれば，あなたの持ち分はなくなってしまいます。その一方で，会社の価値が上がると，あなたの持ち分の価値も上がります。こういうわけで，抜け目ない投資家はつねに同じようなアドバイスをします。すなわち，分散，分散，そして分散，ということです。投資する資金のすべてを1つか2つの企業に投資するのではなく，異なる産業分野のさまざまな企業の株式を購入すべきなのです。そうすることで，そのうちの1つが値を下げ始めたとしても，それであなたのすべての資産の価値が落ち込むのをただ眺めていることにはなりません。

　それでは，どの企業を選ぶべきなのでしょうか。ありがたいことに，自分で候補を探すのに何時間も費やす必要はありません。多くの証券会社はインデックス・ファンドと呼ばれるものを提供しています。これらのファンドは，ダウ＝ジョーンズやS＆P 500などの主要な株式市場指数のいずれかにある企業の株式を集めたものです。インデックス・ファンドは，それほど莫大な財産はもたらしませんが，安定した成長をもたらす堅実な投資です。実際，インデックス・ファンドは，市場で優位に立つことができると主張する専門家よりも，よりよい運用実績を残すことがよくあります。

解答と解説

解答

(1) ②　　(2) ④　　(3) ①　　(4) ①

解説

(1) 第1段落の第1～3文の内容から考えて，2が正解。1は architecture（建築）について本文に記述がないため，誤り。3・4のような記述も本文中にない。特に4のような本文に根拠のない比較には注意したい。

設問・選択肢の和訳

(1)『アメリカン・ゴシック』という絵画を特別なものにさせたものの1つは何か。

× 1　20世紀のアメリカの建築の独特な見方を示した。

○ 2　20世紀の中西部の田園地帯の伝統的な価値観を示す力強いイメージがあった。

× 3　中西部の田園地帯における農民と隣人との間の非友好的な関係を示していた。

× 4　その年代のほかの絵画よりも保守的なスタイルで描かれていた。

---

(2) 第2段落の第4文の内容に一致する4が正解。3は第2段落第5文にヨーロッパ旅行中に印象派について学んだと書かれているため，誤り。

設問・選択肢の和訳

(2) 本文によると，グラント・ウッドについて正しいのは次のうちどれか。

× 1　彼は子供の頃，いつも家から出ていくことを夢見ていた。

× 2　彼は独自の美術学校を設立した時に有名になった。

× 3　彼は外国に旅する前に印象派について勉強した。

○ 4　彼は高校を卒業する前，金属関連の仕事をし始めた。

---

(3) 第3段落の第1・3文の内容に一致する1が正解。2は，第3段落第5文の typical clothing を clothes that were in fashion と書き換えたと考えたとしても，第2段落第1文から『アメリカン・ゴシック』という絵画が描かれたのは1930年だということがわかるので，本文中の 18th-century America という部分と一致しない。3は，「アメリカの環境とヨーロッパのルネサンス芸術に刺激を受けた」という本文の内容と異なる。また，4のような記述はない。

設問・選択肢の和訳

(3)『アメリカン・ゴシック』という絵画の特徴の1つは何か。

○ 1　絵に描かれた人々だけでなく建物も本物のモデルがあった。

× 2　絵に描かれている人々は絵が描かれた時に流行していた洋服を着ている。

× 3　彼はアメリカとヨーロッパの環境に刺激を受けた時に絵を描いた。

× 4　地元の農夫とその娘は絵のモデルになることに同意した。

---

(4) 第4段落の第4文の内容に一致する1が正解。その文に a documentary about

Grant Wood とあり，第 2 段落の第 1 文からグラント・ウッドは『アメリカン・ゴシック』という絵画のモデルではなく，それを描いた画家であることがわかるため，4 は誤り。2 も同じ文から，誤り。3 については記述がない。

設問・選択肢の和訳

(4) アイオワ州エルドンを訪れる人々は…することができる

○ 1 『アメリカン・ゴシック』という絵画に感化された絵画を見る。

× 2 『アメリカン・ゴシック』という絵画の家のデザインについてドキュメンタリーを見る。

× 3 博物館で『アメリカン・ゴシック』という絵画の独自の模倣作品を描いてみる。

× 4 『アメリカン・ゴシック』という絵画のモデルのドキュメンタリーを見る。

語句

〈第 1 段落〉

□ provide a glimpse into ～	～を垣間見る機会を提供する
□ bald	(形) はげ頭の
□ stern expression	厳しい表情
□ characterize	(動) ～を特徴づける
□ barn	(名) 納屋
□ distinct	(形) 明確な，異なった
□ context	(名) 背景，場面

〈第 2 段落〉

□ humble	(形) 質素な
□ apprentice	(名) 見習い
□ metal shop	金属工場
□ Impressionism	(名) 印象派
□ renewed	(形) 新たな，再生された

〈第 4 段落〉

□ commemorate	(動) ～を記念する
□ feature	(動) ～を呼び物にする，特集する

構造確認 ※誤読した部分の確認に使用してください。

⇒別冊 p.14 ~ 16

第1段落 『アメリカン・ゴシック』は20世紀のアメリカ中西部の田園地帯の生活を垣間見せる絵画だ。

① The famous *American Gothic* painting provides a glimpse ⟨into life ⟨in the
　　　　　　　S　　　　　　　　　　V　　　　　O
20th-century rural American Midwest⟩⟩.

有名な『アメリカン・ゴシック』という絵画は《《20世紀のアメリカ中西部の田園地帯での》生活を》垣
間見せてくれます。

② (On display ⟨at the Art Institute ⟨of Chicago⟩⟩), it features a bald farmer and
　　　　　　　　　　　　　　　　　　　　　　　　　S　　V　　　　　O
his blonde daughter ⟨with stern expressions on their faces⟩.　　　注1

(《《シカゴの》美術館に》展示中の)，その絵画は《顔に険しさを浮かべた》はげ頭の農場主とその金髪
の娘を描いています。

③ This couple represents the conservative, traditional values ⟨that
　　　S　　　　V　　　　　　　　　　　　　O
characterized rural life ⟨at the time⟩⟩.
　　V'　　　　　O'

この2人は《《当時の》農村生活を特徴づける》保守的で伝統的な価値観を表しています。

④ (Behind the farmer and his daughter) sit a red barn and a simple white
　　　　　　　　　　　　　　　　　　　　　V　　　　　　　　　　S
house ⟨with a distinct style of window⟩.　　　注2

(この農場主と彼の娘の背後には) 赤い納屋と《独特の形をした窓がある》簡素な白い家があります。

⑤ The image is striking, and it (quickly) became popular (both in its original
　　S①　　V①　C①　　　S②　　　　　V②　　　C②
form and through its imitation ⟨in many different contexts⟩).

そのイメージはとても印象深いので，その絵画は (元の作品と《異なる設定での多くの》模倣作品の両
方で) (たちまち) 有名になりました。

第2段落 『アメリカン・ゴシック』で名声と尊敬を集める前のウッドはつつましい生活を送っていた。

① <u>American Gothic</u> <u>was painted</u> (by Grant Wood) (in 1930).
  S   V

『アメリカン・ゴシック』は (1930年に) (グラント・ウッドによって) 描かれました。

② (Before its exhibition ⟨at the Art Institute ⟨of Chicago⟩⟩, ⟨which <u>brought</u> <u>him</u>
                    V' O'①

<u>widespread fame and respect</u>⟩), <u>Wood</u> <u>lived</u> <u>a humble life</u>. 👉注3
   O'②   S V O

(⟨彼に幅広い名声と尊敬をもたらした⟩, ⟨⟨シカゴの⟩美術館での⟩その絵画の展示の前), ウッドはつつましい生活を送っていました。

③ <u>He</u> <u>was born</u> (in rural Iowa), and <u>his father</u> <u>died</u> (when <u>he</u> <u>was</u> <u>ten years old</u>).
 S① V①   S② V②   S' V' C'

彼は (アイオワ州の田園地帯で) 生まれ, (彼が10歳の時に) 父親が亡くなりました。

④ <u>He</u> <u>was</u> <u>an artist</u> (from a very young age), (starting his career (as an
 S V C

apprentice ⟨in a metal shop⟩) and going on to art school ⟨in Minneapolis⟩

(after his high school graduation)). 👉注4

彼は (とても若い頃からの) 芸術家で, (((⟨金属工場での⟩見習いとして) 働き始め, (高校卒業後に) ⟨ミネアポリスの⟩美術学校に進学しました)。

⑤ <u>He</u> <u>traveled</u> (to Europe) (to study various styles of painting, Impressionism
 S V

in particular), (before [moving back to Iowa]).

彼は ([アイオワに戻る] まで), (特に印象派の, さまざまな絵画スタイルを学ぶために) (ヨーロッパへ) 旅をしました。

⑥ (Back home), <u>he</u> <u>felt</u> <u>a renewed love</u> ⟨for Midwestern life⟩ and <u>started to</u>
     S V① O①   V②

<u>create</u> <u>images</u> ⟨of his surroundings⟩, ⟨which (soon) <u>resulted in</u> <u>the painting</u>
   O②   V'

⟨of American Gothic⟩⟩.

(故郷に戻って), 彼は⟨中西部の生活に対して⟩改めて愛着を感じて⟨自分の周囲に⟩見えるものを描き始め, ⟨(まもなく)⟨『アメリカン・ゴシック』という⟩絵画を生み出しました⟩。

① The small white house 〈behind the farmer and his daughter〉 is a real house
   S   V   C
〈in the small town of Eldon, Iowa〉.

〈農場主と彼の娘の背後にある〉小さな白い家は〈アイオワ州，エルドンという小さな町に〉実在する
家です。

② (When Grant Wood saw this house), he decided to paint it and to include (in
         S'   V'   O'   S   V   O
his painting) the kind of people 〈that he thought would live in it〉.
                                                      V'

（グラント・ウッドがこの家を見た時），彼はそれを描き，〈そこに暮らしているだろうと彼が考えた〉
ような人たちを（その絵の中に）含めることにしました。

③ Grant Wood used real people (as models 〈for the painted couple〉).
     S   V   O

グラント・ウッドは（〈絵に描く男女の〉モデルとして）実在の人たちを使いました。

④ The farmer was modeled (by Wood's dentist), and the daughter (by Wood's
     S①   V   S②
younger sister, Nan).

農場主は（ウッドのかかりつけの歯科医が）モデルで，その娘は（ウッドの妹のナンが）モデルになり
ました。

⑤ The clothes 〈worn (by the painted couple)〉 represent typical clothing 〈from
     S   V   O
18th-century America〉.

〈（描かれた男女が）着ている〉服は〈18世紀のアメリカの〉典型的な服装を表しています。

⑥ Wood's painting style, (while inspired (by his American surroundings)),
     S   V'
was influenced (by Renaissance art 〈that he had studied (during his trips
     V
〈to Europe〉)〉).
                                                                    ◀注5

ウッドの絵画スタイルは，（（アメリカの風景に）刺激を受けているものの），（〈〈ヨーロッパの〉旅行
中に）彼が学んだ〉ルネッサンス芸術による）影響を受けていました。

第4段落 それは今でも20世紀のアメリカ中西部の田園地帯を描いた絵画の中で最も有名なものである。

① (Today), *American Gothic* remains one ⟨of the most well-known paintings
　　　　　　　　　　S　　　　　　V　　　C
⟨of the 20th-century rural American Midwest⟩⟩.

(今日でも)，『アメリカン・ゴシック』は ⟪⟨20世紀のアメリカ中西部の田園地帯（を描いた絵画）の中
で⟩最も有名な絵画の⟩1つであり続けています。

② The white house ⟨featured (in the painting)⟩ is still located (in Eldon, Iowa).
　　　S　　　　　　　　　　　　　　　　　　　　　　　V

⟨(この絵画に)登場する⟩白い家は (アイオワ州，エルドンに)今でもあります。

③ Next door is a small museum ⟨commemorating the *American Gothic*
　　　　　　V　　　S
painting and the life ⟨of Grant Wood⟩⟩.　　　　　　　　　注6

その隣には⟨『アメリカン・ゴシック』という絵画と⟨グラント・ウッドの⟩生涯を記念した⟩小さな博
物館があります。

④ The museum has a small room ⟨where visitors can watch a documentary
　　　S①　　V①　　O①　　　　　　　　S'①　　V'①　　O'①
⟨about Grant Wood⟩⟩, and it also has a large exhibit ⟨featuring many ⟨of
　　　　　　　　　　　　　S②　　V②　　O②
the *American Gothic* imitations ⟨that have been created (over the years)⟩⟩⟩.
　　　　　　　　　　　　　　　　　　　　V'②

この博物館には⟨来館者が⟨グラント・ウッドについての⟩ドキュメンタリー映画を見ることができる⟩
小さな部屋があり，⟪⟨⟨(長年にわたって)作られてきた⟩『アメリカン・ゴシック』の模倣作品の⟩多く
を呼び物とする⟩大規模な展示もあります。

⑤ The museum gift shop sells copies ⟨of the *American Gothic* painting⟩ (along
　　　S　　　　　　　V　　O
with several other products).　　　　　　　　　　　　　　注7

この博物館のギフトショップは⟨『アメリカン・ゴシック』という絵画の⟩複製品を (そのほかの品々と
ともに)販売しています。

71

⑥ The museum also has a set of costumes 〈that match the clothing 〈of the
　　　S　　　　　　 V　　　　O　　　　　　　　　　　　V'　　　　O'
American Gothic farmer and his daughter〉〉.

この博物館には《《『アメリカン・ゴシック』の農場主とその娘の》服にそっくりの》衣装セットもあり
ます。

⑦ People can put them on and take their own pictures outside (in front of the
　　S　　　V①　　O①　　　　　V②　　　　　O②
same small house).

人々はそれらを着て，外にある（同じ小さな家の前で）自分の写真を撮ることができます。

⑧ The museum is free (to the public).
　　　S　　　　V　C

この博物館は（誰でも）入場無料です。

注1　with 名詞＋前置詞句 で「～が…の状態になっている」という意味。前置詞句の部分には，形
　　　容詞や分詞が置かれることもある。

注2　Behind から daughter までの場所を表す副詞句が前に出た，倒置構文。主語は a red barn
　　　and a simple white house.

注3　関係代名詞と先行詞の間にカンマがある場合は，関係代名詞節は補足的な情報を付け足すはた
　　　らきをしている。

注4　starting ... and going ... のような分詞構文は，主文に続けて連続的に行う行為を表すことが
　　　ある。

注5　while の直後に現在分詞や過去分詞が置かれ，「…な一方で」のような意味の副詞句になること
　　　がある。while の直後に it was が省略されていると考えるとよい。

注6　Next door という場所を表す副詞句が前に出た倒置構文。主語は a small museum.

注7　along with ～は前置詞のはたらきをする句で，「～とともに」という意味になる。

72

サイトトランスレーション

⇒別冊 p.14 ～ 16

1 The famous *American Gothic* painting provides /	有名な『アメリカン・ゴシック』という絵画は与えてくれます
a glimpse into life /	生活を垣間見ることを
in the 20th-century rural American Midwest. //	20 世紀のアメリカ中西部の田園地帯での。
On display /	展示中の
at the Art Institute of Chicago, /	シカゴ美術館に,
it features /	それは描いています
a bald farmer and his blonde daughter /	はげ頭の農場主とその金髪の娘を
with stern expressions on their faces. //	顔に険しい表情を浮かべた。
This couple represents /	この 2 人は表しています
the conservative, traditional values /	保守的で, 伝統的な価値観を
that characterized /	特徴づけた
rural life /	農村生活を
at the time. //	当時の。
Behind the farmer and his daughter /	この農場主と彼の娘の背後には
sit a red barn and a simple white house /	赤い納屋と簡素な白い家があります
with a distinct style of window. //	独特の形をした窓がある。
The image is striking, /	そのイメージはとても印象深く,
and it quickly became popular /	そしてそれはたちまち有名になりました
both in its original form /	元の作品と両方で
and through its imitation /	そしてその模倣作品を通して
in many different contexts. //	多くの異なる設定での。

2 *American Gothic* was painted /	『アメリカン・ゴシック』は描かれました
by Grant Wood /	グラント・ウッドによって
in 1930. //	1930 年に。
Before its exhibition /	その展示以前には
at the Art Institute of Chicago, /	シカゴ美術館での,
which brought him /	彼にもたらした
widespread fame and respect, /	幅広い名声と尊敬を,
Wood lived /	ウッドは暮らしていました
a humble life. //	つつましい生活を。
He was born /	彼は生まれました
in rural Iowa, /	アイオワ州の田園地帯で,
and his father died /	そして彼の父親は亡くなりました
when he was ten years old. //	彼が 10 歳の時に。
He was an artist /	彼は芸術家でした
from a very young age, /	とても若い頃から,
starting his career /	働き始めて
as an apprentice /	見習いとして
in a metal shop /	金属工場で
and going on to art school /	そして美術学校に進学しました
in Minneapolis /	ミネアポリスの
after his high school graduation. //	高校卒業後に。
He traveled /	彼は旅行しました
to Europe /	ヨーロッパを
to study various styles of painting, /	さまざまな絵画スタイルを学ぶために,

Impressionism /	印象派
in particular, /	特に,
before moving back /	戻る前に
to Iowa. //	アイオワに。
Back home, /	故郷に戻って,
he felt /	彼は感じました
a renewed love /	改めて愛情を
for Midwestern life /	中西部の生活に対して
and started to create /	そして描き始めました
images of his surroundings, /	自分の周囲のイメージを,
which soon resulted /	そのことがまもなく生み出しました
in the painting of *American Gothic*. //	『アメリカン・ゴシック』という絵画を。
3 The small white house /	小さな白い家は
behind the farmer and his daughter /	農場主と彼の娘の背後にある
is a real house /	実在する家です
in the small town /	小さな町に
of Eldon, Iowa. //	アイオワ州, エルドンの。
When Grant Wood saw /	グラント・ウッドが見た時
this house, /	この家を,
he decided /	彼は決めました
to paint it /	それを描くことを
and to include in his painting /	そして彼の絵の中に含めることを
the kind of people /	その種類の人たちを
that he thought /	彼が考えた

would live in it. //	そこに暮らしているであろうと。
Grant Wood used /	グラント・ウッドは使いました
real people /	実在の人たちを
as models /	モデルとして
for the painted couple. //	絵に描く男女の。
The farmer was modeled /	農場主はモデルとして描かれました
by Wood's dentist, /	ウッドのかかりつけの歯科医を,
and the daughter /	そして娘は
by Wood's younger sister, Nan. //	ウッドの妹, ナンを。
The clothes /	その服は
worn by the painted couple /	描かれた男女が着ている
represent typical clothing /	典型的な服装を表しています
from 18th-century America. //	18世紀のアメリカの。
Wood's painting style, /	ウッドの絵画スタイルは,
while inspired /	刺激を受けているものの
by his American surroundings, /	アメリカの風景に,
was influenced /	影響を受けていました
by Renaissance art /	ルネッサンス芸術による
that he had studied /	彼がかつて学んだ
during his trips to Europe. //	ヨーロッパ旅行中に。
4 Today, /	今日でも,
American Gothic remains /	『アメリカン・ゴシック』はあり続けています
one of the most well-known paintings /	最も有名な絵画の1つで

of the 20th-century rural American Midwest. //	20世紀のアメリカ中西部の田園地帯の。
The white house /	その白い家は
featured in the painting /	その絵画に登場する
is still located /	今でもあります
in Eldon, Iowa. //	アイオワ州，エルドンに。
Next door is a small museum /	隣には小さな博物館があります
commemorating /	記念した
the *American Gothic* painting /	『アメリカン・ゴシック』という絵画を
and the life of Grant Wood. //	そしてグラント・ウッドの生涯。
The museum has /	その博物館にはあります
a small room /	1つの小さな部屋が
where visitors can watch /	来館者が見ることができる
a documentary /	ドキュメンタリーを
about Grant Wood, /	グラント・ウッドについての,
and it also has a large exhibit /	そしてそこには大規模な展示もあります
featuring /	呼び物とする
many of the *American Gothic* imitations /	『アメリカン・ゴシック』の模倣作品の多くを
that have been created /	作られてきた
over the years. //	長年にわたって。
The museum gift shop sells /	その博物館のギフトショップは販売しています
copies of the *American Gothic* painting /	『アメリカン・ゴシック』という絵画の複製品を
along with several other products. //	そのほかの品々とともに。
The museum also has a set of costumes /	その博物館には衣装セットもあります

that match the clothing /	服にそっくりの
of the *American Gothic* farmer and his daughter. //	『アメリカン・ゴシック』の農場主とその娘の。
People can put them on /	人々はそれらを着ることができます
and take their own pictures /	そして自分の写真を撮る
outside /	外で
in front of the same small house. //	同じ小さな家の前で。
The museum is free /	その博物館は無料です
to the public. //	誰に対しても。

The American Gothic Painting

The famous *American Gothic* painting provides a glimpse into life in the 20th-century rural American Midwest. On display at the Art Institute of Chicago, it features a bald farmer and his blonde daughter with stern expressions on their faces. This couple represents the conservative, traditional values that characterized rural life at the time. Behind the farmer and his daughter sit a red barn and a simple white house with a distinct style of window. The image is striking, and it quickly became popular both in its original form and through its imitation in many different contexts.

American Gothic was painted by Grant Wood in 1930. Before its exhibition at the Art Institute of Chicago, which brought him widespread fame and respect, Wood lived a humble life. He was born in rural Iowa, and his father died when he was ten years old. He was an artist from a very young age, starting his career as an apprentice in a metal shop and going on to art school in Minneapolis after his high school graduation. He traveled to Europe to study various styles of painting, Impressionism in particular, before moving back to Iowa. Back home, he felt a renewed love for Midwestern life and started to create images of his surroundings, which soon resulted in the painting of *American Gothic*.

The small white house behind the farmer and his daughter is a real house in the small town of Eldon, Iowa. When Grant Wood saw this house, he decided to paint it and to include in his painting the kind of people that he thought would live in it. Grant Wood used real people as models for the painted couple. The farmer was modeled by Wood's dentist, and the daughter by Wood's younger sister, Nan. The clothes worn by the painted couple represent typical clothing from 18th-century America. Wood's painting style, while inspired by his American surroundings, was influenced by Renaissance art that he had studied during his trips to Europe.

Today, *American Gothic* remains one of the most well-known paintings of the 20th-century rural American Midwest. The white house featured in the painting is still located in Eldon, Iowa. Next door is a small museum commemorating the *American Gothic* painting and the life of Grant Wood. The museum has a small room where visitors can watch a documentary about Grant Wood, and it also has a large exhibit featuring many of the *American Gothic* imitations that have been created over the years. The museum gift shop sells copies of the *American Gothic* painting along with several other products. The museum also has a set of costumes that match the clothing of the *American Gothic* farmer and his daughter. People can put them on and take their own pictures outside in front of the same small house. The museum is free to the public.

『アメリカン・ゴシック』という絵画

　有名な『アメリカン・ゴシック』という絵画は 20 世紀のアメリカ中西部の田園地帯での生活を垣間見せてくれます。シカゴ美術館に展示されているこの絵画は，険しい表情をしたはげ頭の農場主とその金髪の娘を描いたものです。この 2 人は，当時の農村生活を特徴づける保守的で伝統的な価値観を表しています。この農場主と彼の娘の背後には，赤い納屋と，独特の形をした窓がある簡素な白い家が立っています。そのイメージはとても印象深いので，この絵画は元の作品と，さまざまに異なる設定での多くの模倣作品の両方で，たちまち有名になりました。

　『アメリカン・ゴシック』は 1930 年にグラント・ウッドによって描かれました。それがシカゴ美術館で展示されると，彼は幅広い名声と尊敬を集めましたが，それ以前のウッドはつつましい生活を送っていました。彼はアイオワ州の田園地帯で生まれ，父親は彼が 10 歳の時に亡くなりました。彼はとても若い頃からの芸術家で，金属工場で見習いとして働き始め，高校卒業後にミネアポリスの美術学校に進学しました。彼は，さまざまな絵画スタイル，特に印象派のスタイルについて学ぶためヨーロッパを旅し，その後，アイオワに戻りました。故郷に戻って，彼は中西部の生活に対して改めて愛着を感じて自分の周囲に見えるものを描き始め，まもなく『アメリカン・ゴシック』という絵画を生み出しました。

　農場主と彼の娘の背後にある小さな白い家は，アイオワ州のエルドンという小さな町に実在する家です。グラント・ウッドがこの家を見た時，彼はそれを描き，その絵の中にそこに暮らしていそうな人たちを含めることにしました。グラント・ウッドは，絵に描く男女のモデルとして実在の人たちを使いました。農場主はウッドのかかりつけの歯科医がモデルで，その娘はウッドの妹のナンがモデルになりました。描かれた男女が着ている服は，18 世紀のアメリカの典型的な服装を表しています。ウッドの絵画スタイルは，アメリカの風景に刺激を受けているものの，彼がヨーロッパ旅行中に学んだルネッサンス芸術の影響を受けていました。

　今日でも『アメリカン・ゴシック』は，20 世紀のアメリカ中西部の田園地帯を描いた絵画の中で，最も有名なものであり続けています。この絵画に登場する白い家は，今でもアイオワ州エルドンにあります。その隣には，『アメリカン・ゴシック』の絵とグラント・ウッドの生涯を記念した小さな博物館があります。この博物館には，来館者がグラント・ウッドについてのドキュメンタリー映画を見ることができる小さな部屋があり，長年にわたって作られてきた『アメリカン・ゴシック』の数多くの模倣作品を呼び物とする大規模な展示もあります。この博物館のギフトショップは，『アメリカン・ゴシック』という絵画の複製品をそのほかの品々とともに販売しています。この博物館には，『アメリカン・ゴシック』の農場主とその娘の服にそっくりの衣装セットもあります。人はそれを着て，外に出て同じ小さな家の前で自分の写真を撮ることができます。この博物館は誰でも入場無料です。

⇒別冊 p.17 ～ 19

Unit 7

解答と解説

解答

(1) ②　(2) ①　(3) ④　(4) ④

解説

(1) 第1段落の第5文の内容から考えて2が正解。1は第1段落第3文にビーバーやアヒルの近縁種ではないと書かれている。3は第1段落の最後から2文目に現在の姿になったのは約10万年前だと書かれているため，誤り。

設問・選択肢の和訳

(1) 第1段落で述べられているカモノハシの特徴について最適なものは次のうちどれか。

× 1 それはビーバーの近縁種で，哺乳類の一種である。

○ 2 かつては近縁種がいたが，そのほとんどがずっと昔に滅びた。

× 3 1億1,000万年もの間，同じ身体的特徴を維持している。

× 4 今日のカモノハシよりもずっと小さい祖先がいる。

(2) 第2段落の第2文の内容に一致する1が正解。2はthat以下の内容に該当する記述が本文中にないため，誤り。3は第2段落第3文に水かきを後ろに引くことができると書かれているが，水中で泳ぐためといった記述はない。4は第2段落第3文に地面を歩くことができると書かれているものの，最も適しているといった記述はない。

設問・選択肢の和訳

(2) 第2段落で述べられているカモノハシについて正しいものは次のうちどれか。

○ 1 哺乳類よりもむしろ鳥に似ているが，実際には哺乳類に属している。

× 2 オーストラリアの多くの哺乳類が持つ，アヒルのような口を持っている。

× 3 つま先の間に水かきがあり，水中で泳ぐために引っ込める。

× 4 水かきのある足を持ち，陸上を歩くのに最も適している。

(3) 第3段落の第5・6文の内容に一致する4が正解。1は第3段落最後の2文に，オスだけ後ろ足から毒を出すとあるため，誤り。2は第3段落第5文に，歯を持たないと書かれているので，誤り。3は第3段落第2文に，暗く濁った水中でもえさを見つけることができると説明されているが，暗闇の方がよく見えるとは書かれていないため，誤り。

設問・選択肢の和訳

(3) カモノハシは…する能力を持っている

× 1 ほかの動物を攻撃するため，すべての足を通じて毒を出す。

× 2 鋭い歯を使って小動物の肉を食べる。

× 3 暗闇の方がよく見え，食べ物を探すのに役立つ。

○ 4 口の中の食べ物をより食べやすくするために石を使う。

（4）第4段落の第1・2文の内容に一致する4が正解。ほかの選択肢は本文に記述がないため，誤り。

設問・選択肢の和訳

（4）本文によると，カモノハシの奇妙な外見は…

×1　広告に使われたとき，一部の科学者によって非難された。

×2　1つには，それによって科学者たちが困惑したために人気になった。

×3　世界中で放映されている一部のアニメ番組で誇張された。

○4　世界中で人気のマスコットのモデルになった。

語句

〈タイトル〉

☐ platypus　　　　　（名）カモノハシ

〈第1段落〉

☐ native to ～　　　　～原産の

☐ duck　　　　　　　（名）アヒル

☐ mammal　　　　　（名）哺乳動物

☐ monotreme　　　　（名）単孔類動物

☐ echidna　　　　　（名）ハリモグラ

〈第2段落〉

☐ mismatched　　　　（形）不適合な

☐ bill　　　　　　　（名）くちばし

☐ furry　　　　　　（形）毛皮で覆われた

☐ leathery　　　　　（形）革のようにしなやかな

☐ toe　　　　　　　（名）つま先

〈第3段落〉

☐ specialized　　　　（形）特殊化した

☐ detect　　　　　　（動）～を見つける

☐ carnivore　　　　　（名）肉食動物

☐ shellfish　　　　　（名）甲殻類

☐ worm　　　　　　（名）蠕虫（ぜんちゅう）

☐ grind up　　　　　～を挽き砕く

☐ stinger　　　　　（名）毒針

☐ venom　　　　　　（名）毒

〈第4段落〉

☐ loveable　　　　　（形）愛らしい

構造確認 ※誤読した部分の確認に使用してください。　　　　　　　　⇒別冊 p.17 ～ 19

第 1 段落　カモノハシは奇妙な外見を持ち，哺乳類の中でも珍しい「単孔目」に属する生き物である。

① There are few creatures 〈whose appearance seems as absurd (as the
　　　V　　　S　　　　　　　　　　S'　　　　V'　　　　C'
platypus)〉.

〈(カモノハシほど) その外見がふざけているように見える〉生き物はほとんどいません。

② (Native (to Australia) and often found (around rivers and lakes)), the animal
　　　　　　　　　　　　　　　　　　　　　　　　　　　　　　　　　　　　　　　S
resembles a beaver 〈wearing a duck mask〉.　　　　　　　　　　　　　　　注1
　　V　　　O

((オーストラリア)原産で(川や湖の周辺に)よく見られる)，その動物は〈カモのお面をかぶった〉ビー
バーのようです。

③ (However), it is not (directly) related (to either animal).
　　　　　　　 S　　V

(しかしながら)，カモノハシは (どちらの動物にも) (直接) 関係はありません。

④ (Rather), it is a member 〈of a rare group 〈of mammals〉 〈called the
　　　　　　 S V　　C
"monotremes"〉〉.　　　　　　　　　　　　　　　　　　　　　　　　　　　　　　　　　　注2

(正しくは)，それは 〈〈「単孔目」と呼ばれる〉〈哺乳類の中でも〉珍しいグループの〉一員です。

⑤ (Along with the platypus), the only other animal 〈alive today〉 〈that belongs
　　　　　　　　　　　　　　　　　　　 S　　　　　　　　　　　　　　　　　 V'①
(to this category)〉 is the echidna, an animal 〈covered (in spines)〉 〈that is
　　　　　　　　　　　V　　 C　　　　　　　　　　　　　　　　　　　　　　　V'②
also native (to Australia) (as well as New Guinea)〉.　　　　　　　　　　　　　注3
　　 C'②

(カモノハシと並んで)，〈(この分類に) 属し〉〈現存する〉もう 1 つの唯一の動物はハリモグラで，〈同
じく (オーストラリアと) (さらにニューギニアが) 原産で〉〈(針に) 覆われた〉動物です。

⑥ (Although monotremes are probably more than 110 million years old),
　　　　　　　　S'　　　　　　V'　　　　　　　　　　　　　　　C'

the platypus is thought to have lived (in its current form) (for around
　　S　　　　　V

100,000 years).

(単孔目はおそらく 1 億 1,000 万年以上前に登場しましたが)，カモノハシは (現在の形態で) (10 万
年くらい) 生き延びてきたと考えられています。

⑦ Fossils show [that (thousands of years ago), the platypus had
　　S　　　V　　O　　　　　　　　　　　　　　　　　　　S'　　　　　V'

other living relatives ⟨that were larger (in size)⟩].
　　　　　O'

化石は [(数千年前に)，カモノハシには⟨(サイズが) より大きな⟩類縁種がいたこと] を示しています。

第2段落 カモノハシは体長約40〜50cmで短い茶褐色の毛で覆われ，矛盾したいくつかの特徴を持つ。

① The modern platypus is small, about 40 to 50 cm in length, and covered (in
　　　　　　S　　　　　V① C①　　　　　　　　　　　　　　　　　　　　V②

short, dark brown fur).

現代のカモノハシは小さく，体長は約40〜50センチメートルで，(短い茶褐色の毛皮で) 覆われてい
ます。

② It is a mammal ⟨with mismatched features⟩: its duck-like mouth, or bill,
　S①V①　　C①　　　　　　　　　　　　　　　　　　　S②

and webbed feet look (more like they belong to a bird (than to a furry
　　　　　　　　　V②

creature)).　　　　　　　　　　　　　　　　　　　　　　　　　　　　　▶注4

それは⟨矛盾に満ちたいくつかの特徴を持つ⟩哺乳類です，アヒルのような口，もしくはくちばしと，
水かきのある足は ((毛皮で覆われた生物にというよりも) 鳥類に属するように) 見えます。

③ (However), the platypus bill is softer and more leathery (than a duck's), and
　　　　　　　S①　　　　V①　　　　　C①

the webbing ⟨between its toes⟩ can be pulled back (to help it walk (on
　　S②　　　　　　　　　　　　　　　V②

land)).

(しかしながら)，カモノハシのくちばしは (アヒルよりも) 柔らかくて革のようにしなやかで，⟨足指
の間の⟩水かきは引っ込められることができ (それで (陸地を) 歩きやすくなります)。

④ Its tail looks (like a beaver's), but it is thicker and covered (in short fur).
　　S① 　V①　　　　　　　　　　　　　S② V② 　C② 　　　　　V③

注5

その尾は（ビーバーのもののように）見えますが，より厚みがあり（短い毛皮で）覆われています。

⑤ (When the first dead platypus was sent (from Australia) (to England) (in the
　　　　　　　　　S'① 　　　　　　V'①
late 18th century)), British naturalist George Shaw assumed [it was a joke
　　　　　　　　　　　　　　　　S 　　　　　　　　　V 　　　OS② V'② 　C②
or a hoax, (put together (from parts of different animals))].

((18世紀後半に) カモノハシの最初の標本が (オーストラリアから) (イギリスに) 送られた時)，イギリスの動物学者のジョージ・ショーは [それが冗談か悪ふざけで，((いくつかの異なる動物のパーツを) つなぎ合わされている)] と考えました。

⑥ Shaw believed [that such a strange-looking creature could not possibly be
　　S 　　V 　　　O 　　　　　　　　　S' 　　　　　　　　　　　　V'
real].
C'

ショーは [そのような奇妙な姿の生物がまさか本物であるはずがない] と思ったのです。

第3段落 カモノハシは行動と能力も奇妙で，例えば肉食だが歯はなく，卵を産むがミルクを分泌する。

① The behavior and abilities ⟨of the platypus⟩ are as unique (as its
　　　　　　S 　　　　　　　　　　　　　　　　　V 　　C
appearance).

⟨カモノハシの⟩行動と能力は（その外観と）同様に奇妙です。

② Its bill is covered (in specialized sensors ⟨that can detect food (even in dark,
　　S 　　V 　　　　　　　　　　　　　　　　　　　　　V' 　　O'
muddy water)⟩).

そのくちばしは（⟨（暗くて濁った水の中でも）食べ物を感知できる⟩特殊なセンサーで）覆われています。

③ It is a carnivore, ⟨which means [it eats flesh]⟩.
　S V 　　C 　　　　　　　　V' 　　O'

カモノハシは肉食動物で，⟨それは [肉を食べること] を意味します⟩。

86

④ The diet 〈of the platypus〉 consists (mostly of small animals 〈such as
　S　　　　　　　　　　　　　V
shellfish, worms, and insects〉).

〈カモノハシの〉食べ物は（主に〈貝，蠕虫，昆虫などの〉小動物から）なっています。

⑤ (However), the platypus has no teeth 〈for chewing〉.
　　　　　　　　S　　　　V　　O

（しかし），カモノハシは〈噛むための〉歯がまったくないのです。

⑥ (Instead), it fills its cheeks (with small stones 〈that it uses (to help grind up
　　　　　　S　V　　O　　　　　　　　　　　　　　S'　V'
its food)〉).

（その代わりに），カモノハシは〈〈（食べ物をすりつぶすために）使う〉小さな石を）頬に蓄えています。

⑦ (Even though female platypuses lay eggs (like a bird or a reptile)), they also
　　　　　　　　　　S'　　　　V'　O'　　　　　　　　　　　　　　　　S
produce milk (to feed their young).
　V　　O

（メスのカモノハシは（鳥や爬虫類のように）卵を産むにもかかわらず），（子を養うために）ミルクを
分泌もします。

⑧ The platypus loves sleeping—it spends half of its day (doing so) and spends
　　S①　　　　V①　　O①　　S②　V②　　O②　　　　　　　　　　　　V③
the other half (looking for food).
　O③

カモノハシは眠ることが大好きです—1日の半分を（そうして）過ごし，残り半分の時間は（食べ物を
探すことに）費やします。

⑨ The male platypus is also venomous, which is an extremely rare trait (for a
　　S　　　　　V　　　　C　　　V'　　　　　　C'
mammal).

さらにオスのカモノハシは毒を持っていますが，このことは（哺乳類としては）とても珍しい特徴で
す。

87

⑩ It has a sharp stinger (on each back leg) 〈that can deliver its painful venom〉.
　S　V　　O　　　　　　　　　　　　　　　　　V'　　　　O'

オスは (後ろ足のそれぞれに)〈痛みをもたらす毒を放出することができる〉鋭い爪があります。

第4段落 カモノハシの奇妙な性質は科学者を困惑させる一方で,世界中で人気者となるのに役立った。

① (While the platypus' unusual nature had scientists confused (for many
　　　　　　　　　S'　　　　　　　　　V'　　　O'　　　C'
years)), it has also helped make the animal popular (among the general
　　　　S　V　　　　　　　　　　　　O　　　　C
public) (throughout the world).

(カモノハシの奇妙な性質は (長年にわたって) 科学者たちを困惑させてきましたが),そのことはまた
(世界中の) (一般の人々の間で) その動物の人気を高めることに役立ちました。

② Loveable platypus characters have been used (in cartoons), (in
　　　　　　S　　　　　　　　　V
advertising), and (as mascots).

愛らしいカモノハシのイラストは (漫画で),(広告で),そして (マスコットとして) 使われてきまし
た。

③ There is a platypus character (on an animated TV show 〈in America〉), and
　　V①　　　　S①
popular mascots 〈based (on the unusual animal)〉 have been created (for
　　S②　　　　　　　　　　　　　　　　　　　V②
organizations 〈in Australia and Japan〉).

(〈アメリカの〉テレビアニメ番組には) カモノハシのキャラクターが登場し,〈(この奇妙な動物に) 基
づいた〉人気マスコットが (〈オーストラリアや日本の〉企業のために) 作られています。

注1 Native の前には，being が省略されたと考えるとよい。分詞構文の動詞が being である場合はこれが省略され，形容詞や過去分詞が先頭に出ることがある。

注2 rather は「むしろ…（と言える）」という意味で，前に書いてあることよりも適した説明などをその直後で紹介する場合に用いられる。

注3 alive という形容詞は直前の animal という名詞を修飾している。また，that ... category の関係代名詞節も同様に animal を修飾している。

注4 like はもともと前置詞で，直後には名詞が置かれることが多いが，接続詞として直後に節が置かれることもある。「…するように」という意味になる。

注5 beaver's の直後には tail が省略されていると考えるとよい。主語の Its tail との比較対象は，beaver という「動物」ではなく，beaver's tail（ビーバーの尻尾）でなければならない。

注6 which は前の文の内容全体を先行詞としている。このような場合はカンマを使った非制限用法を用いる。

注7 help という動詞は原形不定詞を伴って用いることが多く，help V の形で「V するのに役立つ」という意味になる。help to V というように to を使うこともできる。

サイトトランスレーション

⇒別冊 p.17 ～ 19

1 There are few creatures /	生き物はほとんどいません
whose appearance seems /	その外見が…のように思える
as absurd as the platypus. //	カモノハシほどふざけている。
Native to Australia /	オーストラリア原産で
and often found /	そしてよく見られる
around rivers and lakes, /	川や湖の周辺で,
the animal resembles a beaver /	その動物はビーバーに似ています
wearing a duck mask. //	カモのお面をかぶった。
However, /	しかしながら,
it is not directly related /	それは直接関係ありません
to either animal. //	どちらの動物にも。
Rather, /	正しくは,
it is a member /	それは一員です
of a rare group of mammals /	哺乳類の中でも珍しいグループの
called the "monotremes." //	「単孔目」と呼ばれる。
Along with the platypus, /	カモノハシと並んで,
the only other animal alive today /	もう1つの現存する唯一の動物は
that belongs to this category /	この分類に属している
is the echidna, /	ハリモグラです,
an animal /	動物
covered in spines /	針に覆われた
that is also native /	それも原産です

to Australia as well as New Guinea. //	ニューギニアと同様にオーストラリアの。
Although monotremes are probably more than 110 million years old, /	単孔目はおそらく1億1,000万年以上前から存在しますが,
the platypus is thought /	カモノハシは考えられています
to have lived in its current form /	現在の形態で生き延びてきたと
for around 100,000 years. //	10万年くらいの間。
Fossils show /	化石は示しています
that thousands of years ago, /	数千年前に,
the platypus had /	カモノハシにはいました
other living relatives /	類縁種が
that were larger in size. //	サイズがより大きな。
❷ The modern platypus is small, /	現代のカモノハシは小さいです,
about 40 to 50 cm in length, /	体長は約40〜50センチメートル,
and covered /	そして覆われています
in short, dark brown fur. //	短い, 茶褐色の毛皮で。
It is a mammal /	それは哺乳類です
with mismatched features: /	矛盾したいくつかの特徴を持つ,
its duck-like mouth, /	そのアヒルのような口,
or bill, and webbed feet /	あるいはくちばし, そして水かきのある足は
look more like they belong to a bird /	それらが鳥類に属するようにもっと見えます
than to a furry creature. //	毛皮で覆われた生物にというよりも。
However, /	しかし,
the platypus bill /	カモノハシのくちばしは
is softer and more leathery /	柔らかくて革のようにしなやかです

than a duck's, /	アヒルのものよりも,
and the webbing /	そして水かきは
between its toes /	足指の間の
can be pulled back /	引っ込められることができます
to help it walk on land. //	陸地を歩きやすくできます。
Its tail looks like a beaver's, /	その尾はビーバーのものに似ています,
but it is thicker /	しかしそれはより厚みがあります
and covered /	そして覆われています
in short fur. //	短い毛皮で。
When the first dead platypus was sent /	カモノハシの最初の標本が送られた時
from Australia to England /	オーストラリアからイギリスに
in the late 18th century, /	18世紀後半に,
British naturalist George Shaw assumed /	イギリスの動物学者のジョージ・ショーは考えました
it was a joke or a hoax, /	それは冗談か悪ふざけであると,
put together /	つなぎ合わされていて
from parts of different animals. //	異なる動物のパーツを。
Shaw believed /	ショーは確信しました
that such a strange-looking creature /	そのような奇妙な姿の生物が
could not possibly be real. //	まさか本物であるはずがないと。
3 The behavior and abilities of the platypus /	カモノハシの行動と能力は
are as unique as its appearance. //	その外観と同様に奇妙です。
Its bill is covered /	そのくちばしは覆われています
in specialized sensors /	特殊なセンサーで
that can detect food /	食べ物を感知できる

even in dark, muddy water. //	暗くて，濁った水の中でさえも。
It is a carnivore, /	それは肉食動物で，
which means /	意味します
it eats flesh. //	それが肉を食べることを。
The diet of the platypus consists /	カモノハシの食べ物はなっています
mostly of small animals /	主に小動物から
such as shellfish, worms, and insects. //	貝，蠕虫，昆虫などの。
However, /	しかし，
the platypus has no teeth /	カモノハシは歯がまったくありません
for chewing. //	噛むための。
Instead, /	その代わりに，
it fills its cheeks /	それはその頬をいっぱいにします
with small stones /	小さな石で
that it uses /	それは使います
to help grind up its food. //	食べ物をすりつぶすために。
Even though female platypuses lay eggs /	メスのカモノハシは卵を産むにもかかわらず
like a bird or a reptile, /	鳥や爬虫類のように，
they also produce milk /	ミルクを分泌もします
to feed their young. //	子を養うために。
The platypus loves sleeping /	カモノハシは眠ることが大好きです
—it spends half of its day /	——1日の半分を費やします
doing so /	そうすることに
and spends the other half /	そして残りの半分を費やします
looking for food. //	食べ物を探すことに。

The male platypus is also venomous, /	さらにオスのカモノハシは毒を持っています，
which is an extremely rare trait /	このことはとても珍しい特徴です
for a mammal. //	哺乳類としては。
It has a sharp stinger /	それは鋭い爪を持っています
on each back leg /	後ろ足のそれぞれに
that can deliver its painful venom. //	痛みをもたらす毒を放出することができます。
4 While the platypus' unusual nature had scientists confused /	カモノハシの奇妙な性質は科学者たちを困惑させてきましたが
for many years, /	長年にわたって，
it has also helped make the animal popular /	それはまたこの動物の人気を高めることに役立ちました
among the general public /	一般の人々の間で
throughout the world. //	世界中の。
Loveable platypus characters have been used /	愛らしいカモノハシのイラストは使われてきました
in cartoons, in advertising, and as mascots. //	漫画で，広告で，そしてマスコットとして。
There is a platypus character /	カモノハシのキャラクターがあります
on an animated TV show /	テレビアニメ番組には
in America, /	アメリカの，
and popular mascots based on the unusual animal /	そしてその奇妙な動物に基づいた人気マスコットが
have been created for organizations /	企業用に作られています
in Australia and Japan. //	オーストラリアや日本で。

The Weird and Wonderful Platypus

There are few creatures whose appearance seems as absurd as the platypus. Native to Australia and often found around rivers and lakes, the animal resembles a beaver wearing a duck mask. However, it is not directly related to either animal. Rather, it is a member of a rare group of mammals called the "monotremes." Along with the platypus, the only other animal alive today that belongs to this category is the echidna, an animal covered in spines that is also native to Australia as well as New Guinea. Although monotremes are probably more than 110 million years old, the platypus is thought to have lived in its current form for around 100,000 years. Fossils show that thousands of years ago, the platypus had other living relatives that were larger in size.

The modern platypus is small, about 40 to 50 cm in length, and covered in short, dark brown fur. It is a mammal with mismatched features: its duck-like mouth, or bill, and webbed feet look more like they belong to a bird than to a furry creature. However, the platypus bill is softer and more leathery than a duck's, and the webbing between its toes can be pulled back to help it walk on land. Its tail looks like a beaver's, but it is thicker and covered in short fur. When the first dead platypus was sent from Australia to England in the late 18th century, British naturalist George Shaw assumed it was a joke or a hoax, put together from parts of different animals. Shaw believed that such a strange-looking creature could not possibly be real.

The behavior and abilities of the platypus are as unique as its appearance. Its bill is covered in specialized sensors that can detect food even in dark, muddy water. It is a carnivore, which means it eats flesh. The diet of the platypus consists mostly of small animals such as shellfish, worms, and insects. However, the platypus has no teeth for chewing. Instead, it fills its cheeks with small stones that it uses to help grind up its food. Even though female platypuses lay eggs like a bird or a reptile, they also produce milk to feed their young. The platypus loves sleeping — it spends half of its day doing so and spends the other half looking for food. The male platypus is also venomous, which is an extremely rare trait for a mammal. It has a sharp stinger on each back leg that can deliver its painful venom.

While the platypus' unusual nature had scientists confused for many years, it has also helped make the animal popular among the general public throughout the world. Loveable platypus characters have been used in cartoons, in advertising, and as mascots. There is a platypus character on an animated TV show in America, and popular mascots based on the unusual animal have been created for organizations in Australia and Japan.

奇妙で不思議なカモノハシ

　カモノハシほど，その外見がふざけているように思える生き物はいません。オーストラリア原産で，川や湖の周辺によく見かけるこの動物は，カモのお面をかぶったビーバーのようです。しかしながら，カモノハシはどちらの動物にも直接関係はありません。正しくは，カモノハシは「単孔目」と呼ばれる哺乳類の中でも珍しいグループの1つです。カモノハシと並んで，この分類に属し，現存するもう1つの唯一の動物は針に覆われたハリモグラで，これもオーストラリアとニューギニアが原産です。単孔目は，おそらく1億1,000万年以上前に登場しましたが，カモノハシは現在の形態で10万年くらい生き延びてきたと考えられています。化石の示すところでは，カモノハシには数千年前に，体がより大きな類縁種がいました。

　現代のカモノハシは小さく，体長は約40〜50センチメートルで，短い茶褐色の毛皮で覆われています。カモノハシは，矛盾に満ちたいくつかの特徴を持つ哺乳類です。例えば，アヒルのような口，もしくはくちばしと，水かきのある足は，毛皮で覆われた生物にというよりも，鳥類に属するように見えます。ただし，カモノハシのくちばしはアヒルのよりも柔らかくて革のようにしなやかで，足指の間の水かきは陸地を歩きやすくなるように引っ込めることができます。その尾はビーバーのものに似ていますが，より厚みがあり，短い毛皮で覆われています。18世紀後半に，カモノハシの最初の標本がオーストラリアからイギリスに送られた時，イギリスの動物学者のジョージ・ショーは，それが冗談か悪ふざけで，いくつかの異なる動物のパーツがつなぎ合わされていると考えました。ショーは，そのような奇妙な姿の生物がまさか本物であるはずがないと思ったのです。

　カモノハシの行動と能力は，その外観と同様に奇妙です。そのくちばしは，暗くて濁った水の中でも食べ物を感知できる特殊なセンサーを備えています。カモノハシは肉食動物で，つまり肉を食べるということです。カモノハシの食べ物は，主に貝，蠕虫，昆虫などの小動物からなっています。しかし，カモノハシは噛むための歯がまったくありません。その代わりに，小さな石を頬に蓄えて食べ物をすりつぶすために使います。メスのカモノハシは鳥や爬虫類のように卵を産む一方で，子を養うためにミルクを分泌もします。カモノハシは眠ることが大好きで，1日の半分を眠って過ごし，残り半分の時間は食べ物を探すことに費やします。なお，オスのカモノハシは毒を持っていますが，このことは哺乳類としてはとても珍しい特徴です。オスは後ろ足のそれぞれに鋭い爪があり，痛みをもたらす毒を放出することができます。

　カモノハシの奇妙な性質は，長年にわたって科学者たちを困惑させてきましたが，そのことはまた，世界中の一般の人々の間でこの動物の人気を高めることに役立ちました。愛らしいカモノハシのイラストは，漫画や広告で，マスコットとして使われてきました。アメリカのテレビアニメ番組には，カモノハシのキャラクターが登場し，この奇妙な動物に基づいた人気マスコットが，オーストラリアや日本の企業用に作られています。

⇒別冊 p.20 ～ 22

解答と解説

解答

(1) ④   (2) ②   (3) ①   (4) ②

解説

(1) 第 1 段落の最後の文の内容に一致する 4 が正解。1・2 は，後半の内容が本文に書かれていないため，誤り。3 は，第 1 段落最後の文の内容に合っていない。

設問・選択肢の和訳

(1) フラウ・トロフィアが公衆の面前で踊り始めた時，ストラスブールの住人はどのように反応したか。

×1 彼女の熱心な踊りを楽しみ，音楽を演奏してもっと踊らせようとした。

×2 彼女のダンスに困惑し，彼女を見つめたりそばを歩いたりするのを避けようとした。

×3 彼女の熱心な踊りに感激し，彼女を見るために 6 日間とどまった。

○4 最初のうちは彼女の異様なダンスを楽しんだが，最終的には恐怖を感じた。

(2) 第 2 段落の第 5 文の内容に一致する 2 が正解。1 は前半が，3 は全体的に，第 5 文の内容に一致しない。4 は，亡くなった人がいたことが原因でダンス熱が終わったという記述がないため，誤り。

設問・選択肢の和訳

(2) 踊り始めた後に市民に何が起こったか。

×1 とても楽しんだので，踊りをする人の数がさらに増加した。

○2 望んだように体をコントロールすることができなかった。

×3 踊るのにあまりに忙しかったので，誰も踊りを止めるための助けを求めなかった。

×4 ダンス熱は大半の人が病気または疲労によって命を落としたため，終わった。

(3) 第 3 段落の第 3・4 文の内容に一致する 1 が正解。2・3 の内容は本文に記述がないため，誤り。4 は，第 4 文の後半に diseases と書かれているものの，ダンス熱の後に病気が流行したのではなく，病気などのストレスの多い出来事がダンス熱を引き起こした可能性について言及しているので，誤り。

設問・選択肢の和訳

(3) さまざまなダンス熱の類似点は何か。

○1 それらが起きたのは，自然災害が中世ヨーロッパで起きた時のようなストレスの多い出来事の後だった。

×2 ダンス熱の影響を受けた人々は，恐怖をもたらす悪霊に襲われたと言っていた。

×3 中世ヨーロッパの，踊っていた人々の大部分は，宗教的談話の力を通じて治されたと信じていた。

×4 ダンス熱が終わった後で，それぞれの町が病気の大流行を経験した。

(4) 第 3 段落の内容に一致する 2 が正解。1 は前半部分が，ほかの選択肢はすべて本文

中に該当する記述がないため，誤り。

(4) ダンス熱を引き起こした可能性の1つは何か。

× 1　主に霊への信仰によって引き起こされた精神的疲労がストラスブールの人々の間で一般的なものとなった。

○ 2　多くの市民が命を落とした結果として引き起こされた高レベルのストレスによって人々は扇動された。

× 3　死の呪いを免れる唯一の方法は集まって踊ることだと信じられていた。

× 4　ストラスブールの人々が市場で頻繁に売られていたキノコによって引き起こされた幻覚を経験した。

語句

〈第1段落〉

□ span	(動) 〜に及ぶ

〈第2段落〉

□ take over 〜	〜を乗っ取る
□ dance away 〜	踊って〜を追い払う
□ stroke	(名) 脳卒中
□ heart attack	心臓発作
□ exhaustion	(名) 極度の疲労

〈第3段落〉

□ cathedral	(名) 大聖堂
□ medieval	(形) 中世の
□ persistent	(形) 持続する，なかなか収まらない
□ stem from 〜	〜から起こる

□ failing crop	不作
□ outbreak	(名) 突然の発生，まん延
□ combined with 〜	〜と相まって
□ curse	(名) のろい

〈第4段落〉

□ mass hysteria	集団ヒステリー
□ prior	(形) 前もっての，事前の
□ spirit	(名) 幽霊，悪霊，精霊
□ ergot	(名) 麦角菌
□ toxic	(形) 有毒な
□ fungus	(名) 菌

〈設問・選択肢〉

□ terrorize	(動) 〜を怖がらせる
□ be[become] agitated	扇動される

構造確認 ※誤読した部分の確認に使用してください。　　　　　　⇒別冊 p.20 ~ 22

第1段落 ストラスブールの町には何世紀にもわたって科学者と歴史家を困惑させてきた謎がある。

① (In the northeast of France) lies the city ⟨of Strasbourg⟩, ⟨known (for its rich
history ⟨spanning 2,000 years⟩)⟩.　　　　　　　　　　　　　注1

（フランスの北東部に），〈（〈2,000 年にわたる〉豊かな歴史で）知られる〉〈ストラスブールの〉町があ
ります。

② (Behind Strasbourg's elegant halls and charming homes), (however), lies
a mystery ⟨that has baffled both scientists and historians (for centuries)⟩.　　注2

（しかし），（ストラスブールの優美な建築物や魅力的な家々の陰には），〈（何世紀にもわたって）科学
者と歴史家を困惑させてきた〉謎があります。

③ It starts with a woman ⟨known simply (as "Frau Troffea")⟩.

それは〈（「フラウ・トロフィア」として）だけ知られる〉1 人の女性から始まります。

④ (One day in July 1518), Frau Troffea walked out (into the streets ⟨of
Strasbourg⟩) and began to dance.

（1518 年 7 月のある日），フラウ・トロフィアは（〈ストラスブールの〉町の中に）歩み出て踊り始めま
した。

⑤ There was no music playing, and (soon) her fervent dancing caught
the attention ⟨of people ⟨around her⟩⟩.

音楽の伴奏はありませんでした，そして（まもなく）彼女の激しい踊りは〈〈周囲にいた〉人たちの〉注
目を集めました。

⑥ Their amusement ⟨at this odd display ⟨by the local woman⟩⟩ (soon) turned
　　　S   V

(to horror) (when she continued dancing (into the night)—and only stopped
　　　　　　　　　S'   V'①   V'②

(six days later)).

《《その土地の女性による》奇妙な姿の》おかしさは，（彼女が（夜になっても）踊り続けた時，（すぐに）
（恐怖に）変わり——ようやく（6日後に）（踊りを）やめました）。

第2段落 1人の女性が始めた奇妙な踊りに約400人の市民が加わり死者も出たが，それは突然終わった。

① But the dancing did not end (with Frau Troffea).
　　　　　S   V

しかし，この踊りは（フラウ・トロフィアで）終わりませんでした。

② (During the days ⟨that she had been dancing⟩), 34 more people came down
　　　　　　　　　　　　S'   V'   S   V

(to dance (in the streets ⟨of Strasbourg⟩)).

《彼女が踊り続けていた》日々の間に），さらに34人が（（《ストラスブールの》町中で）踊る）ように
なりました。

③ (Within a month), approximately 400 people had joined (in this dancing
　　　　　　　　　　　　　　　　　　S   V

fever).

（1か月以内に），およそ400人が（このダンス熱に）加わりました。

④ No one knew [why it began], and no one knew [how to stop them].
　　S① V① O① S' V'   S②   V②   O②

誰も［それがなぜ始まったか］を知らず，そして誰も［彼らを止める方法］がわかりませんでした。

⑤ The dancers themselves did not seem to enjoy [what had taken over
　　　　S①   V①   O①   V'①

their bodies]; they cried and begged (for help) (while they danced).
　O'①   S②   V②   S'② V'②

踊っている人たち自身も［自分の体を突き動かしているもの］を楽しんでいないようでした，彼らは
（踊りながら）泣いて（助けを）求めました。

⑥ The city provided extra dance halls and musicians (to encourage its citizens
   S① V① O②
to dance away the fever), but (for some) the experience proved fatal:
                                              S② V② C②
citizens 〈of the city〉 continued to dance (until they died (from strokes, heart
S③   V③   S' V'
attacks, or exhaustion)).

市は追加のダンスホールと楽隊を用意して(住民に気が済むまで踊ることを奨励しました)が，その対応が(一部の人には)命取りになりました，〈その市の〉住民は((脳卒中，心臓発作，あるいは極度の疲労で)死ぬまで)踊り続けたのです。

⑦ (During one month), it was recorded [that about 15 people died (every
                       S   V   O   S'   V'
day)].

注4

(1か月の間に)，[(毎日)およそ15人が死んだこと]が記録されています。

⑧ And then, (just as suddenly as it began), the dancing came (to an end).
                                S'   V'   S   V

注5

その後，(それが始まったのと同じくらい突然に)，この踊りは(終わりを)迎えました。

第3段落 ストレスの多い社会状況が呪いの力への信仰と結びつきダンス熱を発生させた可能性がある。

① (While these accounts seem strange), there is no doubt that the dancing
            S'①   V'①   C'①   V   S   S②
fever 〈of 1518〉 (actually) occurred.
                           V'②

注6

(このような話は奇妙に思えますが)，〈1518年の〉ダンス熱が(実際に)発生したことは疑いの余地がありません。

② Many documents were produced (at the time 〈of the fever〉); historians have
  S①   V①   S②   V②
access 〈to notes 〈from physicians〉 and the texts 〈of religious speeches
O②
〈given at the Strasbourg cathedral〉〉, as well as local and regional records
〈that describe the event (in great detail)〉〉.

注7

(〈その(ダンス)熱の〉時に)多くの文書が作られました，歴史家は《〈医師の〉メモや《〈ストラスブール大聖堂で行われた〉宗教的な談話の〉文面，さらに〈この事件を(きわめて詳細に)説明した〉地元や地域の記録を〉入手(利用)できます。

③(Indeed), this dancing fever was recorded (several more times) (in medieval
　　　　　　 　S　　　　　 V
Europe).

(実は), このようなダンス熱は (中世ヨーロッパで) (さらに何度か) 記録されています。

④ Similar circumstances might have led to the sudden and persistent
　 　　S　　　　　 　V
dancing, 〈such as stressful events 〈stemming from failing crops, natural

disasters, or an outbreak 〈of disease〉〉〉, (combined (with beliefs 〈in the

power 〈of curses〉〉).

《《凶作, 自然災害, あるいは〈病気の〉発生からくる〉ストレスを生む出来事などの》, 似たような状況
が (《《呪いの〉力の〉信仰と結びついて), その突発的で持続的な踊りをもたらした可能性があります。

⑤Attempts 〈at [curing the dancers (with more music)]〉 usually only worsened
　 　S　　　　　　　　　　　　　　　　　　　　　　　　　　　　　　　　　　 V
the situation, (as music invited more people to join (in the dancing)).
　　 O　　　　　　 S'　　 V'　　　 O'

〈[(音楽を追加して) 踊る人を治す] という〉試みはたいてい状況を悪化させるだけでした, (音楽はさ
らに多くの人たちを (踊りに) 加わるように促したのです)。

第4段落 ダンス熱の突然の発生と終息の原因についてはさまざまに研究されているが解決されていない。

① Some researchers believe [that the dancing fever 〈of 1518〉 was a form of
　 　　S　　　　　 V　　　 O　　　　 S'　　　　　　　　　　　　 V'　　 C'
mass hysteria, 〈resulting from the high levels 〈of stress 〈experienced (by

the people 〈of Strasbourg〉)〉〉 and 〈further worsened (by their religious

beliefs)〉〉〉].

研究者の中には [〈1518年の〉ダンス熱は《《《《〈ストラスブールの〉人たちが) 抱えていた〉ストレス
の〉高レベルを原因としていて), 〈〈彼らの宗教的信仰によって) さらに悪化した〉〉集団ヒステリーの
一形態だった] と信じている人もいます。

103

② (Indeed), the inhabitants 〈of Strasbourg〉 had prior belief and fear 〈of
                S   V   O

spirits〉〈that could explain this dancing curse〉.
              V'   O'

(確かに),〈ストラスブールの〉住民は〈この踊りの呪いを説明できそうな〉〈霊に対する〉以前からの
信仰と恐れを持っていました。

③ Other modern theories 〈about the phenomenon〉 point to the ingestion 〈of
               S   V

ergot, a toxic fungus 〈that can cause hallucinations〉〉.
                        V'   O'

〈この現象に関する〉別の新たな説は《《幻覚を引き起こす可能性のある〉有毒の菌である，麦角菌の〉
摂取を指摘しています。

④ But (even with all the research 〈conducted (on the topic)〉), no final
                                                      S

explanation 〈for the dancing fever 〈in Strasbourg〉〉 has yet been found.
                                                    V

しかし《《(この問題について) 行われた〉すべての研究にもかかわらず),《《ストラスブールの〉ダンス
熱に関する〉最終的な説明はまだ見つかっていません。

⑤ The cause 〈of the sudden dancing〉 — and its sudden disappearance — is
          S   V

a mystery 〈that may never be solved〉.
        C   V'

〈いきなり踊り出す〉原因——そしてその突然の終息——は〈決して解決されることがないかもしれな
い〉謎なのです。

注1　In … France までの場所を表す副詞句が前に出た倒置構文。この文の主語は the city。

注2　①の文と同様の倒置構文。主語は a mystery。

注3　疑問詞＋節 や，疑問詞＋ to 不定詞 の形は，名詞のはたらきをする部分を作る。ここでは，両
　　　方とも knew という動詞の目的語となっている。

注4　この文の it は形式主語で，that 以下の名詞節を指している。

注5　just as S V は「ちょうど S が V するように」という意味で様態を表す。

注6　There is no doubt S V は「S が V することへの疑いはない」という意味の構文。

注7　A as well as B は「B と同様に A も」という意味。この文では，notes と the texts が A に
　　　当たり，local and regional records が B に当たる。

注8　such as は，具体例を示す場合に使われる表現。ここでは，主語の Similar circumstances
　　　の例を示すために使われている。

注9　further は「さらに」という意味の副詞で，ここでは直後の過去分詞 worsened を修飾している。

104

サイトトランスレーション

⇒別冊 p.20 ~ 22

1 In the northeast of France /	フランスの北東部に
lies the city of Strasbourg, /	ストラスブールの町があります,
known for its rich history /	豊かな歴史で知られる
spanning 2,000 years. //	2,000 年にわたる。
Behind Strasbourg's elegant halls and charming homes, /	ストラスブールの優美な建築物や魅力的な家々の陰には,
however, /	しかし,
lies a mystery /	謎があります
that has baffled /	困惑させてきた
both scientists and historians /	科学者と歴史家を
for centuries. //	何世紀にもわたって。
It starts with a woman /	それは 1 人の女性から始まります
known simply as "Frau Troffea." //	「フラウ・トロフィア」としてだけ知られる。
One day /	ある日
in July 1518, /	1518 年 7 月の,
Frau Troffea walked out /	フラウ・トロフィアは歩み出しました
into the streets of Strasbourg /	ストラスブールの町中に
and began to dance. //	そして踊り始めました。
There was no music playing, /	音楽の伴奏はありませんでした,
and soon /	そしてまもなく
her fervent dancing caught the attention /	彼女の激しい踊りは注目を集めました
of people around her. //	彼女の周囲の人たちの。

Their amusement /	彼らのおかしさは
at this odd display /	この奇妙な姿に対する
by the local woman /	その土地の女性による
soon /	すぐに
turned to horror /	恐怖に変わりました
when she continued dancing /	彼女が踊り続けた時
into the night /	夜になっても
— and only stopped /	そしてようやく終わりました
six days later. //	6日後に。
2 But the dancing did not end /	しかしその踊りは終わりませんでした
with Frau Troffea. //	フラウ・トロフィアで。
During the days /	日々の間に
that she had been dancing, /	彼女が踊り続けていた,
34 more people came down /	さらに34人が出てきました
to dance /	踊るために
in the streets of Strasbourg. //	ストラスブールの町中に。
Within a month, /	1か月以内に,
approximately 400 people had joined /	およそ400人が加わりました
in this dancing fever. //	このダンスに。
No one knew /	誰もわかりませんでした
why it began, /	なぜそれが始まったかを,
and no one knew /	そして誰もわかりませんでした
how to stop them. //	それを止める方法を。

The dancers themselves did not seem to enjoy /	踊っている人たち自身も楽しんでいないようでした
what had taken over /	乗っ取ったものを
their bodies; /	彼らの体を,
they cried /	彼らは泣きました
and begged for help /	そして助けを求めました
while they danced. //	踊りながら。
The city provided /	市は用意しました
extra dance halls and musicians /	追加のダンスホールと楽隊を
to encourage its citizens /	市民に奨励しました
to dance away the fever, /	熱が冷めるまで踊ることを,
but for some /	しかし一部の人には
the experience proved fatal: /	その経験が命取りになりました,
citizens of the city continued to dance /	市の住民は踊り続けました
until they died /	彼らが死ぬまで
from strokes, heart attacks, or exhaustion. //	脳卒中, 心臓発作, あるいは極度の疲労で。
During one month, /	1 か月の間に,
it was recorded /	それは記録されていました
that about 15 people died /	およそ 15 人が死んだことが
every day. //	毎日。
And then, /	そしてその後,
just as suddenly as it began, /	それが始まったのと同じくらい突然に,
the dancing came to an end. //	その踊りは終わりになりました。
3 While these accounts seem strange, /	これらの説明は奇妙に思えますが,

107

there is no doubt /	疑いの余地はありません
that the dancing fever of 1518 /	1518年のダンス熱が
actually occurred. //	実際に発生したことに。
Many documents were produced /	多くの文書が作られました
at the time of the fever; /	その熱の時に,
historians have access to notes from physicians /	歴史家は医師のメモにアクセスできます
and the texts of religious speeches /	そして宗教的な談話の文面に
given at the Strasbourg cathedral, /	ストラスブール大聖堂で行われた,
as well as local and regional records /	さらに地元や地域の記録も
that describe the event /	その出来事を説明した
in great detail. //	きわめて詳細に。
Indeed, /	実は,
this dancing fever was recorded /	このダンス熱は記録されました
several more times /	さらに何度か
in medieval Europe. //	中世ヨーロッパで。
Similar circumstances might have led /	似たような状況がもたらした可能性があります
to the sudden and persistent dancing, /	その突発的で持続的な踊りを,
such as stressful events /	ストレスを生む出来事などの
stemming from /	…から生じる
failing crops, natural disasters, or an outbreak of disease, /	凶作, 自然災害, あるいは病気の発生,
combined with beliefs /	信仰と結びついて
in the power of curses. //	呪いの力への。
Attempts /	試みは

at curing the dancers /	踊る人を治すことへの
with more music /	音楽で
usually only worsened the situation, /	たいてい状況を悪化させるだけでした，
as music invited /	音楽は促しました
more people /	さらに多くの人たちを
to join in the dancing. //	踊りに加わるように。
4 Some researchers believe /	研究者の中には信じている人もいます
that the dancing fever of 1518 /	1518年のダンス熱は
was a form of mass hysteria, /	一種の集団ヒステリーだったと，
resulting from the high levels of stress /	高レベルのストレスを原因とする
experienced by the people of Strasbourg /	ストラスブールの人たちによって経験された
and further worsened /	そしてさらに悪化した
by their religious beliefs. //	彼らの宗教的信仰によって。
Indeed, /	確かに，
the inhabitants of Strasbourg /	ストラスブールの住民は
had prior belief /	前から信仰を持っていました
and fear of spirits /	そして霊への恐れを
that could explain this dancing curse. //	この踊りの呪いを説明できそうな。
Other modern theories /	別の現代の理論は
about the phenomenon /	その現象についての
point to the ingestion of ergot, /	麦角菌の摂取を指摘しています，
a toxic fungus /	有毒の菌
that can cause hallucinations. //	幻覚を引き起こす可能性のある。
But even with all the research /	しかしすべての研究にもかかわらず

conducted on the topic, /	その問題について行われた,
no final explanation /	最終的な説明はない
for the dancing fever /	ダンス熱に対する
in Strasbourg /	ストラスブールでの
has yet been found. //	まだ見つけられている。
The cause /	原因は
of the sudden dancing /	突然踊ることの
— and its sudden disappearance /	—— そしてその突然の終息
— is a mystery /	—— 謎です
that may never be solved. //	決して解決されることがないかもしれない。

The Mysterious Dancing Fever of 1518

In the northeast of France lies the city of Strasbourg, known for its rich history spanning 2,000 years. Behind Strasbourg's elegant halls and charming homes, however, lies a mystery that has baffled both scientists and historians for centuries. It starts with a woman known simply as "Frau Troffea." One day in July 1518, Frau Troffea walked out into the streets of Strasbourg and began to dance. There was no music playing, and soon her fervent dancing caught the attention of people around her. Their amusement at this odd display by the local woman soon turned to horror when she continued dancing into the night — and only stopped six days later.

But the dancing did not end with Frau Troffea. During the days that she had been dancing, 34 more people came down to dance in the streets of Strasbourg. Within a month, approximately 400 people had joined in this dancing fever. No one knew why it began, and no one knew how to stop them. The dancers themselves did not seem to enjoy what had taken over their bodies; they cried and begged for help while they danced. The city provided extra dance halls and musicians to encourage its citizens to dance away the fever, but for some the experience proved fatal: citizens of the city continued to dance until they died from strokes, heart attacks, or exhaustion. During one month, it was recorded that about 15 people died every day. And then, just as suddenly as it began, the dancing came to an end.

While these accounts seem strange, there is no doubt that the dancing fever of 1518 actually occurred. Many documents were produced at the time of the fever; historians have access to notes from physicians and the texts of religious speeches given at the Strasbourg cathedral, as well as local and regional records that describe the event in great detail. Indeed, this dancing fever was recorded several more times in medieval Europe. Similar circumstances might have led to the sudden and persistent dancing, such as stressful events stemming from failing crops, natural disasters, or an outbreak of disease, combined with beliefs in the power of curses. Attempts at curing the dancers with more music usually only worsened the situation, as music invited more people to join in the dancing.

Some researchers believe that the dancing fever of 1518 was a form of mass hysteria, resulting from the high levels of stress experienced by the people of Strasbourg and further worsened by their religious beliefs. Indeed, the inhabitants of Strasbourg had prior belief and fear of spirits that could explain this dancing curse. Other modern theories about the phenomenon point to the ingestion of ergot, a toxic fungus that can cause hallucinations. But even with all the research conducted on the topic, no final explanation for the dancing fever in Strasbourg has yet been found. The cause of the sudden dancing — and its sudden disappearance — is a mystery that may never be solved.

1518年の奇妙なダンス熱

　フランスの北東部に，2,000年にわたる豊かな歴史で知られるストラスブールの町があります。しかし，ストラスブールの優美な建築物や魅力的な家々の陰には，何世紀にもわたって科学者と歴史家を困惑させてきた謎が隠されています。それは「フラウ・トロフィア」としてだけ知られる1人の女性から始まります。1518年7月のある日，フラウ・トロフィアはストラスブールの町中に歩み出て踊り始めました。音楽の伴奏はなく，まもなく彼女の激しい踊りは周囲にいた人たちの注目を集めました。彼らは，この土地の女性の奇妙な姿をおもしろがっていましたが，彼女が夜になっても踊り続けていると，それがすぐに恐怖に変わりました。踊りが終わったのは，ようやく6日後のことでした。

　しかし，この踊りはフラウ・トロフィアだけで終わりませんでした。彼女が踊り続けていた日々の間に，34人がストラスブールの町中で踊るようになりました。1か月も経たないうちに，およそ400人がこの熱狂的な踊りに加わりました。誰も，なぜそれが始まったかを知らず，そして彼らを止める方法もわかりませんでした。踊っている人たち自身も，自分の体を突き動かしているものを楽しんでいないようでした。彼らは踊りながら泣いて助けを求めました。市は追加のダンスホールと楽隊を用意し，市民に気が済むまで踊ることを奨励しましたが，そのような対応が一部の人には命取りになりました。この市の住民は，脳卒中，心臓発作，あるいは極度の疲労で死ぬまで踊り続けたのです。1か月の間に，毎日およそ15人が死んだことが記録されています。そして，それが始まったのと同じくらい突然に，この踊りは終わりを迎えました。

　このような話は奇妙に思えますが，1518年のダンス熱が実際に発生したことは疑いの余地がありません。この事件の発生時に多くの文書が作られました。歴史家には，医師のメモや，ストラスブール大聖堂で行われた宗教的な談話の文面，さらにこの事件を詳細に説明した地元や周辺地域の記録が手に入ります。実は，このようなダンス熱は中世ヨーロッパでさらに何度か記録されています。凶作，自然災害，あるいは病気の発生からくる，ストレスを生む出来事などの，似たような状況が呪いの力への信仰と結びついて，この突発的で持続的な踊りの原因となった可能性があります。音楽を追加して踊る人を治そうとする試みは，たいてい状況を悪化させるだけでした。音楽は，さらに多くの人たちを踊りに加わるように促したからです。

　研究者の中には，1518年のダンス熱はストラスブールの人たちが抱えていた強いストレスを原因とする集団ヒステリーで，彼らの宗教的信仰によってさらに悪化したのだと考えている人もいます。確かに，ストラスブールの住民は，この踊りの呪いを説明できそうな霊に対する信仰と恐れを前から持っていました。この現象に関する別の新たな説は，幻覚を引き起こす可能性のある有毒な菌である麦角菌の摂取を指摘しています。しかし，この問題について行われた数多くの研究にもかかわらず，ストラスブールのダンス熱に関する最終的な説明はまだ見つかっていません。いきなり踊り出す原因——そしてその突然の終息——は，決して解決されることがないかもしれない謎なのです。

⇒別冊 p.23 ～ 25

解答と解説

解答

(1) ①　　(2) ④　　(3) ③　　(4) ③

解説

(1) 第3段落の第1・2文の内容から，それ以前は金属で作られていたわけではないとわかるので，1が正解。4は，第1段落の第1文～3文で産業革命によって錠前の必要性が増大したことは書かれているものの，第6文で，物理的な錠前の発想は大昔からあると書かれているため，誤り。

設問・選択肢の和訳

(1) 本文によると，物理的な錠前は…

○1 歴史を通してつねに金属で作られていたわけではありません。

×2 開くのがより大変になっているので最近ではデジタルロックに取って代わられつつある。

×3 とても使用するのが複雑なので日常生活において使うのに便利ではない。

×4 人々が持ち物を安全に保管したいと思っていた産業革命の間にデザインされた。

(2) 第2段落の最後の文の内容に一致する4が正解。1・3は，本文にそのような記述はないため，誤り。2は，第2段落の最後から2文目に何世紀も前からあると書かれているので，誤り。

設問・選択肢の和訳

(2)「ダイヤル錠」の特徴の1つは…である

×1 主に上流階級の人々によって使用されていた。

×2 人々はほんのわずかな期間しか使うことがなかった。

×3 ジムや学校のロッカーに使うために発明された。

○4 使用者が操作するのに鍵に頼ることがない。

(3) 第3段落の第3文以降には，さまざまな種類の錠前とその改良の歴史が述べられている。そのことをまとめている3が正解。ほかの選択肢は本文に記述がないため，誤り。

設問・選択肢の和訳

(3) 産業革命の間，…

×1 その時以来，誰も開けることができていない錠前が発明された。

×2 ピッキングの技術が向上するにつれて窃盗の件数が増加した。

○3 より多くの種類の錠前が開発され，それらは開けるのがより困難だった。

×4 一般人の間では，まだ木製の錠前の方が金属製のものより人気があった。

(4) 第4段落の第7・8文の内容に一致する3が正解。1・2のような記述は本文中にないため，誤り。4は，第4段落の最終文にカードキーをなくしてもすぐに再発行できると書かれているものの，自分で発行することができるとは書かれていないため，誤り。

(4) デジタル革命のため，…

× 1　鍵がデータベースを使用しているため，より安全になった。

× 2　多くの人々がキーホルダーを携帯しているので，鍵をなくす人が減った。

○ 3　錠前を開けるのに，鍵が物理的に錠前に触れる必要はない。

× 4　たとえ人々がカードキーをなくしたとしても，自分で新しいカードキーを発行することができる。

語句

〈第 1 段落〉

□ material possession　物質的な所有物

□ theft　(名) 窃盗，盗難

□ sophisticated　(形) 高性能の，精緻な

〈第 2 段落〉

□ release　(動) ～を解除する

□ fastener　(名) 留め具

□ warded　(形) 突起のある

□ block　(動) ～を妨害する，阻止する，塞ぐ

□ combination lock　ダイヤル錠

〈第 3 段落〉

□ exclusively　(副) 独占的に，もっぱら

〈第 4 段落〉

□ within reach　手の届く範囲に

□ bolt　(名) スライド錠

構造確認 ※誤読した部分の確認に使用してください。

⇒別冊 p.23 ~ 25

第1段落 錠前は現代生活の必需品の1つだが，その機能は理解されておらず当たり前の物となっている。

① (Since the Industrial Revolution enabled the spread ⟨of manufactured
goods⟩ (throughout the world)), the average person has more material
possessions (than ever before).

(産業革命が (世界中への)⟨工業製品の⟩普及を可能にして以降)，一般の人でも (かつてないほど) 多くの物的財産を所有しています。

② People ⟨owning these items⟩ (naturally) desire to keep them safe (from
theft).

⟨こうした品々を所有する⟩人々は (当然) それらを (盗難から) 安全に守っておきたいと思います。

③ Locks have (consequently) become a basic necessity ⟨of modern life⟩.

(その結果)，錠前は ⟨現代生活の⟩基本的な必需品になっています。

④ People lock their homes and their cars, their offices and their stores, their
personal diaries, and more.

人々は自分の家や車，オフィスや店舗，個人的な日記，そのほかいろいろなものに錠をかけます。

⑤ There are also digital locks ⟨for phones, computers, and bank accounts⟩.

⟨電話やコンピューター，銀行口座のための⟩デジタルロック (電子錠) もあります。

⑥ (While the concept ⟨of a physical lock⟩ is ancient), most people do not
understand [how these devices work].

(⟨物理的な錠前の⟩概念は非常に古いものですが)，大半の人々は [これらの装置がどのようにしてそ

の機能を果たすのか] を理解していません。

⑦ **(Furthermore)**, **(because sophisticated locks have become so cheap and**
　　　　　　　　　　　　　　　　　　　　　　S'　　　　　　　　　　　V'　　　　　C'

common), they are often taken for granted.
　　　　　　　S　　V

注2

（さらに），（高性能の錠前でも非常に安価で一般的なものになっているので），ごく当たり前のものと
考えられています。

第2段落 錠前は数千年前から存在しており，何世紀にもわたって現代まで使われ続けている種類もある。

① The oldest known locks were created (thousands of years ago) (in the
　　　　　　　　　　S　　　　　　　　V

ancient Assyrian city ⟨of Nineveh⟩, ⟨which eventually became part of Iraq⟩).
　　　　　　　　　　　　　　　　　　　　　　　　　　　　V'　　　　　C'

現在知られているものの中で最古の錠前は（⟨後にイラクの一部となった⟩, ⟨ニネベという⟩古代アッ
シリアの都市で）（数千年前に）作られました。

② These locks were made (of wood) and required a key ⟨to lift a series of
　　　　S　　　　　V①　　　　　　　　　　V②　　O②

pins⟩ (to release the fastener).

これらの錠前は（木で）作られていて（留め具を外すために）⟨一連のピンを持ち上げるための⟩鍵が必
要でした。

③ The "warded lock", ⟨found (in ancient China and Rome)⟩, was a popular lock
　　　　S　　　　　　　　　　　　　　　　　　　　　　　　V　　　　C

⟨that can still be seen (today)⟩.
　　　　V'

注3

⟨（古代中国とローマで）発見された⟩「ウォード錠」は，⟨（今日）でも見られる⟩広く普及した錠前です。

④ The inside ⟨of the lock⟩ has many differently shaped "teeth", and the shape
　　　S①　　　　　　　V①　　　　　　　　O①　　　　　　　　　　　　　S②

⟨of the key⟩ must match them (in order to turn (without [being blocked])).
　　　　　　　　V②　　O②

⟨錠前の⟩内側にはさまざまな形をしたたくさんの「歯」があり，⟨鍵の⟩形は（（[抵抗を受けること] な
く）回転させるために）それらに一致していなければなりません。

117

⑤ The "combination lock" is another design ⟨that has been around (for many
     S   V   C   V'

centuries)⟩.

「ダイヤル錠」は⟨(何世紀にもわたって) 身近に存在してきた⟩もう 1 つの型です。

⑥ This type of lock requires people to input a specific code (by turning a dial),
   S①   V① O①

and (today) it is commonly found (on gym and school lockers).
     S②V②

この種の錠前では人々は (ダイヤルを回して) 特定のコードを入力する (数字を揃える) 必要があり,
(今日では) (スポーツジムや学校のロッカーに) 広く見られます。

第3段落 9世紀後半までには錠前は金属製となり,産業革命の間にはより複雑な設計の物が製造された。

① (By the late 9th century), people had managed to create locks ⟨made
             S   V   O

(entirely) (out of metal)⟩.

注4

(9 世紀後半までには),人々は⟨(すべてが) (金属で) できた⟩錠前を作ることができるようになって
いました。

② (From then on), metal locks and keys were used (almost exclusively).
         S   V

(それ以後),(ほぼ例外なく) 金属製の錠前と鍵が使われていました。

③ (During the Industrial Revolution), locking devices were manufactured (at
                S   V

greater volumes) and (with increasingly more complicated designs).

(産業革命の間),施錠装置は (より大量に) そして (次第にもっと複雑な設計のものが) 製造されまし
た。

④ The "tumbler lock" was one such design, and several variations ⟨of it⟩ were
   S①   V①   C①   S②   V②

developed.

「タンブラー錠」はそうして設計されたものの 1 つで,⟨それについて⟩いくつかの種類が開発されまし
た。

⑤ A man 〈named Joseph Bramah〉 developed a similar lock 〈that he claimed
    S   V   O   S'   V'
no one could pick〉.

〈ジョセフ・ブラマーという名の〉男は〈誰も開けることができないと彼が主張した〉同種の錠前を開
発しました。

⑥ (Indeed), it was so secure that it took 67 years (before an American
          S① V①   C①   S② V②   O②   S'
locksmith proved him wrong).
          V'   O'   C'

(実際)，それはとても堅固なものだったので，(アメリカの錠前師が彼が間違っていることを証明す
るまでに) 67 年かかりました。

⑦ Inventors also came up with other new features (during the Industrial
    S   V   O
Revolution), 〈such as markers 〈indicating [whether someone had
                                            S'   V'
attempted to open the lock (with an incorrect key)]〉〉.
         O'

何人かの発明家も (産業革命の間に)，〈例えば〈[誰かが (正しくない鍵で) 錠前を開こうとしたかどう
か] を示す〉マーカーなどの〉別の新しい機能を考案しました。

第 4 段落 鍵の紛失に備えてさまざまな物が使われてきたが，錠前は現在デジタル革命を経験している。

① (Since ancient times), one 〈of the biggest issues 〈in lock design〉〉 has been
                          S   V
the key itself.
    C

(大昔から)，〈〈錠前の設計での〉最大の問題の〉1 つは鍵そのものです。

② Keys can be lost, and they can be inconvenient (to carry or hold on to).
    S① V①   S②   V②   C②

鍵は紛失するかもしれず，(持ち運びや保管が) 面倒なことがありえます。

③ Wealthy Romans often wore their keys (as rings) (on their fingers) (to keep
       S   V   O

them safe and easily within easy reach (at all times)).

裕福なローマ人たちは鍵を (((いつでも) 安全で簡単に手の届くところに置いておくために) しばしば
(指輪として) (指に) 装着しました。

④ (Later), keyrings were often used (to fasten keys (to belts and clothing)).
          S   V

(後には), (鍵を (ベルトや服に) 固定するために) キーホルダーがよく使われました。

⑤ (Today), (however), locks are undergoing a digital revolution.
                  S   V   O

(しかし), (今日), 錠前はデジタル革命を経験しています。

⑥ Some locks can be opened (with a key card ⟨that fits right (into your
      S   V   V'

wallet)⟩).

錠前の中には (⟨(財布の中に) ぴったり収まる⟩ カードキーで) 開けられるものがあります。

⑦ (When one of these key cards is put near a lock), it sends a digital signature
              S'①   V'①   S V   O

⟨that is compared (against a signature ⟨stored (in a database)⟩)⟩.
      V'②

(こういったカードキーの 1 つが錠前の近くに差し出されると), それが ⟨(⟨(データベースに) 保存さ
れている⟩ 署名と) 照合される⟩ デジタル署名を送信します。

⑧ (If the signature matches), a motor causes a lock's bolt to slide (out of
         S'   V'   S   V   O

place), (allowing a door to be opened).

(その署名が一致すると), モーターが錠前のボルトを (所定の位置から) スライドさせ, (ドアが開け
られるようになります)。

⑨ And (if a key card is lost, (like at a hotel)), a new card can be issued
　　　　　 S'　　　　 V'　　　　　　　　　　　　　 S　　　　　 V

(quickly).

また((ホテルなどで)カードキーが紛失された場合は),(すぐに)新しいカードを発行することができます。

注1　since S V は「S が V して以来」という意味に加えて,「S が V するので」という意味で使うことができ,理由を表す。

注2　furthermore は「さらに」という意味で,前出の内容にさらに情報を追加する場合に使われるつなぎ言葉。

注3　主語の The "warded lock" を直後の過去分詞 found 以下が修飾している。修飾部分が 2 つのカンマで挟まれて,主語と述語の間に挿入される形となっている。

注4　9 世紀後半という過去の時点までの完了を表すために,過去完了形が使われている。

注5　so 形容詞[副詞] that S V は「非常に…なので S は V する」という意味の構文。

注6　whether S V は「S が V するかどうか」という意味の,名詞のはたらきをする節を作る。

注7　この文での be used to V は,「V するために用いられる」という意味で,use(使用する)という動詞が受動態で使われているものである。

注8　like は「〜のように」という意味の前置詞として用いられ,直後に名詞がくるのが普通だが,この文のように前置詞句が置かれることもある。

サイトトランスレーション

⇒別冊 p.23 ～ 25

1 Since the Industrial Revolution enabled /	産業革命が可能にして以降
the spread of manufactured goods /	工業製品の普及を
throughout the world, /	世界中での,
the average person has /	一般人は持っています
more material possessions /	多くの物的財産を
than ever before. //	かつてないほど。
People /	人々は
owning these items /	これらの品々を所有する
naturally desire /	当然望みます
to keep them safe /	それらを安全に守っておきたいと
from theft. //	盗難から。
Locks have consequently become a basic necessity /	その結果として錠前は基本的な必需品になっています
of modern life. //	現代生活の。
People lock /	人は錠をかけます
their homes and their cars, /	彼らの家や車に,
their offices and their stores, /	オフィスや店舗に,
their personal diaries, /	個人的な日記に,
and more. //	そのほかいろいろなものに。
There are also digital locks /	デジタルロック（電子錠）もあります
for phones, computers, and bank accounts. //	電話, コンピューター, 銀行口座のための。
While the concept of a physical lock is ancient, /	物理的な錠前の概念は大昔から存在しますが,

most people do not understand /	大半の人々は理解していません
how these devices work. //	これらの装置がどのようにしてその機能を果たすのか。
Furthermore, /	さらに,
because sophisticated locks have become /	高性能の錠前がなっているので
so cheap and common, /	非常に安価で一般的に,
they are often taken for granted. //	それらはしばしば当たり前と考えられています。
2 The oldest known locks were created /	最も古いと知られている錠前は作られました
thousands of years ago /	数千年前に
in the ancient Assyrian city /	古代アッシリアの都市で
of Nineveh, /	ニネべという,
which eventually became /	後になりました
part of Iraq. //	イラクの一部に。
These locks were made of wood /	これらの錠前は木製でした
and required a key /	そして鍵を必要とします
to lift a series of pins /	一連のピンを持ち上げるための
to release the fastener. //	留め具を外すための。
The "warded lock," /	「ウォード錠」は,
found in ancient China and Rome, /	古代中国とローマで発見された,
was a popular lock /	広く普及した錠前でした
that can still be seen today. //	それは今日でも見られます。
The inside of the lock has /	錠前の内側にはあります
many differently shaped "teeth," /	多くのさまざまな形をした「歯」が,
and the shape of the key must match them /	そして鍵の形はそれらに一致していなければなりません

in order to turn /	回転させるために
without being blocked. //	妨害されることなく。
The "combination lock" /	「ダイヤル錠」は
is another design /	もう1つの型です
that has been around for many centuries. //	何世紀にもわたって身近に存在してきた。
This type of lock requires /	この種の錠前は必要とします
people /	人々に
to input a specific code /	特定のコードを入力することを
by turning a dial, /	ダイヤルを回すことで，
and today it is commonly found /	そして今日よく見られます
on gym and school lockers. //	スポーツジムや学校のロッカーなどで。
3 By the late 9th century, /	9世紀後半までには，
people had managed to create /	人々は作り出せるようになっていました
locks /	錠前を
made entirely out of metal. //	すべて金属でできた。
From then on, /	それ以後，
metal locks and keys were used /	金属製の錠前と鍵が使われました
almost exclusively. //	ほとんど例外なく。
During the Industrial Revolution, /	産業革命の間，
locking devices were manufactured /	錠前は製造されました
at greater volumes /	より大量に
and with increasingly more complicated designs. //	そして次第にもっと複雑な設計をして。
The "tumbler lock" was one such design, /	「タンブラー錠」はそうして設計されたものの1つでした，

and several variations of it /	そしてそのいくつかの種類が
were developed. //	開発されました。
A man named Joseph Bramah /	ジョセフ・ブラマーという名の男は
developed a similar lock /	同種の錠前を開発しました
that he claimed /	彼は主張しました
no one could pick. //	誰も開けることができないと。
Indeed, /	実際,
it was so secure /	それはとても堅固でした
that it took 67 years /	なので 67 年かかりました
before an American locksmith proved him wrong. //	アメリカの錠前師が彼が間違っていることを証明するまでに。
Inventors also came up with other new features /	発明家たちも別の新しい機能を考案しました
during the Industrial Revolution, /	産業革命の間に,
such as markers indicating /	示すマーカーなどを
whether someone had attempted /	誰かがしようとしたかどうかを
to open the lock /	錠前を開くことを
with an incorrect key. //	正しくない鍵で。
4 Since ancient times, /	大昔から,
one of the biggest issues /	最大の問題の 1 つは
in lock design /	錠前の設計で
has been the key itself. //	鍵そのものでした。
Keys can be lost, /	鍵は紛失することもありえます,
and they can be inconvenient /	そして面倒なこともありえます
to carry /	持ち運ぶことが

or hold on to. //	あるいは保管することが。
Wealthy Romans often wore /	裕福なローマ人たちはしばしば装着しました
their keys /	彼らの鍵を
as rings on their fingers /	指輪として指に
to keep them safe /	それらを安全に保つために
and easily within easy reach /	そして簡単に手が届くように
at all times. //	いつでも。
Later, /	後になると,
keyrings were often used /	キーホルダーがよく使われました
to fasten keys /	鍵を固定するために
to belts and clothing. //	ベルトや服に。
Today, /	今日では,
however, /	しかし,
locks are undergoing a digital revolution. //	錠前はデジタル革命を経験しています。
Some locks can be opened /	錠前の中には開けられるものがあります
with a key card /	カードキーで
that fits right into your wallet. //	財布の中にぴったり収まる。
When one of these key cards is put near a lock, /	これらのカードキーの1つが錠前の近くに差し出されると,
it sends a digital signature /	それはデジタル署名を送信します,
that is compared /	照合されます
against a signature /	署名と
stored in a database. //	データベースに保存されている。
If the signature matches, /	その署名が一致すると,

a motor causes a lock's bolt /	モーターが錠前のボルトに…させます
to slide out of place, /	所定の位置からスライドするように,
allowing a door /	ドアを可能にします
to be opened. //	開けられることを。
And if a key card is lost, /	そしてカードキーが紛失された場合は,
like at a hotel, /	ホテルなどで,
a new card can be issued /	新しいカードが発行されます
quickly. //	すぐに。

The History of Locks

Since the Industrial Revolution enabled the spread of manufactured goods throughout the world, the average person has more material possessions than ever before. People owning these items naturally desire to keep them safe from theft. Locks have consequently become a basic necessity of modern life. People lock their homes and their cars, their offices and their stores, their personal diaries, and more. There are also digital locks for phones, computers, and bank accounts. While the concept of a physical lock is ancient, most people do not understand how these devices work. Furthermore, because sophisticated locks have become so cheap and common, they are often taken for granted.

The oldest known locks were created thousands of years ago in the ancient Assyrian city of Nineveh, which eventually became part of Iraq. These locks were made of wood and required a key to lift a series of pins to release the fastener. The "warded lock," found in ancient China and Rome, was a popular lock that can still be seen today. The inside of the lock has many differently shaped "teeth," and the shape of the key must match them in order to turn without being blocked. The "combination lock" is another design that has been around for many centuries. This type of lock requires people to input a specific code by turning a dial, and today it is commonly found on gym and school lockers.

By the late 9th century, people had managed to create locks made entirely out of metal. From then on, metal locks and keys were used almost exclusively. During the Industrial Revolution, locking devices were manufactured at greater volumes and with increasingly more complicated designs. The "tumbler lock" was one such design, and several variations of it were developed. A man named Joseph Bramah developed a similar lock that he claimed no one could pick. Indeed, it was so secure that it took 67 years before an American locksmith proved him wrong. Inventors also came up with other new features during the Industrial Revolution, such as markers indicating whether someone had attempted to open the lock with an incorrect key.

Since ancient times, one of the biggest issues in lock design has been the key itself. Keys can be lost, and they can be inconvenient to carry or hold on to. Wealthy Romans often wore their keys as rings on their fingers to keep them safe and easily within easy reach at all times. Later, keyrings were often used to fasten keys to belts and clothing. Today, however, locks are undergoing a digital revolution. Some locks can be opened with a key card that fits right into your wallet. When one of these key cards is put near a lock, it sends a digital signature that is compared against a signature stored in a database. If the signature matches, a motor causes a lock's bolt to slide out of place, allowing a door to be opened. And if a key card is lost, like at a hotel, a new card can be issued quickly.

錠前の歴史

産業革命が工業製品を世界中に普及させることを可能にして以降，一般の人でもかつてない
ほど多くの物的財産を所有しています。そうした品々を所有する人たちは当然，それらを盗難か
ら安全に守っておきたいと思います。その結果，錠前は現代生活の基本的な必需品となっていま
す。人は自分の家や車，オフィスや店舗，個人的な日記，そのほかいろいろなものに錠をかけま
す。携帯電話やコンピューター，銀行口座のためのデジタルロック（電子錠）もあります。物理
的な錠前の概念は大昔から存在しますが，大半の人たちはこれらの装置がどのようにしてその
機能を果たすのか理解していません。さらに，高性能の錠前でも非常に安価で一般的なものに
なっているので，ごく当たり前のものと考えられています。

現在知られているものの中で最古の錠前は，数千年前に古代アッシリアの都市ニネベで作ら
れましたが，そこは後にイラクの一部となったところです。その錠前は木製で，留め具を外すの
に一連のピンを持ち上げるための鍵が必要でした。古代中国とローマで発見された「ウォード錠」
は，広く普及した錠前で，今でも見られます。錠前の内側には，さまざまな形をしたたくさんの
「歯」があり，鍵の形は，抵抗を受けることなく歯を回転させるためにその歯に一致していなけ
ればなりません。「ダイヤル錠」は，何世紀にもわたって身近に存在してきたもう1つの型です。
この種の錠前では，人はダイヤルを回して特定のコードを入力する（正しい数字を揃える）必要
があり，今日では広くスポーツジムや学校のロッカーなどに使われています。

9世紀後半までには，人はすべてが金属でできた錠前を作ることができるようになっていま
した。それ以後，ほぼ例外なく金属製の錠前と鍵が使われていました。産業革命の間，錠前はよ
り大量に，そして次第にもっと複雑な設計のものが製造されました。「タンブラー錠」は，そう
して設計されたものの1つで，いくつかの種類が開発されました。ジョセフ・ブラマーという
名の男は，同種の錠前を開発し，（鍵がなければ）誰も開けることができないと主張しました。実
際，それはとても堅固だったので，アメリカの錠前師がそうでないことを証明するまでに67年
かかりました。何人かの発明家も産業革命の間に別の新しい機能を考案し，その例としては，誰
かが正しくない鍵で錠前を開こうとしたかどうかがわかるマーカーなどがありました。

大昔から，錠前の設計で最大の問題の1つは，鍵そのものでした。鍵は紛失することもあり
えるし，持ち運びや保管が面倒なこともありえます。裕福なローマ人たちは，しばしば鍵を指輪
として指に装着し，安全でいつでも簡単に手の届くところに置いておこうとしました。後になる
と，鍵をベルトや服に固定するためにキーホルダーがよく使われるようになりました。しかし，
今日では，錠前はデジタル革命を経験しています。錠前の中には，財布の中にぴったり収まる
カードキーで開けられるものがあります。そのようなカードキーの1つが錠前の近くに差し出
されるとデジタル署名が送信され，それがデータベースに保存されている署名と照合されます。
その署名が一致すると，モーターが錠前のボルトを所定の位置からスライドさせ，ドアが開け
られるようになります。また，ホテルなどでカードキーを紛失した場合は，すぐに新しいカード
を発行することができます。

Column リーディングに強くなるには

　リーディングの力をつけるために最も大切なことは，ズバリ「英語を読むこと」です。

　よく外国人が日本人の英語学習に関して不思議に思うことがあります。それは，リーディングができるようになりたいと言いながら，単語を覚えたり，文法や構文を学んだり，日本語で書かれた解説を勉強してばかりいることです。もちろん，それらはすべて大切なことではあるのですが，やはり英語を読む練習を重ねなければ，読めるようになるはずはありません。

　その練習には，しっかりと読み，音読やリスニングで固めるような「精読」と，純粋に読書として楽しむ「多読」とがあります。精読に関しては，本書のような教材を使用するのが最も効率的でしょう。一方，多読に関しては，現在の自分のレベルよりも，少々低めの素材を選ぶことをお勧めします。また，多読する場合，細かいことがわからなくても追求せずに読み進めましょう。多少の知らない単語があっても，ストーリーを追いながら読書を楽しむことが重要です。英語に触れる時間を少しでも増やしていくのが，多読の役割です。

　英語でのウェブサーフィンも最高の多読練習です。皆さんの趣味は何ですか？　例えば，写真を撮ることが趣味の人は，英語の写真関係のサイトを見てはどうでしょうか。もちろん，難しい語彙も出てくると思いますが，知っている単語をつまみながら，内容を推測しましょう。ウェブサイトには，多くのイラストや写真が使われていることが多いので，飽きることなく英語に触れることができると思います。

　このように，リーディングの力をつけるためには，さまざまな練習を通して，たくさんの英文を読むことが大切なのです。

⇒別冊 p.26 ～ 28

解答と解説

解答

(1) ④　　(2) ②　　(3) ①　　(4) ①

解説

(1) 第1段落の最後から3番目の文中の the opposite is true に着目する。「その逆が正しい」とは，前文の内容から考えて「シェルパ族の方が非シェルパ族よりも（酸素を運ぶ働きをする）赤血球が少ない」ということ。したがって，4が正解。1は前半，2は後半，3は全体が本文の記述と違っている。

設問・選択肢の和訳

(1) 研究者たちはシェルパ族について何を理解するのに苦労したか。

×1 より高い確率で脳浮腫や肺水腫が起こるにもかかわらず，彼らは高地で元気に動くことができた。

×2 彼らは高地ではスタミナ十分だったが，低い高度では病気になる傾向があった。

×3 呼吸するのに苦労すると苦情を言うけれど，大半のシェルパ族はほかの登山者と同じくらいの量の酸素を得ているように思われた。

○4 彼らの方が赤血球の数が少ないのに，ほかの登山者よりも高度をあまり苦にしない。

(2) 第2段落の最後の3つの文の内容に一致する2が正解。第2段落によれば，シェルパ族と非シェルパ族との差は，ミトコンドリアのサイズではなくその働き方である。したがって，1・3は誤り。4のような記述はない。

設問・選択肢の和訳

(2) シェルパ族の細胞についてアンドリュー・マーレーは何を発見したか。

×1 それらは非シェルパ族の細胞よりもはるかに大きく，より活発なミトコンドリアを含んでいる。

○2 それらのミトコンドリアの方が，酸素からエネルギーを作り出す効率がはるかに高かった。

×3 シェルパ族の登山者の細胞中のミトコンドリアのサイズは，5,300メートルの高度で大幅に増加した。

×4 シェルパ族のミトコンドリアは，集中的な運動の間，ほかの人たちよりもよく機能した。

(3) 第3段落の最後の文にあるとおり，シェルパ族の能力は遺伝によると考えられる。そう判断できるのは，その前に述べられているように高地での実験と低地での実験結果の間に，シェルパ族の酸素の処理能力の点で差がないからである。したがって，1が正解であり，ほかの選択肢は誤り。

設問・選択肢の和訳

(3) 実験に参加したシェルパ族は高度の低い場所で暮らしていたので，…

○1 高地で発揮される彼らの高い能力は，それらが生来のものであることを示唆している。

×2 彼らの細胞は高地で暮らすシェルパ族の細胞ほどの量の酸素を取り込めなかった。

×3 シェルパ族が高地で発揮する高い能力は，そのライフスタイルのせいだと研究者たちは信じている。

×4 非シェルパ族に勝る彼らの遺伝的な強みは，活動量が減った暮らし方のために弱まっているかもしれない。

---

(4) 第4段落の最後の文中の this does not happen to the same degree in Sherpas' bodies に着目する。this は2つ前の文の tries to compensate by producing more red blood cells（より多くの赤血球を作り出すことで埋め合わせをしようとする）を指している。つまり，シェルパ族の体内では赤血球の生産の度合いが低いので，血液が濃くならなくて済む。したがって，1が正解。2は本文に記述がなく，3・4は本文の内容に反する。

設問・選択肢の和訳

(4) 科学者たちは，…によって集中治療室の患者を助けたいと思っている

○1 シェルパ族が非シェルパ族より効率的に赤血球を使える理由を知ること。

×2 肺の病気，心臓発作，がんに苦しむシェルパ族の細胞の反応のしかたを比較すること。

×3 シェルパ族の血液が高地ではより濃くなる理由を見つけること。

×4 シェルパ族の血液を使用して，体内に十分な酸素が流れていることを確認すること。

語句

〈第1段落〉

□ stamina	（名）スタミナ，体力
□ altitude	（名）高度，標高，（通例，複数形で）高地
□ swell	（動）膨張する
□ fluid	（名）液体，体液
□ deadly	（形）致命的な
□ be immune to ～	～に免疫がある，～を免れる
□ red blood cell	赤血球
□ puzzling	（形）当惑させる

〈第2段落〉

□ mitochondria	（名）ミトコンドリア

□ convert A into B	AをBに変換する
□ it's not A,（but）it's B that counts	重要なのはAでなくBである（強調構文）

〈第3段落〉

□ genetic	（形）遺伝的な

〈第4段落〉

□ intensive care unit	集中治療室
□ hypoxia	（名）低酸素症
□ organ	（名）臓器
□ compensate	（動）埋め合わせをする
□ mechanism	（名）仕組み

⇒別冊 p.26 ～ 28

構造確認 ※誤読した部分の確認に使用してください。

第 1 段落 シェルパ族は血液の酸素を運ぶ能力が低いにもかかわらず，高地で活動することができた。

① The Sherpa people live (in the Himalaya Mountains ⟨in Nepal⟩).
　　　　 S　　　　　　 V

シェルパ族の人々は（《ネパールの》ヒマラヤ山脈に）住んでいます。

② (Ever since the Sherpa Tenzing Norgay and Sir Edmund Hillary of England
　　　　　　　　　　　　　　　　　　　　 S'
made the first successful climb ⟨to the top ⟨of Mt. Everest⟩⟩), Sherpas
　 V'　　　　 O'　　　　　　　　　　　　　　　　　　　　　　 S
have been known (for their amazing stamina and ability ⟨to survive (at high
　　 V
altitudes)⟩). 注1

（シェルパ族のテンジン・ノルゲイとイギリスのサー・エドモンド・ヒラリーが《《エベレストの》頂上への》登山に初めて成功して以来），シェルパ族は（《《高地で》生存できる》そのすばらしい体力と能力で）知られています。

③ Most climbers have trouble (breathing (at high altitudes)) (due to the lack ⟨of
　　　 S①　　 V①　 O①
oxygen ⟨in the air⟩⟩), and (in serious cases) they can suffer from swelling
　　　　　　　　　　　　　　　　　　　　　　 S②　　 V②
⟨of the brain⟩ or fluid ⟨in the lungs⟩, ⟨both of which can be deadly⟩. 注2
　　　　　　　　　　　　　　　　　　　 S'　 V'　　 C'

大半の登山者は（《《空気中の》酸素》不足で）（《高地では》呼吸することに）苦労しており，《深刻な場合には》〈脳〉浮腫や〈肺〉水腫を発症し，〈そのどちらも命取りになりかねません〉。

④ (While Sherpas are not immune (to these dangers)), they experience them
　　　　 S'　　 V'　　 C'　　　　　　　　　　　　 S　　 V　　 O
(less frequently).

（シェルパ族も（これらの危険を）免れるわけではありませんが），そうなる確率は（より低い）のです。

⑤ It was once believed [that Sherpas must have more red blood cells
　 S　 V　　　　　　　　　 S'　　　　 V'　　　　　 O'
(because those are the cells ⟨that carry oxygen⟩)].

[（赤血球は《酸素を運ぶ》細胞であることから）シェルパ族はより多くの赤血球を持っているに違いない]とかつて信じられていました。

⑥ It was discovered, (however), [that the opposite is true].
　S　　V　　　　　　　　　　　　　　　　S'　　V'　C'

(しかしながら)，[事実はその反対であること] がわかりました。

⑦ (Since it appeared that Sherpa's blood had less ability ⟨to carry oxygen⟩),
　　　　　　S'①　　V'①

it did not seem to make sense [that they were able to perform (so well) (at
S　　　　　　V　　　　　　　　　S'②　　　　　V'②

high altitudes)].

(シェルパ族の血液は《酸素を運ぶ》能力が低いようなので)，[彼らが (高地で) (非常にうまく) 活動
できるの] は道理に合わないと思われました。

⑧ This was highly puzzling (to researchers).
　S　V　　　　　　C

このことは (研究者たちにとって) 大いに謎でした。

第2段落 シェルパ族のミトコンドリアは非シェルパ族よりも多くの酸素をエネルギーに変換できた。

① (To solve the mystery), researcher Andrew Murray ⟨of the University ⟨of
　　　　　　　　　　　　　　　　　　　S

Cambridge⟩⟩ studied a group ⟨of non-Sherpas⟩ and a group ⟨of Sherpas
　　　　　　　V　　　　O

⟨who all lived (at low altitudes)⟩⟩.
　　　V'

(その謎を解明するために)，《《ケンブリッジ》大学の》研究者アンドリュー・マーレーは《非シェルパ
族の》グループと《《全員 (標高の低い場所に) 住んでいる》シェルパ族の》グループを調査しました。

② He took them (up to 5,300 meters, an altitude ⟨where many people start to
　S　V①　O①　　　　　　　　　　　　　　　　　　　S'①　　　　V'①

feel sick⟩), and studied [how their bodies reacted (to the high altitude)].
　C'①　　　　V②　　O②　　S'②　　　V'②

彼は (《多くの人たちが気分が悪くなり始める》標高である，5,300 メートル地点まで) 彼らを連れて
いき，[彼らの体が (高い標高に) どう反応するのか] を調べました。

③ All human cells contain mitochondria, and these are responsible (for
　S①　　　　V①　　O①　　　　　　S②　V②　　C②

[producing energy]).

人間のすべての細胞はミトコンドリアを含んでおり，それらが ([エネルギーの生成] を) 担っていま
す。

135

④ Murray found [that (although the amounts ⟨of mitochondria⟩ were similar),
   _S   _V   _O

the Sherpa's mitochondria were able to convert much more oxygen (into
───────────────────────── ─────────── ───────────────
         S'   V'   O'

energy) (than the mitochondria of non-Sherpas)].

マーレーは [(⟨ミトコンドリアの⟩量は変わらないものの)，シェルパ族のミトコンドリアは (非シェ
ルパ族のミトコンドリアよりも) はるかに多くの酸素を (エネルギーに) 変換できること] を発見しま
した。

⑤ Murray says, "This shows [that it's not [how much oxygen you've got]; it's
   _{S①} _{V①} _{S②}   _{V②}   _{O② S'① V'①   C'①}   _{S'②}

[what you do with it] that counts]".
─────────────────
      _{C'②}

マーレーは述べています，「これは [[あなたがどれくらいの酸素を取り込んだか] ではない，重要なの
は [あなたがそれをどう処理するか] だということを示している」と。

⑥ (In total), Sherpas' mitochondria produced over 30 percent more energy.
                ──────────────────── ──────── ───────────────────
                        S   V   O

(全体として)，シェルパ族のミトコンドリアは 30 パーセント以上もエネルギーを多く生み出してい
ました。

第3段落 シェルパ族の細胞は低い標高でも高い標高の時と同じ量の酸素を大気中から取り入れられた。

① The Sherpas ⟨in the experiment⟩ had been living (in a city ⟨at a much lower
   ──────────   ───────────────
      _{S①}   _{V①}

altitude ⟨than other Sherpas⟩⟩), and they were eating exactly the same
                                          ──── ────────── ───────────────
                                          _{S②}   _{V②}   _{O②}

foods ⟨as the non-Sherpas⟩.
─────
  _{O②}

⟨実験における⟩シェルパ族は (⟨⟨ほかのシェルパ族よりも⟩はるかに標高の低いところにある⟩町に)
住んでおり，⟨非シェルパ族と⟩まったく同じものを食べていました。

② This was done (to make the two groups as similar as possible).
   ──── ─────────
    S   V

これは (その 2 つのグループを，できるだけ同じものにするため) でした。

③ (Also), (before the experiment began), the same tests were conducted (on

　　　　　　　　　　S'① 　　　　V'① 　　　　　　　　　S　　　　　　V

the Sherpas) (while they were still living (at a low altitude)).

　　　　　　　　　　　S'② 　V'②

（また），（その実験が始まる前に），（シェルパ族に）同様の検査が（まだ彼らが（標高の低いところで）
生活している間に）行われました。

④ The researchers discovered [that the Sherpas' cells were able to get just as

　　　S　　　　　　V　　　　　　O　　　　　　S'　　　　　　　　V'　　　　　　O'

much oxygen (from the air) (at a low altitude) (as they were at a high

altitude)].

研究者たちは［シェルパ族の細胞は（低い標高でも）（高い標高にいる時と）まったく同じ量の酸素を
（大気中から）取り入れられるということ］を発見しました。

⑤ This suggests [that the differences are genetic (rather than being acquired

　　S　　　V　　　　O　　　　　S'　　　　　V'　　C'

(during an individual's lifetime))].　　　　　　　　　　　　　　　　注8

このことは［その違いが（（個人の生涯の間に）獲得されるものではなく）遺伝的なものであること］を
示しています。

第4段落 シェルパ族の細胞の仕組みを知ることが ICU にいる患者の生存率上昇に役立つかもしれない。

① (Every year) (in the UK), one ⟨out of every five people ⟨admitted to the

　　　　　　　　　　　　　　　　S①

intensive care unit ⟨of a hospital⟩⟩⟩ dies, and one ⟨of the main reasons⟩ is

　　　　　　　　　　　　　　　　　　　　　V①　　　　　S②　　　　　　　　　　　V②

hypoxia, or a lack ⟨of oxygen ⟨in the body's organs⟩⟩.　　　　　　注9

　　　　　C②

（イギリスでは）（毎年），⟨⟨⟨病院の⟩集中治療室に運ばれてくる⟩5人のうち⟩1人が亡くなりますが，
⟨その主な理由の⟩1つが低酸素症，すなわち⟨⟨体の臓器中の⟩酸素⟩不足です。

② (In patients ⟨suffering from diseases ⟨that cause hypoxia⟩, ⟨including lung

illnesses, heart attacks, and cancer⟩⟩), the body tries to compensate (by

　　　　　　　　　　　　　　　　　　　　　　S　　　　　V

producing more red blood cells).

（⟨⟨肺の病気や心臓発作，がんなどの⟩，⟨低酸素症を引き起こす⟩病気を患っている⟩患者において
は），体は（より多くの赤血球を生成することによって）補おうとします。

③ (However), this causes the blood to become thicker and can cause it to
               S   V①   O①   V② O②
flow less well.

(しかし)，これが血液の濃度をよりいっそう上げ，その流れを悪くすることがあります。

④ (Since this does not happen (to the same degree) (in Sherpas' bodies)),
          S'①   V'①

scientists hope [that [learning about the mechanisms ⟨that make their cells
    S   V   O   S'②

more efficient⟩] could help to improve the chances ⟨of survival ⟨for patients
                       V'②   O'②

⟨in ICUs⟩⟩⟩].
                                                注10

(このようなことは (シェルパ族の体では) (同じ程度には) 起こらないので)，科学者たちは [[⟨彼らの
細胞をより効率的にしている⟩ 仕組みについて知ること] が ⟪⟪集中治療室にいる⟩ 患者の⟩ 生存の⟩
チャンスを高めることに役立つかもしれない] と期待しています。

サイトトランスレーション

1 The Sherpa people live / シェルパ族は住んでいます

in the Himalaya Mountains / ヒマラヤ山脈に

in Nepal. // ネパールの。

Ever since / 以来

the Sherpa Tenzing Norgay and / シェルパ族のテンジン・ノルゲイと

Sir Edmund Hillary of England / イギリスのサー・エドモンド・ヒラリーが

made the first successful climb / 初めて登ることに成功して

to the top of Mt. Everest, / エベレストの頂上まで,

Sherpas have been known / シェルパ族は知られています

for their amazing stamina / そのすばらしい体力で

and ability to survive / そして生存できる能力

at high altitudes. // 高地で。

Most climbers have trouble / 大半の登山者は苦労しています

breathing at high altitudes / 高地で呼吸することに

due to the lack of oxygen / 酸素不足で

in the air, / 空気中の,

and in serious cases / そして深刻な場合には

they can suffer / 彼らは苦しむことがあります

from swelling of the brain or fluid in the lungs, / 脳浮腫や肺水腫に,

both of which can be deadly. // そのどちらも命に関わります。

While Sherpas are not immune to these dangers, / シェルパ族もこうした危険を免れるわけではありませんが,

139

they experience them less frequently. //	彼らはさほど頻繁にはそういう体験をしません。
It was once believed /	かつて考えられていました
that Sherpas must have /	シェルパ族は持っているに違いないと
more red blood cells /	より多くの赤血球を
because those are the cells /	なぜならそれらは細胞だからです
that carry oxygen. //	酸素を運ぶ。
It was discovered, /	わかりました,
however, /	しかしながら,
that the opposite is true. //	その反対のことが正しいと。
Since it appeared /	…のようなので
that Sherpa's blood had less ability /	シェルパ族の血液は能力が低いということ
to carry oxygen, /	酸素を運ぶ,
it did not seem to make sense /	それは道理に合わないと思われました
that they were able to perform /	彼らが活動できるのは
so well /	非常にうまく
at high altitudes. //	高地で。
This was highly puzzling /	このことは大いに謎でした
to researchers. //	研究者たちにとって。
2 To solve the mystery, /	その謎を解明するために,
researcher Andrew Murray /	研究者アンドリュー・マーレーは
of the University of Cambridge /	ケンブリッジ大学の
studied /	調査しました
a group of non-Sherpas /	非シェルパ族のグループを
and a group of Sherpas /	そしてシェルパ族のグループ

who all lived /	いずれも全員が住んでいる
at low altitudes. //	標高の低い場所に。
He took them /	彼は彼らを連れていきました
up to 5,300 meters, /	5,300 メートル地点まで,
an altitude /	標高
where many people start to feel sick, /	多くの人々が気持ち悪くなり始めるところ,
and studied /	そして調べました
how their bodies reacted /	彼らの体がどう反応するのかを
to the high altitude. //	高い標高に。
All human cells contain /	人間のすべての細胞は含んでいます
mitochondria, /	ミトコンドリアを,
and these are responsible /	そしてこれらが担っています
for producing energy. //	エネルギーの生成を。
Murray found /	マーレーは見つけました
that although the amounts of mitochondria were similar, /	ミトコンドリアの量は似ているが, (…ことを)
the Sherpa's mitochondria were able to convert /	シェルパ族のミトコンドリアは変換できる
much more oxygen /	はるかに多くの酸素を
into energy /	エネルギーに
than the mitochondria of non-Sherpas. //	非シェルパ族のミトコンドリアよりも。
Murray says, /	マーレーは述べています,
"This shows /	「これは示しています
that it's not how much oxygen you've got; /	(問題は) 人がどれくらいの酸素を取り込んだかではない,

it's what you do with it /	それをどう処理するかである
that counts." //	重要なのは」と。
In total, /	全体として,
Sherpas' mitochondria produced /	シェルパ族のミトコンドリアは生み出しました
over 30 percent more energy. //	30 パーセント以上も多くのエネルギーを。
3 The Sherpas in the experiment /	実験に参加したシェルパ族は
had been living /	住んでいました
in a city at a much lower altitude /	はるかに標高の低い町に
than other Sherpas, /	ほかのシェルパ族よりも,
and they were eating /	そして彼らは食べていました
exactly the same foods /	まったく同じ食べ物を
as the non-Sherpas. //	非シェルパ族と。
This was done /	これはなされました
to make the two groups as similar as possible. //	2つのグループをできるだけ同じものにするために。
Also, /	また,
before the experiment began, /	この実験が始まる前に,
the same tests were conducted /	同じ検査が行われました
on the Sherpas /	シェルパ族に
while they were still living /	彼らがまだ生活している間に
at a low altitude. //	標高の低いところで。
The researchers discovered /	研究者たちは発見しました
that the Sherpas' cells were able to get /	シェルパ族の細胞は取り入れることができることを
just as much oxygen /	まったく同じ量の酸素を
from the air /	大気中から

at a low altitude /	低い標高において
as they were at a high altitude. //	彼らが高い標高にいる時と。
This suggests /	このことは示しています
that the differences are genetic /	この違いが遺伝的なものであることを
rather than being acquired /	獲得されるものではなく
during an individual's lifetime. //	個人の生涯の間に。
4 Every year /	毎年
in the UK, /	イギリスでは，
one out of every five people /	5人のうち1人が
admitted to the intensive care unit /	集中治療室に運ばれてくる
of a hospital /	病院の
dies, /	亡くなります，
and one of the main reasons is hypoxia, /	そしてその主な理由の1つが低酸素症です，
or a lack of oxygen /	あるいは酸素不足
in the body's organs. //	体の臓器中の。
In patients /	患者の場合
suffering from diseases /	病気を患っている
that cause hypoxia, /	低酸素症を引き起こす，
including lung illnesses, heart attacks, and cancer, /	肺の病気，心臓発作，そしてがんを含む，
the body tries to compensate /	体は補おうとします
by producing /	生成することによって
more red blood cells. //	より多くの赤血球を。
However, /	しかし，

this causes the blood to become thicker /	これが血液をより濃くします
and can cause it /	そしてそれを導くこともあります
to flow less well. //	流れが悪くなるように。
Since this does not happen /	このようなことは起こらないので
to the same degree /	同じ程度には
in Sherpas' bodies, /	シェルパ族の体では,
scientists hope /	科学者たちは期待しています
that learning about the mechanisms /	仕組みについて知ることが
that make their cells more efficient /	彼らの細胞をより効率的にしている
could help to improve /	上げることに役立つかもしれない
the chances of survival /	生存の可能性を
for patients in ICUs. //	集中治療室にいる患者の。

Secrets of the Sherpas

The Sherpa people live in the Himalaya Mountains in Nepal. Ever since the Sherpa Tenzing Norgay and Sir Edmund Hillary of England made the first successful climb to the top of Mt. Everest, Sherpas have been known for their amazing stamina and ability to survive at high altitudes. Most climbers have trouble breathing at high altitudes due to the lack of oxygen in the air, and in serious cases they can suffer from swelling of the brain or fluid in the lungs, both of which can be deadly. While Sherpas are not immune to these dangers, they experience them less frequently. It was once believed that Sherpas must have more red blood cells because those are the cells that carry oxygen. It was discovered, however, that the opposite is true. Since it appeared that Sherpa's blood had less ability to carry oxygen, it did not seem to make sense that they were able to perform so well at high altitudes. This was highly puzzling to researchers.

To solve the mystery, researcher Andrew Murray of the University of Cambridge studied a group of non-Sherpas and a group of Sherpas who all lived at low altitudes. He took them up to 5,300 meters, an altitude where many people start to feel sick, and studied how their bodies reacted to the high altitude. All human cells contain mitochondria, and these are responsible for producing energy. Murray found that although the amounts of mitochondria were similar, the Sherpa's mitochondria were able to convert much more oxygen into energy than the mitochondria of non-Sherpas. Murray says, "This shows that it's not how much oxygen you've got; it's what you do with it that counts." In total, Sherpas' mitochondria produced over 30 percent more energy.

The Sherpas in the experiment had been living in a city at a much lower altitude than other Sherpas, and they were eating exactly the same foods as the non-Sherpas. This was done to make the two groups as similar as possible. Also, before the experiment began, the same tests were conducted on the Sherpas while they were still living at a low altitude. The researchers discovered that the Sherpas' cells were able to get just as much oxygen from the air at a low altitude as they were at a high altitude. This suggests that the differences are genetic rather than being acquired during an individual's lifetime.

Every year in the UK, one out of every five people admitted to the intensive care unit of a hospital dies, and one of the main reasons is hypoxia, or a lack of oxygen in the body's organs. In patients suffering from diseases that cause hypoxia, including lung illnesses, heart attacks, and cancer, the body tries to compensate by producing more red blood cells. However, this causes the blood to become thicker and can cause it to flow less well. Since this does not happen to the same degree in Sherpas' bodies, scientists hope that learning about the mechanisms that make their cells more efficient could help to improve the chances of survival for patients in ICUs.

シェルパ族の秘密

シェルパ族の人々はネパールのヒマラヤ山脈に住んでいます。シェルパ族のテンジン・ノルゲイとイギリスのサー・エドモンド・ヒラリーがエベレストの初登頂を達成して以来，シェルパ族は，高地で生存できるそのすばらしい体力と能力で知られています。大半の登山者は，空気中の酸素不足で呼吸することが難しくなり，深刻な場合には脳浮腫や肺水腫を発症し，そのどちらも命取りになりかねません。シェルパ族も，そうした危険を免れるわけではありませんが，そうなる確率はより低いのです。かつて，シェルパ族は，より多くの赤血球を持っているに違いないと考えられていました。というのは，赤血球は酸素を運ぶ細胞だからです。しかしながら，事実はその反対であることがわかりました。シェルパ族の血液は酸素を運ぶ能力が低いようなので，彼らが高地で非常にうまく活動できるのは道理に合わないと思われました。このことは，研究者たちにとって大きな謎でした。

この謎を解明するために，ケンブリッジ大学の研究者アンドリュー・マーレーは，いずれも全員が標高の低い場所に住んでいる非シェルパ族のグループとシェルパ族のグループを調査しました。マーレーは，彼らを多くの人が気分が悪くなり始める標高の 5,300 メートル地点まで連れていき，彼らの体が高い標高にどう反応するのかを調べました。人間のすべての細胞はミトコンドリアを含んでおり，それがエネルギーの生成を担っています。マーレーは，ミトコンドリアの量は変わらないものの，シェルパ族のミトコンドリアは非シェルパ族のミトコンドリアよりも，はるかに多くの酸素をエネルギーに変換できることを発見しました。マーレーはこう述べています。「これが示すのは，重要なのは，人がどれくらいの酸素を取り込んだかではない。重要なのは，その酸素をどう利用するかなのだ」と。全体として，シェルパ族のミトコンドリアは 30 パーセント以上もエネルギーを多く生み出していました。

実験に参加したシェルパ族は，ほかのシェルパ族よりも，はるかに標高の低い町に住んでおり，非シェルパ族とまったく同じものを食べていました。そうしたのは，この 2 つのグループを，できるだけ同じものにするためでした。また，この実験が始まる前に，これと同様の検査が，まだシェルパ族が標高の低いところで生活している間に行われました。研究者たちは，シェルパ族の細胞は，低い標高でも高い標高にいる時とまったく同じ量の酸素を大気中から取り入れることができることを発見しました。このことは，この違いが個人の生涯の間に獲得されるものではなく，遺伝的なものであることを示しています。

イギリスでは毎年，病院の集中治療室に運ばれてくる 5 人のうち 1 人が亡くなりますが，その主な理由の 1 つが低酸素症，すなわち体の臓器中の酸素不足です。肺の病気や心臓発作，がんなどの低酸素症を引き起こす病気を患っている患者の場合，体はより多くの赤血球を生成することによってそれを補おうとします。しかし，これが血液の濃度をよりいっそう上げ，その流れを悪くすることがあります。このようなことは，シェルパ族の体ではそれほど起こらないので，科学者たちは，シェルパ族の細胞をより効率的にしている仕組みについて知ることが，集中治療室にいる患者の生存率を高めることに役立つかもしれないと期待しています。

⇒別冊 p.29 ~ 31

解答と解説

解答

(1) ①　　(2) ④　　(3) ③　　(4) ①

解説

(1) 第1段落の第1~5文の内容に一致する1が正解。2は前半が本文と異なる。3は第1段落最終文に大きな飛躍を遂げたと書かれているが，完全に理解したわけではないので，誤り。4は第1段落第4文に反している。

設問・選択肢の和訳

(1) 本文によると，科学者は…

○1　なぜ人によって時間の認識が異なるのかを知るために研究を行った。

×2　休暇中の人を観察することで，時間の認識について大発見をした。

×3　時間の認識の背後にあるメカニズムを完全に理解した。

×4　人々が時計を見つめた時に，時間がより早く過ぎると感じるということを確かめた。

(2) 第2段落の第4・5文には，ネズミが鼻で正しい答えを示した場合にほうび（餌）を与えられたということが述べられている。このことを言い換えてまとめている4が正解。ほかの選択肢は本文にそのような記述がないため，誤り。

設問・選択肢の和訳

(2) 時間の認識の実験において，マウスは…

×1　より多くの報酬を受け取るためにより一生懸命働こうということを示した。

×2　適切に訓練を受けなかったので，科学者は誤った結論に至った。

×3　科学者から報酬を受け取った時，ドーパミンが増加した。

○4　適切な音の長さを示したら，報酬を受け取った。

(3) 第3段落の第1~3文には，特定の部位における神経活動と時間の感じ方についての関係が述べられている。また，その実験の結果が期待の持てるものであったことが述べられている。これをまとめて言い換えている3が正解。ほかの選択肢は本文にそのような記述がないため，誤り。

設問・選択肢の和訳

(3) 本文によると，実験の結果は…

×1　マウスの大半がどのくらい時間が経過していたかについて短く見積もることを証明した。

×2　科学者が光遺伝学を使用した時，時間が早く過ぎるようだと示した。

○3　神経活動が時間の認識に関連していることを示したので，有望だった。

×4　脳のニューロンは刺激がまったくない時でさえも反応を引き起こされるという発見に至った。

(4) 第4段落の最後の2文の内容から考えて，1が正解。2・3は本文の内容と異なる。4は，第1段落第4文に授業に退屈した学生は，時計を見つめるかもしれないと書かれ

ているが，これが精神的な刺激を作り出すかどうかについては言及されていない。

(4) 本文に基づいて得られる結論の1つは何か。

○1　ニューロンが刺激された時に人々は時間がより早く経過すると感じる。

×2　忙しくすることには脳内のニューロンを刺激する効果がまったくない。

×3　活動の量は時間の認識と関連がない。

×4　頻繁に時計を見ることはより精神的な刺激を作り出す手助けとなるだろう。

語句

〈第1段落〉

□ second hand　　秒針

□ reason behind　　〜の背後にある理由

□ time perception　　時間の感じ方

□ eternity　　（名）永遠

□ achieve a breakthrough　　大きな飛躍を遂げる

〈第2段落〉

□ put together　　〜をまとめて結論を出す

□ process　　（動）〜を処理する

〈第3段落〉

□ promising　　（形）有望な

□ underestimate　　（動）〜を過小評価する

□ neural activity　　神経活動

□ fly by　　（時間が）速く過ぎる

□ neural stimulation　　神経への刺激

□ assessment　　（名）判断，評価

□ optogenetics　　（名）光遺伝学

□ manipulate　　（動）〜を操作する

□ overestimate　　（動）〜を過大評価する

□ radically　　（副）根本的に

□ trigger　　（動）〜を引き起こす

〈第4段落〉

□ implication　　（名）暗示，意味

□ crawl　　（動）這うように（ゆっくり）進む

〈設問・選択肢〉

□ demonstrate that 〜　　〜を実証する

構造確認 ※誤読した部分の確認に使用してください。

⇒別冊 p.29 ~ 31

第1段落 楽しいか退屈かで時間の進み方が違って感じられることの科学的根拠が長年研究されてきた。

① People often say [that time "flies" (when they are enjoying themselves), but
    S   V   O   S'①   V'①

it "drags" (when they are bored)].
S'② V'②

人はしばしば [(楽しんでいる時には) 時間が「飛ぶように過ぎる」, しかし (退屈している時には) そ
れは「のろのろと進む」] と言います。

② (On vacation), (for example), it can feel like hardly any time has gone by
                           S   V

(between the time ⟨you first arrive (at the destination)⟩ and the time ⟨you

have to leave⟩).

注1

(例えば), (休暇中には), (⟨⟨(目的地に) 最初に到着する⟩時刻と⟨帰らなければならない⟩時刻の間に
は) 時間がほとんど過ぎていないかのように感じることがあります。

③ But (at less interesting moments, ⟨like during a boring class ⟨at school⟩⟩),

time seems to move (at a slow pace).
 S   V

ところが (⟨⟨⟨学校での⟩退屈な授業中のように⟩, あまりおもしろくない時には), 時間が (ゆっくりと)
進んでいるように思えます。

④ A bored student might feel like every minute lasts an hour (while staring at
     S   V

the clock), (hoping [the second hand will move faster]).

退屈している学生は ([秒針がもっと速く動いてくれること] を望んで), (時計を見つめている間は) 毎
分が 1 時間続くように感じるかもしれません。

⑤ (For years), researchers have tried to find the scientific reason ⟨behind this
           S   V   O

difference ⟨in time perception⟩⟩ (by [studying the brain]).

(長年), 研究者は ([脳を研究すること] によって) ⟨⟨時間の感覚の⟩この違いの背後にある⟩科学的な
根拠を見つけようと努めてきました。

150

⑥ And (after [what may have felt like an eternity]), scientists may have
            V'   S   V
achieved a breakthrough.
         O

そして（[永遠のように感じられたかもしれないこと]の後に），科学者たちは大きな進展を成し遂げた
ようです。

第2段落 ポルトガルのチームがネズミを使って心が時間をどのように経験するのかの研究をまとめた。

① (In 2016), a team ⟨of researchers ⟨in Portugal⟩⟩ put together a study ⟨using
                S   V   O
mice⟩ (to help understand the way ⟨time is experienced (by the mind)⟩⟩).

(2016 年)，《《ポルトガルの》研究者の》チームは（《(心が) 時間を経験する》やり方を理解するのに役
立てようとして）《ネズミを使った》研究をまとめました。

② Scientists often use rodents (to analyze brain functions) (because they
        S   often V   O   S'
share a similar brain structure (with humans)).
  V'   O'

科学者はしばしば齧歯類動物を使って（脳機能を分析します），（なぜならそれらは (人間と) 似た脳構
造を持っているからです）。

③ (In their experiment), the scientists first taught the mice [how to judge the
                              S   V   O   O
amount ⟨of time ⟨that had passed (between two sounds)⟩⟩].
                              V'

(それらの実験で)，科学者たちはまずネズミに [《《(2 つの音の間に) 経過する》時間の》量の判断の方
法] を教えました。

④ The mice (then) had to indicate (with their noses) [whether a sound was
     S   V   O   S'   V'
longer or shorter (than 1.5 seconds)].
     C'

(その後で) ネズミは [音が (1.5 秒より) 長いか短いか] を (鼻で) 示さなければなりませんでした。

⑤ (When they gave the correct answer), they were given a reward.
      S'   V'   O'   S   V   O

(ネズミは正しく答えられたら)，ほうび (の餌) を与えられました。

⑥ (While the mice provided their responses), the scientists observed
  S'① V'① O'① S V

dopamine neurons (in a specific area ⟨of the brain⟩ ⟨which is known (for its
  O V'②

role ⟨in [processing time]⟩)⟩).

(ネズミが反応を示している間に), 科学者たちは (⟨⟨⟨[時間を処理する] 上での⟩ その役割で) 知られ
ている⟩⟨脳の⟩特定の部位で) ドーパミン神経細胞を観察しました。

第3段落 ネズミの時間の判断は脳神経細胞への刺激により変えられる可能性があると結論づけられた。

① The results ⟨of the initial experiment⟩ were promising.
  S V C

⟨最初の実験の⟩結果は期待が持てるものでした。

② The researchers observed [that (when the mice underestimated the amount
  S V

⟨of time ⟨that had passed⟩⟩), there was greater neural activity (in that
  V' S'

specific area)].   注5

研究者たちは [(ネズミが⟨⟨経過した⟩時間の⟩量を実際より短いと見積もった時), (その特定の部位
で) 前よりも活発な神経活動があったこと] に気づきました。

③ (In other words), time seemed to fly by (when the brain was stimulated).
  S V S' V'

(言い換えれば), (脳が刺激された時は) 時間は飛ぶように過ぎると感じられたのです。

④ (In order to provide more support ⟨for this finding⟩), the scientists attempted
  S V

to show a causal link ⟨between neural stimulation and time assessment⟩.
  O

(⟨この発見を⟩さらに補強するために), 科学者たちは⟨神経への刺激と時間の判断 (認識) の間の⟩因
果関係を示そうと試みました。

⑤ (By using a technique ⟨called "optogenetics"⟩), researchers (directly)
  S

manipulated brain neurons (using light) and found [that (with increased
  V① O① V② O②

stimulation), the mice underestimated the amount ⟨of time ⟨that passed
  S' V' O'

152

by〉〉, (whereas they overestimated the passing 〈of time〉 (when there was

no stimulation))]. 注6

(〈「光遺伝学」と呼ばれる〉技術を使うことで), 研究者たちは (光を使って) 脳神経細胞を (直接) 操作
し, [(刺激が増えると), ネズミは〈〈経過した〉時間の〉量を短いと見積もり, ((刺激がまったくない
時は)〈時間の〉経過を長いと見積もる) こと] がわかりました。

⑥ The researchers concluded [that the mice's judgment 〈of time〉 could be
　　　　　S　　　　　　　　V　　　　　　O　　　　　　　　　　　　S'　　　　　　　　V'

(radically) altered (through the direct manipulation 〈of brain neurons〉 or

external stimulations 〈that trigger similar activity 〈in the neurons〉〉)].

研究者たちは [〈時間に関する〉ネズミの判断は (〈〈脳神経細胞の〉直接的な操作や〈〈神経細胞に〉同様
の活動を引き起こす〉外部からの刺激を通して) (根本的に) 変えられる可能性がある] と結論づけまし
た。

第4段落 この研究結果は人間の脳が時間の経験をどのように処理するのかを理解する手がかりとなる。

① The researchers admit [that a limitation 〈of the study〉 is their inability 〈to
　　　　　S　　　　　　　　V　　　　O　　　　　　　　　　　　　S'　　　　　V'　　　　　C'
know the actual feelings 〈of the animals〉〉].

研究者たちは [〈この研究の〉限界は〈〈動物の〉実際の感覚を知ることが〉できないことだ] と認めてい
ます。

② They could only interpret the mice's behavior (to make conclusions 〈about
　　　S　　　　　　V　　　　　　　　　　O
[how the mice perceived time]〉).
　　　S'　　　　V'　　　　O'

彼らはネズミの行動を解釈することでしか (〈[ネズミが時間をどのように認識しているか] について
の〉結論を出すこと) ができませんでした。

③ (Still), the results have exciting implications: the findings point to a deeper
　　　　　　　S①　　　V①　　　　　　O①　　　　　　　S②　　　V②
understanding 〈of [how the human brain processes time experiences]〉.
　　　　　　　　　　　　　S'　　　　　　V'　　　　　O'

(それでも), この結果は興味深い意味を持ちます, この発見は〈[人間の脳が時間の経験をどのように
処理するのか] についての〉より深い理解への手がかりとなります。

153

④ It explains, (for example), [why time would seem to pass (more quickly)
(when there are plenty of activities ⟨to stimulate the mind⟩), (whereas time
crawls by (slowly) (when a person is bored (in class) (without mental
stimulation)))].

それは，（例えば），[[⟨心を刺激するような⟩活動がたくさんある時には）なぜ時間が（より速く）進む
ように感じられるのか，（それに対し（（授業中に）（精神的な刺激がなくて）退屈している時には）なぜ
時間が（ゆっくりと）這うように進む）のか］を説明しています。

⑤ (In other words), it could all be related (to the neurons ⟨in our brain⟩).

（言い換えれば），そうしたことはすべて（⟨私たちの脳の⟩神経細胞に）関係しているのかもしれません。

⑥ So, (to make time go faster (in a boring class)), find an activity ⟨that
stimulates your neurons⟩ — it just might trick your mind (into [perceiving time
(as moving faster)]).

ですから，（（退屈な授業中に）時間を早く進ませるためには），⟨あなたの神経細胞を刺激する⟩活動を
見つけるとよいでしょう——そうすれば（［時間を（より速く進んでいると）認識する］ように）まさに
あなたの心を錯覚させることができるかもしれません。

注1 it feels like S V は「S が V するように感じる」という意味の構文。like はもともと前置詞で，
直後に名詞が置かれるが，この構文のように接続詞として用いられて直後に節が置かれる場合
もある。

注2 what は，関係代名詞で「…なもの」「…なこと」という意味で用いられる。

注3 the way S V は「S が V する方法」という意味の構文。how S V とも言い換えることができる。

注4 indicate の目的語は whether 以下の節。whether S V は「S が V するかどうか」という意
味の名詞節となる。

注5 過去完了形は，基準となる主文の過去時点までの完了や，過去よりももっと前のことを過去と
区別するために用いられる。ここでは，過去時点までの完了を表すために用いられている。

注6 whereas は while よりも少々堅い言い方で，「…するが」「…する一方で」という意味になる。

注7 in other words は「別の言い方をすれば」という意味で，直前の内容を具体的にわかりやすく
言い換える場合などに用いられる。

サイトトランスレーション

⇒別冊 p.29 ～ 31

1 People often say /	人はしばしば言います
that time "flies" /	時間が「飛ぶように過ぎる」
when they are enjoying themselves, /	楽しんでいる時には,
but it "drags" /	しかしそれは「のろのろと進む」
when they are bored. //	退屈している時には。
On vacation, /	休暇中は,
for example, /	例えば,
it can feel like hardly any time has gone by /	ほとんど時間が過ぎていないように感じられます
between /	…の間には
the time you first arrive /	最初に到着した時刻
at the destination /	目的地に
and the time you have to leave. //	そして帰らなければならない時刻。
But at less interesting moments, /	ところがあまりおもしろくない時に,
like during a boring class /	退屈な授業中のように
at school, /	学校での,
time seems to move /	時間が進んでいるように思えます
at a slow pace. //	ゆっくりと。
A bored student might feel like /	退屈している学生は感じるかもしれません
every minute lasts an hour /	毎分が 1 時間続いている
while staring at the clock, /	時計を見つめている間,
hoping the second hand will move faster. //	秒針がもっと速く動いてくれることを望んで。
For years, /	長年,

researchers have tried to find /	研究者は見つけようと努めてきました
the scientific reason behind this difference /	この違いの背後にある科学的な根拠を
in time perception /	時間の感覚の
by studying the brain. //	脳を研究することによって。
And after what may have felt like an eternity, /	そして永遠のように感じられたかもしれないことの後に、
scientists may have achieved a breakthrough. //	科学者たちは大きな進展を成し遂げたようです。
2 In 2016, /	2016年、
a team of researchers /	研究者チームは
in Portugal /	ポルトガルの
put together a study /	研究をまとめました
using mice /	ネズミを使った
to help understand the way /	方法を理解するのに役立てようとして
time is experienced /	時間が経験される
by the mind. //	心の中で。
Scientists often use /	科学者は使うことが多い
rodents /	齧歯類動物を
to analyze brain functions /	脳機能を分析するために
because they share /	なぜならそれらは共有しているからです
a similar brain structure /	似た脳構造を
with humans. //	人間と。
In their experiment, /	その実験で、
the scientists first taught /	科学者たちはまず教えました
the mice /	ネズミに

how to judge /	どう判断するかを
the amount of time /	時間の量を
that had passed between two sounds. //	2つの音の間に経過する。
The mice then had to indicate /	ネズミはその後で示さなければなりませんでした
with their noses /	鼻で
whether a sound was longer or shorter /	音が長いか短いかを
than 1.5 seconds. //	1.5秒より。
When they gave the correct answer, /	正しく答えられた時は,
they were given a reward. //	報酬を与えられました。
While the mice provided /	ネズミが提供した時
their responses, /	反応を,
the scientists observed /	科学者たちは観察しました
dopamine neurons /	ドーパミン神経細胞を
in a specific area of the brain /	脳の特定の部位の
which is known /	知られている
for its role /	役割を持つことで
in processing time. //	時間を処理する上での。
3 The results /	その結果は
of the initial experiment /	最初の実験の
were promising. //	期待が持てるものでした。
The researchers observed /	研究者たちは観察しました
that when the mice underestimated /	ネズミが短く見積もった時
the amount of time /	時間の量を
that had passed, /	経過した,

there was greater neural activity /	より活発な神経活動があった
in that specific area. //	その特定の部位で。
In other words, /	言い換えれば,
time seemed to fly by /	時間は飛ぶように過ぎると思われました
when the brain was stimulated. //	脳が刺激された時は。
In order to provide /	与えるために
more support /	さらなる裏付けを
for this finding, /	この発見に,
the scientists attempted to show /	科学者たちは示そうと試みました
a causal link /	因果関係を
between neural stimulation and time assessment. //	神経への刺激と時間の判断との間の。
By using a technique /	技術を使うことで
called "optogenetics," /	「光遺伝学」と呼ばれる,
researchers directly manipulated /	研究者たちは直接操作しました
brain neurons /	脳神経細胞を
using light /	光を使って
and found /	そしてわかりました
that with increased stimulation, /	刺激が増えると,
the mice underestimated /	ネズミは実際より短いと見積もりました
the amount of time /	時間の量を
that passed by, /	経過した,
whereas they overestimated /	反対に実際より長いと見積もりました
the passing of time /	時間の経過を
when there was no stimulation. //	刺激がまったくない時は。

The researchers concluded /	研究者たちは結論づけました
that the mice's judgment of time /	ネズミの時間の判断は
could be radically altered /	根本的に変えられる可能性がある
through the direct manipulation /	直接的な操作を通して
of brain neurons /	脳神経細胞の
or external stimulations /	あるいは外部からの刺激
that trigger similar activity /	同様の活動を引き起こす
in the neurons. //	神経細胞に。
4 The researchers admit /	研究者たちは認めています
that a limitation of the study /	この研究の限界は
is their inability to know /	知ることができないことである
the actual feelings /	実際の感覚を
of the animals. //	動物の。
They could only interpret /	彼らは解釈することができたにすぎません
the mice's behavior /	ネズミの行動を
to make conclusions /	結論を出すのに
about how the mice perceived /	ネズミがどのように認識しているかについての
time. //	時間を。
Still, /	それでも,
the results have exciting implications: /	その結果は興味深い意味を持ちます,
the findings point /	その発見は手がかりとなります
to a deeper understanding /	より深く理解することへの
of how the human brain processes /	人間の脳がどのように処理するのかを
time experiences. //	時間の経験を。

It explains, /	それは説明しています,
for example, /	例えば,
why time would seem to pass /	時間が進むように感じられる理由を
more quickly /	より速く
when there are plenty of activities /	活動がたくさんある時には
to stimulate the mind, /	心を刺激するような,
whereas time crawls by /	反対に時間が這うように進む
slowly /	ゆっくりと
when a person is bored /	人が退屈している時には
in class /	授業中に
without mental stimulation. //	精神的な刺激がなく。
In other words, /	言い換えれば,
it could all be related /	そうしたことはすべて関係しているのかもしれません
to the neurons /	神経細胞に
in our brain. //	私たちの脳の。
So, /	ですから,
to make time go faster /	時間をより早く進ませるためには
in a boring class, /	退屈な授業中に,
find an activity /	活動を見つけましょう
that stimulates your neurons /	あなたの神経細胞を刺激する
— it just might trick /	それがまさにだましてくれるかもしれません
your mind /	あなたの心を
into perceiving time /	時間を錯覚するように
as moving faster. //	より速く進んでいると。

The Speed of Time

People often say that time "flies" when they are enjoying themselves, but it "drags" when they are bored. On vacation, for example, it can feel like hardly any time has gone by between the time you first arrive at the destination and the time you have to leave. But at less interesting moments, like during a boring class at school, time seems to move at a slow pace. A bored student might feel like every minute lasts an hour while staring at the clock, hoping the second hand will move faster. For years, researchers have tried to find the scientific reason behind this difference in time perception by studying the brain. And after what may have felt like an eternity, scientists may have achieved a breakthrough.

In 2016, a team of researchers in Portugal put together a study using mice to help understand the way time is experienced by the mind. Scientists often use rodents to analyze brain functions because they share a similar brain structure with humans. In their experiment, the scientists first taught the mice how to judge the amount of time that had passed between two sounds. The mice then had to indicate with their noses whether a sound was longer or shorter than 1.5 seconds. When they gave the correct answer, they were given a reward. While the mice provided their responses, the scientists observed dopamine neurons in a specific area of the brain which is known for its role in processing time.

The results of the initial experiment were promising. The researchers observed that when the mice underestimated the amount of time that had passed, there was greater neural activity in that specific area. In other words, time seemed to fly by when the brain was stimulated. In order to provide more support for this finding, the scientists attempted to show a causal link between neural stimulation and time assessment. By using a technique called "optogenetics," researchers directly manipulated brain neurons using light and found that with increased stimulation, the mice underestimated the amount of time that passed by, whereas they overestimated the passing of time when there was no stimulation. The researchers concluded that the mice's judgment of time could be radically altered through the direct manipulation of brain neurons or external stimulations that trigger similar activity in the neurons.

The researchers admit that a limitation of the study is their inability to know the actual feelings of the animals. They could only interpret the mice's behavior to make conclusions about how the mice perceived time. Still, the results have exciting implications: the findings point to a deeper understanding of how the human brain processes time experiences. It explains, for example, why time would seem to pass more quickly when there are plenty of activities to stimulate the mind, whereas time crawls by slowly when a person is bored in class without mental stimulation. In other words, it could all be related to the neurons in our brain. So, to make time go faster in a boring class, find an activity that stimulates your neurons — it just might trick your mind into perceiving time as moving faster.

....

時間の速度

　人はしばしば，何かを楽しんでいる時には時間が「飛ぶように過ぎる」と言い，退屈している時は時間が「のろのろと進む」と言います。例えば，休暇中なら，目的地に最初に到着する時刻から帰るべき時刻までの間，時間がほとんど過ぎていないかのように感じることがあります。ところが，学校での退屈な授業中のように，あまりおもしろくない時だと，時間がゆっくりと進んでいるように思えます。退屈している学生は，秒針がもっと速く動いてくれることを望んで時計を見つめている時，毎分が1時間のように感じるかもしれません。研究者は長年，脳を研究することによって，この時間の感覚の違いの背後にある科学的な根拠を見つけようと努めてきました。そして，永遠のように感じられたかもしれない時を経て，科学者たちは大きな進展を成し遂げたようです。

　2016年，ポルトガルの研究者チームは，心が時間を経験する方法を理解するのに役立てよ

うとして，ネズミを使った研究をまとめました。科学者が齧歯類動物を使って脳機能を分析することが多いのは，それらが人間に似た脳構造を持っているためです。その実験で，科学者たちは，まずネズミに2つの音の間の経過する時間の量を判断できるようにする訓練をしました。その後で，ネズミは音が1.5秒より長いか短いかを鼻で示さなければなりませんでした。ネズミは正しく答えられたら，ほうび（の餌）を与えられました。ネズミが反応を示している間に，科学者たちは，時間を処理する役割を担うことがわかっている脳の特定の部位でのドーパミン神経細胞を観察しました。

　最初の実験結果は期待が持てるものでした。研究者たちは，ネズミが経過した時間を実際より短いと見積もった時，その特定の部位で前よりも活発な神経活動があったことに気づきました。言い換えれば，脳が刺激された時は，時間は飛ぶように過ぎると感じられたのです。この発見をさらに補強するために，科学者たちは神経への刺激と時間の判断（認識）との間に因果関係があることを示そうと試みました。「光遺伝学」と呼ばれる技術を使うことで，研究者たちは光を使って脳神経細胞を直接操作し，刺激が増えるとネズミは経過した時間を実際より短いと見積もり，刺激がまったくないと時間の経過を実際より長いと見積もることがわかりました。研究者たちは，ネズミの時間の判断は，脳神経細胞の直接的な操作や，神経細胞に同様の活動を引き起こす外部からの刺激によって根本的に変えられる可能性があると結論づけました。

　研究者たちは，この研究の限界は動物の実際の感覚を知ることができないことだと認めています。彼らはネズミの行動を解釈することでしか，ネズミが時間をどのように認識しているかについての結論を出すことができませんでした。それでも，この結果は興味深い意味を持ちます。すなわち，この発見は人間の脳が時間の経験をどのように処理するのかをより深く理解する手がかりとなります。例えば，なぜ，心を刺激するような活動がたくさんある時には時間がより速く進むように感じられるのに対し，授業中に精神的な刺激がなくて退屈している時には時間がゆっくりと這うように進むのかを説明してくれます。言い換えれば，そうしたことはすべて私たちの脳の神経細胞に関係しているのかもしれません。ですから，退屈な授業中に時間を早く進ませるためには，あなたの神経細胞を刺激する活動を見つけるとよいでしょう——そうすれば，ひょっとすると時間がより速く進んでいるように，あなたの心を錯覚させることができるかもしれません。

解答と解説

(1) ①　　(2) ④　　(3) ④　　(4) ②

(1) 第1段落の最後の文では，カッシーニの長年の探査が人間の宇宙の広大さに対する理解への変革をもたらしたことが述べられている。これを別の言葉で言い換えている1が正解。ほかの選択肢は，カッシーニの任務に関して本文に記述がないため，誤り。

設問・選択肢の和訳

(1) カッシーニの任務は…

○ 1　人々に宇宙の大きさに関して新たな理解を与える手助けをした。

× 2　主要な目的を果たすことができないため，時々非難を受けている。

× 3　衛星の1つを通じて重要なデータを地球に送り続けている。

× 4　地球から発射されたどんな宇宙探査機よりも遠くに移動した。

(2) 第2段落第3・4文に，ホイヘンス着陸船の特徴として，パラシュート降下について述べられている。これをまとめて言い換えている4が正解。1は本文にそのような記述がなく，2・3はカッシーニの行ったことなので，誤り。

設問・選択肢の和訳

(2) ホイヘンス着陸船が重要なのは，…からである

× 1　小惑星帯を越えたところで最初の衛星を発見した。

× 2　潜在的に生命が存在し得る近くの惑星を特定した。

× 3　土星とそのいくつかの衛星についての情報を送り返した。

○ 4　着陸するためにパラシュートを用いた最初の宇宙船だった。

(3) ソーシャルメディアの運動と大衆の支持に関して述べられている第3段落の第2～4文の内容に一致する4が正解。ほかの選択肢は，カッシーニの任務延長に関して本文中に記述がないため，誤り。

設問・選択肢の和訳

(3) どのようにして NASA はカッシーニの任務をこれほど長引かせることができたのか。

× 1　その探査機が非常に多くの貴重なデータを売ることができたので，NASA の予算が増大した。

× 2　任務のために生じた技術を人々は重視した。

× 3　多くの人々がインターネットを通じてカッシーニの任務に進んで寄付をした。

○ 4　強力なソーシャルメディアの運動のためにその任務についての大衆の支持が増大した。

(4) 最終段落の第3文では，NASA は「生物学的な汚染」をしたくなかったと述べられている。これは「外来の物質を落とす」と言い換えることができ，2が正解となる。1は，老朽化していたことは第1文に書かれているが，事故が発生したという記述はない。3・

4 は本文に記述がない。

〔設問・選択肢の和訳〕

(4) なぜカッシーニは土星の表面に激突したのか。

×**1** 老朽化し過ぎたため，その探査機に事故が発生した。

○**2** NASA は外来の物質をどんな土星の衛星にも落とすリスクを冒したくなかった。

×**3** NASA は惑星の表面にある化学物質についてのデータを集めたかった。

×**4** 一般市民は土星が適切な休憩場所であると決定づけた。

〔語句〕

〈タイトル〉

□ space probe	宇宙探査機

〈第 1 段落〉

□ breathtaking	(形) 息を呑むような，見事な
□ Saturn	(名) 土星
□ satellite system	衛星系
□ hail	(動) ～を称賛する
□ tremendous	(形) 非常に大きな
□ unprecedented	(形) 前例のない
□ flawless	(形) 完璧な
□ execution	(名) 遂行
□ sub-mission	(名) 付帯任務
□ fascination with ～	～に魅了されること，～への特別な関心
□ solar system	太陽系
□ inspire	(動) ～を呼び起こす
□ general public	一般大衆
□ exploration	(名) 探査
□ revolutionize	(動) ～に大革命をもたらす

〈第 2 段落〉

□ fix	(動) ～を固定する
□ orbit	(名) 軌道
□ transmit	(動) ～を送る，発信する

□ expansive	(形) 広大な
□ feat	(名) 偉業，功績
□ lander	(名) 着陸船
□ parachute drop	落下傘降下
□ asteroid belt	小惑星帯
□ man-made	(形) 人造の
□ reside	(動) 存在する
□ celestial body	天体
□ give credit to ～	～を称賛する
□ uncover	(動) ～を明らかにする
□ alien life	宇宙生命

〈第 3 段落〉

□ extension	(名) 延長
□ incorporate	(動) ～を取り入れる
□ up-and-coming	(形) 新進の，有望な

〈第 4 段落〉

□ deliberately	(副) 意図的に
□ deem	(動) ～と見なす
□ retire	(動) 撤退する
□ contaminate	(動) ～を汚染する
□ dip ～ into ...	～を…の中に浸す
□ ring system	環系
□ host	(動) ～を主催する
□ grateful	(形) 感謝して

構造確認 ※誤読した部分の確認に使用してください。

⇒別冊 p.32 〜 34

第1段落 カッシーニ宇宙探査機は2017年のミッション終了まで20年近く人々の想像力を刺激してきた。

① The Cassini space probe captured the world's imagination (for nearly twenty
　　　　　　S　　　　　　　V　　　　　　O
years) (with breathtaking images 〈of the planet Saturn and its surrounding

satellite system〉).

カッシーニ宇宙探査機は (〈土星とその周囲の衛星群の〉息をのむような画像によって) (20 年近くに
わたって) 世界の人々の想像力を刺激しました。

② NASA hails its mission (as one 〈of tremendous historical importance〉).
　　S　　V　　　O

NASA は，そのミッションを (〈歴史的に非常に重要なものの〉1 つだと) 称賛しています。

③ The unprecedented data 〈it gathered (over the years)〉, the flawless
　　　　　S
execution 〈of various sub-missions〉, and the fascination 〈with our solar

system〉〈that it was able to inspire (in the general public)〉 are some 〈of the
　　　　　　　　　S'　　　　　　V'　　　　　　　　　V　　C
many reasons 〈it was considered such a success〉〉.

〈それが (長年にわたって) 収集した〉前例のないデータ，〈さまざまな副次的活動の〉完璧な遂行，そ
して〈(一般の人々の間で) 高めることができた〉〈太陽系への〉関心などは《〈それが大成功と見なされ
た〉多くの理由の〉一部です。

④ (On September 15, 2017), the Cassini mission came to an end, (concluding
　　　　　　　　　　　　　　　S　　　　　　V　　　O
nearly two decades of space exploration and revolutionizing [how humans
　　　　　　　　　　　　　　　　　　　　　　　　　　　　　　　　S'
comprehend the vastness 〈of space〉]).
　　V'　　　O'

(2017 年 9 月 15 日に)，(20 年近くに及ぶ宇宙探査を締めくくり，[人間が〈宇宙の〉広大さを理解す
る方法] に大きな変革をもたらして)，カッシーニのミッションは終了しました。

第2段落 カッシーニは土星の最大の衛星タイタンにホイヘンス探査機を着陸させる偉業を成し遂げた。

① NASA launched the Cassini space probe (on October 15, 1997), (sending
　　S　　V　　　　　O

it (on a six-year, 1.2-billion-kilometer journey ⟨through the solar system

towards Saturn⟩)).

NASA は (1997 年 10 月 15 日に) カッシーニ宇宙探査機を打ち上げ，((⟨太陽系を通って土星へと向
かう⟩6 年間にわたる，12 億キロメートルの旅に) 送り出しました)。

② The probe fixed itself (in orbit) (at its final destination) (on July 1, 2004), and
　　　S①　 V①　 O①

it immediately began transmitting data (from the distant planet and its
S②　　　　　V②　　　　O②

expansive moon system) (back to Earth).

この探査機は (2004 年 7 月 1 日に) (最終目的地である) (軌道に) 入り，すぐに (遠方の惑星とその広
大な衛星群からの) データを (地球に) 送信し始めました。

③ (Only a single year into its mission), Cassini accomplished its greatest feat
　　　　　　　　　　　　　　　　　　　S　　　 V　　　　　 O

(by [(successfully) landing the Huygens lander (on Saturn's largest moon,

Titan)]).

(ミッション開始からわずか 1 年のうちに)，カッシーニは ([(土星の最大の衛星である，タイタンに)
ホイヘンス着陸船を (首尾よく) 着陸させる] ことによって) 偉業を成し遂げました。

④ The parachute drop remains mankind's only successful landing ⟨beyond
　　　　　　S①　　　 V①　　　　　　　　C①

our solar system's asteroid belt⟩, and Huygens holds the record (as the
　　　　　　　　　　　　　　　　　　　S②　 V②　　 O②

most distant man-made object ⟨residing (on a foreign celestial body)⟩).

そのパラシュート降下は ⟨私たちの太陽系の小惑星帯を越えて⟩ 着陸をした人類唯一の成功例で，ホ
イヘンスは (⟨⟨(未知の天体に) 置かれている⟩最も遠方の人工物という) 記録を今でも保持しています。

⑤ Credit is also given (to Cassini) (for [discovering new moons ⟨never before
　　　S　 V

observed by NASA⟩] and even [uncovering the potential ⟨for alien life⟩ ⟨on

Saturn's moon Enceladus⟩]).　　　　　　　　　　　　　　　　　　　　　　　　▶注4

これに加えて ([⟨NASA がこれまで観測したことのなかった⟩新たな数個の衛星を発見したこと]，さ
らには [⟨土星の衛星のエンケラドゥスに⟩⟨生命体が存在する⟩可能性を示したこと] から) (カッシー
ニは) 称賛されています。

第3段落 カッシーニのミッションは多くのフォロワーを獲得し支援を受けて予定より長く継続された。

① (Originally), NASA intended to conclude Cassini's mission (after just four
　　　　　　　S① 　　　　　V① 　　　　　　　　O①
years), but extensions 〈granted (to the program) (in 2008 and 2010)〉
　　　　　　　S②
allowed it to continue (well into the age 〈of social media〉).
V② 　O②

(当初)，NASA は (4年間だけで) カッシーニのミッションを終えるつもりでしたが，〈(2008年と
2010年に)(この計画に)認められた〉期限延長によって〈〈ソーシャルメディアの〉時代に入っても〉
活動を続けることができました。

② NASA wisely incorporated the Internet and up-and-coming social media
　　 S　　　　　V　　　　　　　　　　　　O
websites 〈such as Twitter〉 (into Cassini's mission) (to make its images
readily available (to the general public)).
注5

NASA は，インターネットや〈ツイッターのような〉新進のソーシャルメディアのウェブサイトを
(カッシーニのミッションに) 巧みに取り入れ (その画像を (一般の人たちに) 簡単に利用できるよう
に) しました。

③ (Every day) people were granted easy access 〈to knowledge and
　　　　　　　 S① 　　　V① 　　　O①
photographs〉, and Cassini's scientific mission (quickly) gained millions of
　　　　　　　　　　Cassini's scientific mission 　　　　gained　millions of
　　　　　　　　　　　　S② 　　　　　　　　　　　　V② 　　　O②
followers.

人々は (毎日)〈情報や写真に〉簡単にアクセスできるようになり，カッシーニの科学的ミッションは
(たちまち) 数百万人ものフォロワーを獲得しました。

④ The broad and popular support 〈that the probe enjoyed〉 granted NASA
　　　　　　　S 　　　　　　　　　　　S'① 　　V'① 　　　V 　　O
the ability 〈to continue its mission (for an additional ten years) (beyond
　　O
[what it had intended])〉.
　　S'② 　V'②

〈この探査機が受けた〉幅広い一般からの支援で，NASA は〈([意図していた]よりも)(さらに10年
長く) このミッションを続けて〉できることになりました。

168

第4段落 耐用年数と資金面の問題からカッシーニは意図的に土星に衝突させられミッションを終えた。

① (Unfortunately), (due to the machine's age and funding issues 〈back on
Earth〉), NASA announced plans (in 2014) 〈for Cassini to be deliberately
destroyed (by [crashing it into Saturn])〉.
    S   V   O

（残念ながら），（機器の耐用年数と〈地球側での〉資金面の問題から），NASA は（2014年に）〈カッシーニを（[それを土星に衝突させること]で）意図的に破壊するという〉計画を発表しました。

② Cassini did not have enough fuel 〈to escape from Saturn's orbit〉, and
the planet's surface was deemed to be the safest place 〈for the probe to
retire〉.

カッシーニは〈土星の軌道から離脱するのに〉十分な燃料を持っておらず，その惑星の地表は〈探査機が引退するのに〉最も安全な場所であると見なされたのです。

③ NASA did not want to (biologically) contaminate any 〈of Saturn's moons'
surfaces〉 and destroy the potential 〈for life〉.

NASA は〈土星にある衛星群の地表の〉どれをも（生物学的に）汚染して〈生命が存在する〉可能性を台無しにしたくなかったのです。

④ (After 22 months 〈of [dipping Cassini (into Saturn's ring system)]〉 and
[examining the planet (from a closer viewpoint 〈than any other object 〈in
history〉〉)]）), the time 〈for Cassini's retirement〉 finally arrived.

（〈[カッシーニを（土星の輪の中に）投入して]そして[〈〈歴史上の〉ほかのどのような天体よりも〉近い観測地点から）この惑星を調査した]〉22か月間の後で），〈カッシーニの引退の〉時がとうとうやって来ました。

⑤ NASA hosted a "Grand Finale" celebration (on its website), (enabling the
   S   V   O

millions of fans ⟨the probe had attracted (over the years)⟩ to witness its final

moments).

注6

NASA は (そのウェブサイトで)「グランドフィナーレ」という式典を開催し, (⟨その探査機が (長年
にわたって) 魅了してきた⟩数百万人ものファンがその最後の瞬間を目撃することができました)。

⑥ Many ⟨in both NASA and the general public⟩ called the final mission
   S   V   O

"bittersweet", (stating [that (while they were sad that Cassini was no longer
     C

orbiting Saturn), they felt grateful (knowing [that they witnessed such an
                       S'   V'   C'

important moment ⟨in scientific history⟩ and expanded their knowledge

⟨about worlds ⟨beyond our own⟩⟩])]).

注7

⟨NASA 関係者と一般の人たちの⟩多くがその最後のミッションを「ほろ苦いもの」と呼び, ([(カッ
シーニがもはや土星を周回していないことは悲しいことだが), ([⟨科学の歴史上⟩これほど重要な瞬
間を目撃でき, ⟨⟨私たちの外の⟩世界についての⟩知識を広げてくれたこと] に) 感謝している] と述
べました)。

サイトトランスレーション

⇒別冊 p.32 ～ 34

1 The Cassini space probe captured /	カッシーニ宇宙探査機は魅了しました
the world's imagination /	世界の（人々の）想像力を
for nearly twenty years /	20 年近くにわたって
with breathtaking images /	息をのむような画像で
of the planet Saturn and its surrounding satellite system. //	土星とその周囲の衛星群の。
NASA hails /	NASA は称賛しています
its mission /	そのミッションを
as one of tremendous historical importance. //	歴史的に非常に重要なものの 1 つだと。
The unprecedented data /	前例のないデータ
it gathered /	それが収集した
over the years, /	長年にわたって，
the flawless execution /	完璧な遂行
of various sub-missions, /	さまざまな副次的活動の，
and the fascination /	そして興味
with our solar system /	太陽系への
that it was able to inspire /	それは高めることができた
in the general public /	一般の人々の間で
are some of the many reasons /	多くの理由の一部です
it was considered /	それが見なされた
such a success. //	大成功と。
On September 15, 2017, /	2017 年 9 月 15 日に，

the Cassini mission came to an end, /	カッシーニのミッションは終了となりました,
concluding nearly two decades /	約 20 年間を締めくくり
of space exploration /	宇宙探査の
and revolutionizing /	そして大きな変革をもたらした
how humans comprehend /	人間が理解する方法の
the vastness of space. //	宇宙の広大さを。
2 NASA launched /	NASA は打ち上げました
the Cassini space probe /	カッシーニ宇宙探査機を
on October 15, 1997, /	1997 年 10 月 15 日に,
sending it on a six-year, /	それを 6 年の (…に) 送り出しました,
1.2-billion-kilometer journey /	12 億キロメートルの旅
through the solar system /	太陽系を通って
towards Saturn. //	土星へと向かう。
The probe fixed itself /	その探査機は入りました
in orbit /	軌道に
at its final destination /	その最終目的地で
on July 1, 2004, /	2004 年 7 月 1 日に,
and it immediately began transmitting /	そしてそれはすぐに送信し始めました
data /	データを
from the distant planet /	その遠方の惑星から
and its expansive moon system /	そしてその広大な衛星群
back to Earth. //	地球へと。
Only a single year /	わずか 1 年で
into its mission, /	ミッションに入ってから,

Cassini accomplished /	カッシーニは成し遂げました
its greatest feat /	偉業を
by successfully landing /	着陸させることに成功することによって
the Huygens lander /	ホイヘンス着陸船を
on Saturn's largest moon, Titan. //	土星の最大の衛星である，タイタンに。
The parachute drop remains /	そのパラシュート降下は保持しています
mankind's only successful landing /	人類の唯一の着陸成功例を
beyond our solar system's asteroid belt, /	太陽系の小惑星帯を越えた，
and Huygens holds the record /	そしてホイヘンスは記録されています
as the most distant man-made object /	最も遠く離れた人工物として
residing on a foreign celestial body. //	地球外の天体上にある。
Credit is also given /	称賛はまた与えられています
to Cassini /	カッシーニに
for discovering new moons /	新たな数個の衛星を発見したことで
never before observed /	これまで観測されたことのなかった
by NASA /	NASA によって
and even uncovering /	そしてさらには明らかにしたこと
the potential /	可能性を
for alien life /	宇宙生命体が存在する
on Saturn's moon Enceladus. //	土星の衛星のエンケラドゥスに。
3 Originally, /	当初，
NASA intended to conclude /	NASA は終えるつもりでした
Cassini's mission /	カッシーニのミッションを
after just four years, /	4 年間だけで，

but extensions granted to the program /	しかしこの計画に認められた期限延長によって
in 2008 and 2010 /	2008年と2010年に
allowed it to continue well /	それを続けることができました
into the age of social media. //	ソーシャルメディアの時代に入っても。
NASA wisely incorporated /	NASAは巧みに組み込みました
the Internet /	インターネットを
and up-and-coming social media websites /	そして新進のソーシャルメディアのウェブサイト
such as Twitter /	ツイッターなどの
into Cassini's mission /	カッシーニのミッションに
to make its images readily available /	その画像を簡単に利用できるように
to the general public. //	一般の人たちに。
Every day /	毎日
people were granted easy access /	人々は簡単にアクセスできるようになりました
to knowledge and photographs, /	情報や写真に,
and Cassini's scientific mission quickly gained /	そしてカッシーニの科学的ミッションはたちまち獲得しました
millions of followers. //	数百万人ものフォロワーを。
The broad and popular support /	一般からの幅広い支援が
that the probe enjoyed /	その探査機が恵まれた
granted NASA /	NASAに許しました
the ability to continue its mission /	そのミッションを継続できることを
for an additional ten years /	さらに10年間
beyond what it had intended. //	それが予定していたのを超えて。
4 Unfortunately, /	残念ながら,
due to the machine's age /	機械の寿命のため

and funding issues back on Earth, /	そして地球での資金面の問題,
NASA announced plans /	NASA は計画を発表しました
in 2014 for Cassini /	2014 年にカッシーニを
to be deliberately destroyed /	意図的に破壊するという
by crashing it into Saturn. //	土星に衝突させることで。
Cassini did not have enough fuel /	カッシーニは十分な燃料を持っていませんでした
to escape /	離脱するのに
from Saturn's orbit, /	土星の軌道から,
and the planet's surface was deemed /	そしてその惑星の地表は見なされました
to be the safest place /	最も安全な場所であると
for the probe /	その探査機にとって
to retire. //	引退するのに。
NASA did not want to biologically contaminate /	NASA は生物学的に汚染したくありませんでした
any of Saturn's moons' surfaces /	土星のどの衛星の表面も
and destroy /	そして台無しにする
the potential for life. //	生命が存在する可能性を。
After 22 months of dipping Cassini /	カッシーニを 22 か月間投入した後で
into Saturn's ring system /	土星の輪の中に
and examining the planet /	そしてその惑星を調査した
from a closer viewpoint /	より近い観測地点から
than any other object /	ほかのどのような天体よりも
in history, /	歴史上,
the time /	その時が
for Cassini's retirement /	カッシーニの引退の

finally arrived. //	とうとうやって来ました。
NASA hosted /	NASA は開催しました
a "Grand Finale" celebration /	「グランドフィナーレ」という式典を
on its website, /	そのウェブサイトで,
enabling the millions of fans /	数百万人ものファンに可能にしました
the probe had attracted /	その探査機が魅了してきた
over the years /	長年にわたって
to witness its final moments. //	その最後の瞬間を目撃することを。
Many in both NASA and the general public called /	多くの NASA 関係者と一般の人たちの両方が呼びました
the final mission /	最後のミッションを
"bittersweet," /	「ほろ苦いもの」と,
stating /	述べました
that while they were sad /	彼らは悲しんでいましたが
that Cassini was no longer orbiting Saturn, /	カッシーニがもはや土星を周回していないことは,
they felt grateful /	彼らは感謝しています
knowing /	認識して
that they witnessed /	彼らが目撃したことを
such an important moment /	これほど重要な瞬間を
in scientific history /	科学の歴史上
and expanded their knowledge /	そして知識を広げてくれた
about worlds beyond our own. //	私たちの外の世界についての。

The Cassini Space Probe

The Cassini space probe captured the world's imagination for nearly twenty years with breathtaking images of the planet Saturn and its surrounding satellite system. NASA hails its mission as one of tremendous historical importance. The unprecedented data it gathered over the years, the flawless execution of various sub-missions, and the fascination with our solar system that it was able to inspire in the general public are some of the many reasons it was considered such a success. On September 15, 2017, the Cassini mission came to an end, concluding nearly two decades of space exploration and revolutionizing how humans comprehend the vastness of space.

NASA launched the Cassini space probe on October 15, 1997, sending it on a six-year, 1.2-billion-kilometer journey through the solar system towards Saturn. The probe fixed itself in orbit at its final destination on July 1, 2004, and it immediately began transmitting data from the distant planet and its expansive moon system back to Earth. Only a single year into its mission, Cassini accomplished its greatest feat by successfully landing the Huygens lander on Saturn's largest moon, Titan. The parachute drop remains mankind's only successful landing beyond our solar system's asteroid belt, and Huygens holds the record as the most distant man-made object residing on a foreign celestial body. Credit is also given to Cassini for discovering new moons never before observed by NASA and even uncovering the potential for alien life on Saturn's moon Enceladus.

Originally, NASA intended to conclude Cassini's mission after just four years, but extensions granted to the program in 2008 and 2010 allowed it to continue well into the age of social media. NASA wisely incorporated the Internet and up-and-coming social media websites such as Twitter into Cassini's mission to make its images readily available to the general public. Every day people were granted easy access to knowledge and photographs, and Cassini's scientific mission quickly gained millions of followers. The broad and popular support that the probe enjoyed granted NASA the ability to continue its mission for an additional ten years beyond what it had intended.

Unfortunately, due to the machine's age and funding issues back on Earth, NASA announced plans in 2014 for Cassini to be deliberately destroyed by crashing it into Saturn. Cassini did not have enough fuel to escape from Saturn's orbit, and the planet's surface was deemed to be the safest place for the probe to retire. NASA did not want to biologically contaminate any of Saturn's moons' surfaces and destroy the potential for life. After 22 months of dipping Cassini into Saturn's ring system and examining the planet from a closer viewpoint than any other object in history, the time for Cassini's retirement finally arrived. NASA hosted a "Grand Finale" celebration on its website, enabling the millions of fans the probe had attracted over the years to witness its final moments. Many in both NASA and the general public called the final mission "bittersweet," stating that while they were sad that Cassini was no longer orbiting Saturn, they felt grateful knowing that they witnessed such an important moment in scientific history and expanded their knowledge about worlds beyond our own.

カッシーニ宇宙探査機

カッシーニ宇宙探査機は，土星とその周囲の衛星群の息をのむような画像によって，20年近くにわたって世界の人々の想像力を刺激しました。NASA（米航空宇宙局）は，そのミッションを歴史的に非常に重要なものの1つだと称賛しています。それが長年にわたって収集した前例のないデータ，さまざまな副次的活動の完璧な遂行，そして一般の人々の間で高めることができた太陽系への関心などは，それが大成功と見なされた多くの理由の一部です。2017年9月15日に，カッシーニのミッションは終了して20年近くに及ぶ宇宙探査を締めくくり，人間が宇宙の広大さを理解する方法に大きな変革をもたらしました。

NASAは1997年10月15日にカッシーニ宇宙探査機を打ち上げ，太陽系を抜けて土星へと

向かう6年間にわたる12億キロメートルの旅に送り出しました。この探査機は，2004年7月1日に最終目的地である土星の軌道に入り，すぐにこの遠方の惑星とその広大な衛星群からのデータを地球に送信し始めました。ミッション開始からわずか1年のうちに，カッシーニは，土星の最大の衛星であるタイタンに，ホイヘンス着陸船を着陸させることに成功することによって偉業を成し遂げました。このパラシュートによる降下は，私たちの太陽系の小惑星帯を越えて着陸をした人類唯一の成功例で，ホイヘンスは未知の天体に置かれ，地球から最も遠方にある人工物という記録を今でも保持しています。これに加えてカッシーニが称賛されているのは，NASAがこれまで観測したことのなかった新たな数個の衛星を発見し，さらには土星の衛星エンケラドゥスに生命体が存在する可能性を示したからです。

　当初，NASAは4年間だけでカッシーニのミッションを終えるつもりでしたが，2008年と2010年にこの計画に認められた期限延長によって，ソーシャルメディアの時代に入っても活動を続けることができました。NASAは，インターネットやツイッターなど新進のソーシャルメディアのウェブサイトをカッシーニのミッションに巧みに取り入れ，その画像を一般の人たちにも簡単に利用できるようにしました。人々は毎日，情報や写真に簡単にアクセスできるようになり，カッシーニの科学的ミッションは，たちまち数百万人ものフォロワーを獲得しました。この探査機が受けた幅広い一般からの支援のおかげで，NASAは意図していたよりもさらに10年長く，このミッションを継続することができました。

　残念ながら，機器の耐用年数と地球側での資金面の問題から，NASAは2014年にカッシーニを意図的に土星に衝突させることで破壊するという計画を発表しました。カッシーニは土星の軌道から離脱するのに十分な燃料を持っておらず，この惑星の地表は探査機が引退するのに最も安全な場所であると見なされたのです。NASAは，土星にある衛星群の地表を生物学的に汚染して生命が存在する可能性を台無しにしたくなかったのです。カッシーニを土星の輪の中に22か月間投入し，歴史上ほかのどのような天体の場合よりも近い観測地点からこの惑星を調査した後で，カッシーニの引退の時がとうとうやって来ました。NASAは，そのウェブサイトで「グランドフィナーレ」という式典を開催し，この探査機が長年にわたって魅了してきた数百万人ものファンがその最後の瞬間を目撃することができました。多くのNASA関係者と一般の人たちは，この最後のミッションを「ほろ苦いもの」と呼び，カッシーニがもはや土星を周回していないことは悲しいことだが，科学の歴史上これほど重要な瞬間を目撃でき，私たちの外の世界についての知識を広げてくれたことに感謝していると述べました。

⇒別冊 p.35 ～ 37

解答と解説

解答

(1) ④　　(2) ①　　(3) ③　　(4) ①

解説

(1) 第1段落最後の文の主節部分には，「健康と幸福に寄与する」とあり，これとほぼ同内容の4が正解となる。ほかの選択肢はパーマカルチャーの人気の理由としては本文で述べられていないので，誤り。

設問・選択肢の和訳

(1) パーマカルチャーは人気を博している，なぜならそれは…からである

× 1　新しいテクノロジーを使用して，人々があまりお金をかけずに家を建てるのを助ける。

× 2　人々が環境によい材料だけを使って家を建てるのを助けることができる。

× 3　人々が新しい家を購入した後，より少ない固定資産税を支払うようにできる。

○ 4　人々の健康と環境の健全性の両方を向上させる助けとなる。

(2) 第2段落の最後の文では，自給自足と有機物のサイクルについて述べられている。その点と本文で述べられているパーマカルチャーの概念から推測して，1が正解。ほかの選択肢はパーマカルチャーの活用例として本文で述べられている内容には合致しない。

設問・選択肢の和訳

(2) パーマカルチャーを活用するために，人々は…

○ 1　自分の有機果物や野菜を育てるために庭を作ろうとすることができる。

× 2　新しい家を建てる時は，明確に定義された一連のルールに従わなければならない。

× 3　コミュニティが連携してグリーンテクノロジーに投資する必要がある。

× 4　環境の改善に役立つ3つの方法を思いつくべきである。

(3) 第3段落の第7・8文の内容に関連しているが，本文には「すべてのごみ」とは書かれていないので3が正解。この選択肢のように「すべて」，または「だけ」などと言い切っているものは特に，本文としっかり照合するようにしたい。

設問・選択肢の和訳

(3) パーマカルチャーの例ではないのは次のうちどれか。

× 1　廃棄されたかもしれない木材で家を建てること。

× 2　自然光を利用して家の中で食べ物を育てること。

○ 3　植物に栄養を与えるためにすべてのごみを庭に投げ捨てること。

× 4　雨が不足した時に使うために雨水を集めること。

(4) 第4段落の第2文には，パーマカルチャーの課題として労力や資金が必要なことが述べられている。これに合致する1が正解となる。2・3・4は，パーマカルチャーの課

題としては本文で述べられているものではないので，誤り。

(4) パーマカルチャーにはどのような難題がありうるか。

○1 いくつかのパーマカルチャー技術は，十分なお金を持っている人にのみ利用可能である。

×2 電気自動車は環境に適しているが，持続不可能な方法で製造されている。

×3 より古いパーマカルチャー製品を販売している店を人々が見つけるのは非常に困難である。

×4 一部の地域の法律は，人々が最新のパーマカルチャー技術を適用することを禁止している。

語句

〈タイトル〉

□ permaculture	（名）パーマカルチャー，持続型農業

〈第1段落〉

□ from scratch	ゼロから
□ mount	（動）高まる，強くなる
□ emerge	（動）現れる
□ address	（動）（問題に）取り組む，対処する
□ sustainable	（形）持続できる
□ property tax	固定資産税
□ wellbeing	（名）福利

〈第2段落〉

□ care for ~	~を大切にする
□ vague	（形）漠然としている
□ organic farming	有機農業
□ green	（形）環境に優しい
□ waste reduction	廃棄物の削減
□ integrative	（形）統合的な

□ landscaping	（名）造園，景観整備
□ carbon footprint	二酸化炭素排出量

〈第3段落〉

□ driveway	（名）私道
□ pollinate	（動）~に授粉する，受粉する
□ sturdy	（形）頑丈な
□ salvage	（動）回収する
□ gutter	（名）雨どい
□ barrel	（名）樽
□ nourish	（動）~に栄養を与える
□ drought	（名）干ばつ，日照り
□ wherein	（副）その中で
□ spot	（動）~に気づく
□ enclosure	（名）囲い
□ compost	（名）堆肥
□ crush up ~	~を押しつぶす

〈第4段落〉

□ initial investment	初期投資

構造確認 ※誤読した部分の確認に使用してください。　　　　　⇒別冊 p.35 〜 37

第1段落 パーマカルチャーは家を人と周囲の環境にとって持続可能な観点から捉える思考体系である。

① [Buying a home] is not as easy (as [(merely) signing a contract]), and (for
　　　 S① 　　　　　 V① 　 C① 　　
those ⟨who choose to build their homes (from scratch)⟩) there are questions
　　　 　V' 　　　　　 O' 　　　　　　 V② 　 S②
⟨of location, materials, and even [what kind of heating and cooling system
to install]⟩.　　　　　　　　　　　　　　　　　　　　　　　　　🔖注1

【家を購入すること】は（[（単に）契約書にサインをする（だけ）のこと]のように）簡単ではなく，⟨⟨家
を（ゼロから）建設することを選ぶ⟩人には）⟨立地，建材，さらには【どのような冷暖房装置を設置す
るか】といった⟩問題があります。

② (As concerns ⟨for the environment⟩ mount), (however), a concept has
　　 S'① 　　　　　　　　　　　　 V'① 　　　　　　　 S 　 V
emerged ⟨that attempts to address many ⟨of these significant challenges⟩⟩:
　　　　　　　　　 V'② 　　　　 O'② 　
permaculture.　　　　　　　　　　　　　　　　　　　　　　　🔖注2

（しかし），⟨⟨環境への⟩懸念が高まっているので），⟨⟨⟨これらの重要な課題の⟩多くに対処しようとす
る⟩考え方が生まれました，それがパーマカルチャーです。

③ Permaculture is a combination ⟨of the words "permanent" and "culture"⟩,
　　 S① 　　　 V① 　　 C① 　
and it is a system of thinking ⟨about a home⟩ ⟨in a way ⟨that is sustainable
　　 S②V② 　 C② 　　　　　　　　　　　　　　　　　 V' 　 C'
(for the people ⟨in it⟩ and the rest ⟨of the environment⟩)⟩⟩.

パーマカルチャーとは⟨「パーマネント（永遠の）」と「カルチャー（文化）」という言葉の⟩合成で，そ
れは⟨家というものについて⟩⟨⟨⟨⟨そこに住む⟩人たちと（人以外の）その他⟨の環境⟩にとって）持続
可能な⟩観点からの⟩思考体系のことです。

④ (While it doesn't go as far as [helping new homeowners resolve questions
    S'   V'
〈about property taxes and local school systems〉]), it does contribute (to
                                                    S   V
their health and wellbeing).   注3

(それは【新たに住宅を手に入れた人たちが〈固定資産税や地元の学校制度についての〉疑問を解決する役に立つ】まではなりませんが),（その人たちの健康と幸福には）しっかりと寄与してくれます。

第2段落 基本的な目標は，地球に気を配る，人間を大事にする，資源を正しく利用する，の3つである。

① (According to a report 〈written by Kara Greenblott and Kristof Nordin in
2012〉), the three basic goals 〈of permaculture〉 are [to care for the Earth],
        S   V   C
[to care for people], and [to use resources (fairly)].   注4

(〈2012年にカーラ・グリーンブロットとクリストフ・ノルディンによって書かれた〉報告書によると),〈パーマカルチャーの〉3つの基本的な目標は[地球に気を配ること],[人間を大事にすること],そして[資源を(正しく)利用すること]です。

② Those goals are both ambitious and vague, so it's not surprising [that
    S①   V①   C①   S② V②   C②
permaculture refers to a wide range of areas].
    S'   V'   O'

それらの目標は壮大で漠然としているため，[パーマカルチャーが幅広い領域に関わること]は驚くにはあたりません。

③ These areas include organic farming, "green" energy 〈like solar panels〉,
    S   V   O
waste reduction, and integrative landscaping.

こうした分野には有機農業，〈ソーラーパネルのような〉「グリーンな(環境に優しい)」エネルギー，廃棄物の削減，統合的な景観設計などが含まれます。

④ These concepts are not just for people 〈with money to spend〉, (however).
    S   V   C

(ただし)，こうした考え方は〈費やせる資金を持っている〉人たちだけのものではありません。

⑤ (On the contrary), those ⟨living in poverty⟩ can use some principles of
　　　　　　　　　　　　S　　　　　　　　　　　　V　　　　　　　　O
permaculture (to live both cheaply and sustainably), (providing their own

food, managing their own waste, and reducing their carbon footprint). 注5

(むしろ)，〈貧困の中で暮らしている〉人たちはパーマカルチャーのいくつかの原理を利用することで
(安価にも持続可能にも生活をすること)ができ，(自分の食べる食料を調達し，自分の出したごみを
管理し，二酸化炭素排出量を削減すること)ができるのです。

第3段落 パーマカルチャーの原理に基づき建てられる家は実際にはどのような外観と雰囲気になるか。

① So what would a home ⟨built (on the principles ⟨of permaculture⟩)⟩
　　　　　　　　V　　　S
(actually) look and feel like?

それでは〈〈〈パーマカルチャーの〉原理に基づいて)建てられる〉家は(実際には)どのような外観と雰
囲気になるのでしょうか。

② Picture this: (as you enter the driveway), you smell the fragrance of flowers.
　V①　　O①　　　　　　S'　V'　　　　O'　　　　S②　V②　　　　　　O②
　　　　　　　　　　　　　　　　　　　　　　　　　　　　　　　　　　　注6
このように想像してみてください，(あなたが私道に入ると)，花の香りがします。

③ Those flowers aren't just there (to produce a pleasant perfume), (though);
　　　S①　　　　V①
they attract bees, ⟨which pollinate other plants and also produce delicious
S②　V②　　O②　　　　　V'①　　　　　O'①　　　　　　　　V'②　　　O'②
honey (for the owners)⟩.　注7

(しかし)，そうした花は(心地よい香りを生み出すため)だけにあるのではありません，それらはミツ
バチを呼び寄せ，〈それがほかの植物に授粉し，さらに(家主のために)おいしいハチミツを作ってく
れます〉。

④ The house itself is sturdy, (built from thick, recycled wood ⟨salvaged from a
　　　　S　　　　　V　　C
nearby house ⟨that was being rebuilt⟩⟩).
　　　　　　　　　　　　V'

家屋自体は頑丈で，(〈〈建て替え中の〉近くの家から回収された〉分厚い再生木材で作られています)。

⑤ (Under the gutters 〈in the corners 〈of the house〉〉), there are large barrels,
_V _S

〈which collect rainwater 〈that will be used (to nourish the fruit trees (in case
_{V'} _{O'}

of a drought))〉〉.

(《《家の》隅にある》雨どいの下には)，《《(水不足の時に) 果樹に与えるために) 使われる》雨水を集める》，大きな樽があります。

⑥ The inside 〈of the house〉 is bright, (thanks to the large windows 〈in the
_S _V _C

kitchen〉), 〈wherein you see a wall of live herbs and salad greens 〈that
_{S''} _{V''} _{O''}

grow year-round〉〉.

〈家の》中が明るいのは，《《キッチンの》大きな窓のおかげで)，《その中に〈一年中育つ〉生き生きしたハーブとサラダ用の野菜の壁が見えます》。

⑦ (When you enter the backyard), you spot a wooden enclosure 〈that is
_{S'①} _{V'①} _{O'①} _S _V _O _{V'②}

surrounded (by large flies and mosquitos)〉.

(裏庭に出ると)，《(大きなハエや蚊が) 群がる》木製の囲いが目に入ります。

⑧ You look (inside) and see compost: rich, black dirt 〈full of crushed up
_S _{V①} _{V②} _{O②}

eggshells, chicken bones, and orange peels〉〈that help sustain the garden〉.
_{V'} _{O'}

(その中には) 堆肥が見えます，それは《細かく砕いた卵の殻，鶏の骨，オレンジの皮などがたくさん混じった》《菜園を維持するのに役立ってくれる》豊かな，黒い土です。

第4段落 その原則を採用するには多くの計画，研究，資金が必要かもしれないが，完全でなくてもよい。

① The world 〈of permaculture〉 is not without its challenges.
_S _V

〈パーマカルチャーの》世界には課題がないわけではありません。

② (In fact), [using the principles ⟨of permaculture⟩] can require far more
　　　　　　　　　　　S　　　　　　　　　　　　　　　　　　V
planning, research, and, (in some cases), even money.
　　　　　　　　　　　　　　　O

(実際), 【⟨パーマカルチャーの⟩原則を採用すること】ははるかに多くの計画, 研究, そして, (場合
によっては), 資金さえ必要となります。

③ So-called "green technologies", (for instance), are (without a doubt) better
　　　　　　　　S　　　　　　　　　　　　　　　　　　　V①　　　　　　　　　　C①
(for the environment), but can cost more than standard technologies,
　　　　　　　　　　　　　　　V②
((especially) considering the initial investment).　　　　　　　　注10

(例えば), いわゆる「グリーンテクノロジー」は, (間違いなく)(環境にとって)よりよいものですが,
((特に)初期投資を考慮すると), 標準的なテクノロジーよりももっとコストがかかる可能性がありま
す。

④ (For example), [buying an electric car] might not be an option ⟨for someone
　　　　　　　　　　　　　S　　　　　　　　　　V　　　　　　　C
⟨who only has a few thousand dollars ⟨to spend⟩⟩⟩.
　　　　　V'　　　　O'

(例えば), 【電気自動車を購入すること】は⟨⟨⟨払えるのが⟩数千ドルしかない⟩人にとっては⟩選択肢
にならないかもしれません。

⑤ (However), the idea ⟨behind permaculture⟩ is not [to be perfect]; it's about
　　　　　　　　S①　　　　　　　　　　　　　　V①　　　　C①　　　　S②V②　　C②
[trying to be thoughtful (about every detail ⟨of your home's future⟩)] and
[considering [how every decision will affect your family, your community,
and even the Earth itself]].

(しかしながら), ⟨パーマカルチャーの背後にある⟩考え方は【完全であること】を求めるものではあ
りません, それは【((あなたの家の将来の⟩あらゆる細部について) 配慮する努力をする】そして【【す
べての決断があなたの家族, あなたの住む地域, さらに地球そのものにどのように影響するのか】を
考えること】なのです。

注1　those who V は「V する人々」という意味。この those は「人々（the people）」という意味
　　　になる。

注2　as S V は「S が V するので，時，ように，につれて」のような意味になるが，文脈から柔軟
　　　に意味を解釈する。

注3　help ～ V は，原形不定詞を用いた形で，「～が V するのを助ける」という意味になる。help
　　　～ to V というように to 不定詞を用いることもある。

注4　are の補語となっている3つの to 不定詞は，名詞的用法で用いられている。

注5　on the contrary は「それとは反対に」「むしろ」という意味で，直前の内容を否定しながら，
　　　続く内容を紹介する場合に用いる。

注6　この文での this は，直後に続く内容を指している。this は直前の内容を指すことが多いが，こ
　　　の文での this のように直後の内容を指すことがある。

注7　though は「…だけれども」という接続詞として用いられることが多いが，副詞として「でも」「け
　　　れど」という意味で用いられることがある。

注8　wherein は珍しい関係副詞で，where よりも「中で」という in の意味を強調したい場合に用
　　　いられる。

注9　not without ～は「～がないわけではない」という意味で，少し柔らかく「～がある」という
　　　ことを言う場合に用いる。

注10　considering ～は「～を考慮すれば」という意味の分詞構文の慣用表現。

サイトトランスレーション

⇒別冊 p.35 ～ 37

1 Buying a home is not as easy as /	家を購入することは…ほど簡単ではありません
merely signing a contract, /	単に契約書にサインをするだけのこと,
and for those who choose to build their homes /	そして家を建てることを選ぶ人には
from scratch /	ゼロから
there are questions /	問題があります
of location, /	立地の,
materials, /	建材,
and even what kind of heating and cooling system /	そしてさらにはどのような冷暖房装置を
to install. //	設置するか。
As concerns for the environment mount, /	環境への意識が高まるにつれて,
however, /	しかし,
a concept has emerged /	考え方が生まれました
that attempts to address /	対処しようとする
many of these significant challenges: /	これらの重要な課題の多くに,
permaculture. //	(それが) パーマカルチャーです。
Permaculture is a combination of the words /	パーマカルチャーは言葉を合成したものです
"permanent" and "culture," /	「パーマネント (永遠の)」と「カルチャー (文化)」という,
and it is a system /	そしてそれは体系です
of thinking about a home /	家について考えることの
in a way /	観点から

that is sustainable /	持続可能な
for the people in it /	そこに住む人たちにとって
and the rest of the environment. //	そして残りの環境。
While it doesn't go as far as helping /	それは役には立つまでではありませんが
new homeowners /	新たに住宅を手に入れた人たちが
resolve questions /	疑問を解決する
about property taxes and local school systems, /	固定資産税や地元の学校制度についての,
it does contribute /	それはしっかりと寄与します
to their health and wellbeing. //	その人たちの健康と幸福に。
2 According to a report /	報告書によると
written by Kara Greenblott and Kristof Nordin /	カーラ・グリーンブロットとクリストフ・ノルディンによって書かれた
in 2012, /	2012 年に,
the three basic goals /	3 つの基本的な目標は
of permaculture /	パーマカルチャーの
are to care for the Earth, /	地球に気を配ることです,
to care for people, /	人間を大事にすること,
and to use resources fairly. //	そして資源を正しく利用すること。
Those goals are both ambitious and vague, /	それらの目標は壮大で漠然としています,
so it's not surprising /	なのでそれは驚くべきことではありません
that permaculture refers to /	パーマカルチャーが関わることは
a wide range of areas. //	幅広い領域に。
These areas include /	これらの分野は含みます

organic farming, /	有機農業,
"green" energy /	「グリーンな (環境に優しい)」エネルギー
like solar panels, /	ソーラーパネルなどの,
waste reduction, /	廃棄物の削減,
and integrative landscaping. //	そして統合的な景観設計。
These concepts are not just for people /	こうした考え方は人々のためだけのものではありません
with money to spend, /	費やせるお金を持っている,
however. //	しかしながら。
On the contrary, /	むしろ,
those living in poverty can use /	貧困の中で暮らしている人たちは利用できます
some principles of permaculture /	いくつかのパーマカルチャーの原理を
to live /	生活をして
both cheaply and sustainably, /	安価にも持続可能にも,
providing /	調達して
their own food, /	自分の食料を,
managing /	管理して
their own waste, /	自分の出したごみを,
and reducing /	そして削減します
their carbon footprint. //	二酸化炭素排出量を。
3 So what would a home built /	それでは建てられる家はどのようになるのでしょうか
on the principles of permaculture /	パーマカルチャーの原理に基づいて
actually look and feel like? //	実際の外観と雰囲気は。
Picture this: /	このように想像してみてください,

as you enter /	あなたが入ると
the driveway, /	私道に,
you smell /	あなたはかぎます
the fragrance of flowers. //	花の香りを。
Those flowers aren't just there /	そうした花は…だけにそこにあるのではありません
to produce a pleasant perfume, /	心地よい香りを生み出すため,
though; /	しかし,
they attract bees, /	それらはミツバチを魅了し,
which pollinate other plants /	それがほかの植物に授粉します
and also produce delicious honey /	そしてさらにおいしい蜂蜜を作ります
for the owners. //	家主のために。
The house itself is sturdy, /	家屋自体は頑丈です,
built from thick, recycled wood /	分厚い, 再生木材で作られています
salvaged from a nearby house /	近くの家から回収された
that was being rebuilt. //	建て替え中の。
Under the gutters /	雨どいの下には
in the corners of the house, /	家の隅にある,
there are large barrels, /	大きな樽があり,
which collect rainwater /	それが雨水を集めます
that will be used to nourish /	栄養を与えるために使われる
the fruit trees /	果樹に
in case of a drought. //	水不足の時に。
The inside of the house /	家の中は
is bright, /	明るいです,

191

thanks to the large windows /	大きな窓のおかげで
in the kitchen, /	キッチンの,
wherein /	その中には
you see a wall /	壁が見えます
of live herbs and salad greens /	生き生きしたハーブとサラダ用の野菜の
that grow year-round. //	一年中育つ。
When you enter /	あなたが入ると
the backyard, /	裏庭に,
you spot /	目に入ります
a wooden enclosure /	木製の囲いが
that is surrounded /	群がる
by large flies and mosquitos. //	大きなハエや蚊が。
You look inside /	その中を覗くと
and see compost: /	堆肥が見えます,
rich, black dirt /	豊かな, 黒い土
full of crushed up eggshells, /	細かく砕いた卵の殻がたくさん混じった,
chicken bones, /	鶏の骨,
and orange peels /	そしてオレンジの皮
that help sustain the garden. //	菜園を維持するのに役立ってくれる。
4 The world of permaculture /	パーマカルチャーの世界は
is not without its challenges. //	課題がないわけではありません。
In fact, /	実際,
using the principles /	原則を利用することは
of permaculture /	パーマカルチャーの

can require /	必要とする可能性があります
far more planning, research, /	はるかに多くの計画，調査が，
and, in some cases, /	そして，場合によっては，
even money. //	お金さえ。
So-called /	いわゆる
"green technologies," /	「グリーンテクノロジー」は，
for instance, /	例えば，
are without a doubt /	間違いありません
better for the environment, /	環境にとってよりよいことは，
but can cost /	しかしコストがかかる可能性があります
more than standard technologies, /	標準的なテクノロジーよりも，
especially /	特に
considering the initial investment. //	初期投資を考慮すると。
For example, /	例えば，
buying an electric car /	電気自動車を購入することは
might not be an option /	選択肢にならないかもしれません
for someone /	人にとっては
who only has a few thousand dollars /	数千ドルしか持たない
to spend. //	払うために。
However, /	しかしながら，
the idea /	考え方は
behind permaculture /	パーマカルチャーの背後にある
is not to be perfect; /	完全である必要はありません，
it's about trying to be thoughtful /	それは考えようとすることです

about every detail /	あらゆる細部について
of your home's future /	あなたの家の将来の
and considering /	そして考えることです
how every decision will affect /	すべての決断がどのように影響するのかを
your family, /	あなたの家族,
your community, /	あなたの住む地域,
and even the Earth itself. //	そして地球そのものにまでも。

Will Permaculture Save the World?

Buying a home is not as easy as merely signing a contract, and for those who choose to build their homes from scratch there are questions of location, materials, and even what kind of heating and cooling system to install. As concerns for the environment mount, however, a concept has emerged that attempts to address many of these significant challenges: permaculture. Permaculture is a combination of the words "permanent" and "culture," and it is a system of thinking about a home in a way that is sustainable for the people in it and the rest of the environment. While it doesn't go as far as helping new homeowners resolve questions about property taxes and local school systems, it does contribute to their health and wellbeing.

According to a report written by Kara Greenblott and Kristof Nordin in 2012, the three basic goals of permaculture are to care for the Earth, to care for people, and to use resources fairly. Those goals are both ambitious and vague, so it's not surprising that permaculture refers to a wide range of areas. These areas include organic farming, "green" energy like solar panels, waste reduction, and integrative landscaping. These concepts are not just for people with money to spend, however. On the contrary, those living in poverty can use some principles of permaculture to live both cheaply and sustainably, providing their own food, managing their own waste, and reducing their carbon footprint.

So what would a home built on the principles of permaculture actually look and feel like? Picture this: as you enter the driveway, you smell the fragrance of flowers. Those flowers aren't just there to produce a pleasant perfume, though; they attract bees, which pollinate other plants and also produce delicious honey for the owners. The house itself is sturdy, built from thick, recycled wood salvaged from a nearby house that was being rebuilt. Under the gutters in the corners of the house, there are large barrels, which collect rainwater that will be used to nourish the fruit trees in case of a drought. The inside of the house is bright, thanks to the large windows in the kitchen, wherein you see a wall of live herbs and salad greens that grow year-round. When you enter the backyard, you spot a wooden enclosure that is surrounded by large flies and mosquitos. You look inside and see compost: rich, black dirt full of crushed up eggshells, chicken bones, and orange peels that help sustain the garden.

The world of permaculture is not without its challenges. In fact, using the principles of permaculture can require far more planning, research, and, in some cases, even money. So-called "green technologies," for instance, are without a doubt better for the environment, but can cost more than standard technologies, especially considering the initial investment. For example, buying an electric car might not be an option for someone who only has a few thousand dollars to spend. However, the idea behind permaculture is not to be perfect; it's about trying to be thoughtful about every detail of your home's future and considering how every decision will affect your family, your community, and even the Earth itself.

パーマカルチャーは世界を救うのか

家を購入することは，単に契約書にサインをするだけですむほど簡単ではなく，家をゼロから建設することを選ぶ人には，立地，建材，さらにはどのような冷暖房装置を設置するかといった問題があります。しかし，環境への意識が高まるにつれて，これらの重要な課題の多くに対処しようとする考え方が生まれました。それがパーマカルチャーです。パーマカルチャーとは，「パーマネント（永遠の）」と「カルチャー（文化）」という言葉を合成したもので，家というものを，そこに住む人たちと周囲の環境にとって持続可能な観点からとらえる思考体系のことです。それは新たに住宅を手に入れた人たちが固定資産税や地元の学校制度について抱く疑問を解決する役には立ちませんが，その人たちの健康と幸福には間違いなく貢献してくれます。

2012 年にカーラ・グリーンブロットとクリストフ・ノルディンによって書かれた報告書によると，パーマカルチャーの 3 つの基本的な目標は，地球に気を配ること，人間を大事にする

こと，そして資源を正しく利用することです。これらの目標は壮大で漠然としているため，パーマカルチャーが幅広い領域に関わることは驚くにはあたりません。そうした分野には，有機農業，ソーラーパネルなどの「グリーンな（環境に優しい）」エネルギー，廃棄物の削減，統合的な景観設計などが含まれます。ただし，こうした考え方は費やせる資金を持っている人だけのものではありません。むしろ，貧困の中で暮らしている人たちは，パーマカルチャーのいくつかの原理を利用すれば，安価に持続可能な生活ができ，そして自分の食べる食料を調達し，自分の出したごみを管理し，二酸化炭素排出量を削減できるのです。

それでは，パーマカルチャーの原理に基づいて建てられる家は，実際にはどのような外観と雰囲気になるのでしょうか。このように想像してみてください。あなたが私道に入ると，花の香りがします。しかし，そうした花は心地よい香りを生み出すためだけにあるのではありません。それはミツバチを呼び寄せ，それがほかの植物に授粉し，さらに家主のためにおいしいハチミツを作ってくれます。家屋自体は頑丈で，建て替え中の近くの家から回収された分厚い再生木材で作られています。家の隅にある雨どいの下には大きな樽があり，それらが水不足の時に果樹に栄養を与えるために使う雨水を集めます。家の中が明るいのはキッチンの大きな窓のおかげで，そこには一年中育つ生き生きしたハーブとサラダ用の野菜が壁一面に見えます。裏庭に出ると，大きなハエや蚊が群がる木製の囲いが目に入ります。その中を覗くと堆肥が見えます。それは細かく砕いた卵の殻，鶏の骨，オレンジの皮などがたくさん混じった豊かな黒い土で，それが菜園を維持するのに役立ってくれます。

パーマカルチャーの世界には課題がないわけではありません。実際，パーマカルチャーの原則を採用するには，普通よりもはるかに多くの計画，研究，そして場合によっては資金さえ必要となります。例えば，いわゆる「グリーンテクノロジー」は，間違いなく環境にとってより好ましいものですが，特に初期投資を考慮すると，標準的なテクノロジーよりもよりコストがかかる可能性があります。例えば，電気自動車を購入することは，数千ドルしか払えない人にとっては選択肢に入らないかもしれません。しかしながら，パーマカルチャーの背後にある考え方は完全であることを求めるものではありません。それは，あなたの家の将来についてあらゆる細部まで配慮する努力をするとともに，すべての決断があなたの家族，あなたの住む地域，そして地球そのものにまでどのように影響するのかを考えることなのです。

⇒別冊 p.38 ～ 40

解答と解説

解答

(1) ①　　(2) ①　　(3) ③　　(4) ④

解説

(1) 第1段落の第4文の内容に一致する1が正解。2・3は本文中に記述がない。4は第1段落の第3文にアメリカで何千人もの人がジェットコースターでけがをしていることが書かれている点，第4文に何百万人もの人が何の事故もなくジェットコースターに乗っていると書かれている点に一致しない。

設問・選択肢の和訳

(1) ジェットコースターに関して正しいのは次のうちどれか。

○ 1　現代科学技術のおかげで，ジェットコースターに関連した事故の件数は減少してきた。

× 2　大人に比べて子供はジェットコースターに乗っている間にけがをしやすい。

× 3　ジェットコースターが高ければ高いほど人々は事故に巻き込まれやすい。

× 4　世界中で何百万人もの人が毎年ジェットコースターの事故でけがをしている。

(2) 第2段落の第5・6文の内容に一致する1が正解。2・3は本文中に記述がない。4は，第5文に新しいジェットコースターには車輪付きの台車が備わっていたことが書かれているが，安全性についての記述は本文にないため，誤り。

設問・選択肢の和訳

(2) 氷の滑り台の人気が低下した理由は…からである

○ 1　人々は車輪付きの台車がついたジェットコースターに一年中乗れた。

× 2　とても滑りやすく危険だったので多くの人は乗りたがらなかった。

× 3　製作に多くの時間がかかり，維持するのに費用がかかり過ぎた。

× 4　新しいジェットコースターは安全性を高める車輪付きの台車を備えていた。

(3) 第3段落の第4文には，木材と違い柔軟な鉄の特徴について述べられている。このことと合致する3が正解となる。ほかの選択肢は，鉄の利点として本文中に同様の記述がない。

設問・選択肢の和訳

(3) ジェットコースターを作るのに鉄を使う利点は次のうちどれか。

× 1　木材よりも鉄のジェットコースターを作る方がずっと安い。

× 2　とても滑らかなのでコースターがずっと速く走ることができる。

○ 3　木製よりも多くのタイプの形を作ることができる。

× 4　コースターがより高い位置まで行くことができ，よりよい眺めを提供する。

(4) 第4段落の第3・4文の内容に一致する4が正解。1は，第4文に建造物の高さ制限に関する現地の法に違反していたと書かれているが，法律を変更したという記述はな

いため，誤り。2・3 は本文中に記述がない。

(4) スカイスクレイパーの建設を巡る論争があったのはなぜか。

×1 地元政府が建物の高さに関する法律を変更した。

×2 地元住民が高い建造物は町の景観を損なうと主張した。

×3 ギネスワールドレコーズ・グループは公式な測定をしなかった。

○4 ジェットコースターはあまりに高すぎたので，地元政府が反対した。

語句

〈第1段落〉

□ ride	(名) 乗り物
□ adrenaline rush	興奮状態
□ significantly	(副) 大いに

〈第2段落〉

□ structure	(名) 建造物
□ ramp	(名) 斜面，スロープ
□ recreate	(動) 〜を再現する
□ engineer	(動) 〜を設計する
□ wheeled	(形) 車輪の付いた
□ carriage	(名) 台車
□ track	(名) 軌道，線路

□ incorporate	(動) 〜を組み込む，取り入れる
□ loop	(名) 環
□ platform	(名) 台，(乗り物の) 乗降場

〈第3段落〉

□ rigid	(形) 柔軟性のない，硬くて (簡単に) 曲がらない
□ bend	(動) 〜を曲げる
□ twists and turns	曲がりくねり，紆余曲折

〈第4段落〉

□ controversy	(名) 論争
□ legal battle	法廷闘争

構造確認 ※誤読した部分の確認に使用してください。

⇒別冊 p.38 ～ 40

第 1 段落 ジェットコースターは人気のある乗り物だが，その 400 年の歴史の中で大きく変化してきた。

① The roller coaster is one ⟨of the most popular amusement park rides ⟨ever
　　　　　 S　　　　　V　C
invented⟩⟩.
　　　　　　　　　　　　　　　　　　　　　　　　　　　　　　　　　　注1

ジェットコースターは《《これまでに発明された》最も人気のある遊園地の乗り物の》1 つです。

② Some eager thrill-seekers even travel (all over the world) (seeking the
　　　　　　　 S　　　　　　　　　　 V
adrenaline rush ⟨provided (by the tallest and fastest coasters)⟩).

スリルを求めることに情熱を持つ人の中には《《最も高さがあって最もスピードの速いコースターに
よって》もたらされる》興奮の極致を求めて）（世界中を）旅する人さえいます。

③ (While thousands of people ⟨in the U.S. alone⟩ are injured (each year) and
　　　　　 S'①　　　　　　　　　　　　　 V'①
some ⟨of them⟩ are (seriously) injured), roller coasters remain a remarkably
 S'②　　　　　 V'②　　　　　　　　　　　 S　　　　　 V　　 C
safe and exciting ride ⟨for children and adults alike⟩.

((毎年)⟨米国だけでも⟩数千人もの人がけがをし，⟨その中には⟩(深刻な) けがをする人もいますが)，
ジェットコースターは⟨子供にとっても大人にとっても等しく⟩相変わらず非常に安全で胸躍る乗り物
です。

④ (In fact), millions of people ride them (each year) (without any incidents),
　　　　　　　 S①　　　　　　 V①　 O①
and (thanks to new computerized controls), they are safer (than ever
　　　　　　　　　　　　　　　　　　　　　 S②　 V②　 C②
before).
　　　　　　　　　　　　　　　　　　　　　　　　　　　　　　　　　　注2

(実際に)，(毎年) 数百万人もの人たちが (何の事故もなく) 乗っており，(新しいコンピューター制御
のおかげで)，(かつてないほど) 安全になっています。

⑤ But (while the modern idea ⟨of a "roller coaster"⟩ is familiar to many),
　　　　　　　　 S'　　　　　　　　　　　　　　 V'　 C'
this ride has changed (significantly) (during the course ⟨of its 400-year-long
 S　　　 V

history⟩).

しかし (⟨「ジェットコースター」についての⟩現代の概念は多くの人にとってなじみ深いものですが)，
この乗り物は (⟨その 400 年の歴史の⟩中で) (大きく) 変化してきました。

第2段落 ジェットコースターは 17 世紀のロシアにあった氷の滑り台に起源があり，欧州に広がった。

① The structures ⟨that we recognize (today) (as "roller coasters")⟩ began (as
　　S　　　　　　　　　S'　　V'　　　　　　　　　　　　　　　　　V
ice slides) (in Russia).

⟨(今日) (「ジェットコースター」として) 私たちが認識している⟩構造物は (ロシアで) (氷の滑り台と
して) 始まりました。

② (During the 17th century), residents ⟨of St. Petersburg⟩ would climb (to the
　　　　　　　　　　　　　　　S　　　　　　　　　　　　　　　V①
top ⟨of special structures⟩) and slide down wooden ramps ⟨that were
　　　　　　　　　　　　　　　V②　　　　　O②　　　　　　V'
covered (with thick sheets ⟨of ice⟩)⟩.　　　　　　　　　　　　　注3

(17 世紀に)，⟨サンクトペテルブルクの⟩住民たちはよく (⟨特別な構造物の⟩頂上に) 登って⟨⟨氷の⟩
厚い板で) 覆われた⟩木製のスロープを滑り降りていました。

③ (Over time), these slides became popular (among European upper-class
　　　　　　　　　S　　　　V①　　C①
people) and were recreated (outside of Russia).
　　　　　　　　V②

(時が経つにつれて)，このような滑り台は (ヨーロッパの上流階級の人々の間で) 人気が高まり (ロシ
ア以外でも) 同様のものが作られました。

④ (By the 18th century), both the Russians and the French had engineered
　　　　　　　　　　　　　　S　　　　　　　　　　　　　　V
a ride ⟨that was similar (to the original ice slides)⟩ ⟨that did not require any
　O　　　V①　　C①　　　　　　　　　　　　　　　　V②　　　O'②
ice⟩.　　　　　　　　　　　　　　　　　　　　　　　　　　注4

(18 世紀までには)，ロシア人とフランス人が⟨氷をまったく必要としない⟩⟨(元の氷の滑り台と) 似
た⟩乗り物を設計しました。

⑤ **The new ride**, 〈called a "coaster"〉, used **wheeled carriages** 〈attached (to
    _S   _V   _O

tracks — 〈similar to train tracks〉) —〉〈that guided riders (up and over a
                                                           _{V'}   _{O'}

series of small hills)〉.

〈「コースター」と呼ばれた〉，その新しい乗り物では，〈(軌道——〈列車の線路のような〉——に) 取り
付けられた〉車輪付きの台車を使って〈それが乗客を (連続する小さな丘を乗り越えて) 運びました〉。

⑥ It could be ridden (at any time 〈of the year〉).
  _S   _V

それは (〈一年中〉いつでも) 乗ることができました。

⑦ (Soon), people began to build **bigger coasters** 〈that incorporated loops and
          _S   _V   _O   _{V'}   _{O'}

higher platforms 〈from which to release the carriages〉〉. 注5

(やがて)，人々は〈ループ軌道や〈車両を解き放つために〉より高さのある乗降場を取り入れた〉より
大規模なコースターを作り始めました。

⑧ **Public demand** 〈for roller coasters〉 continued to grow (throughout the
      _{S①}   _{V①}

years), and coaster designs continued to improve.
               _{S②}   _{V②}

〈ジェットコースターに対する〉一般市民からの要望は (年々) 増え続け，コースターの設計は改善さ
れ続けました。

第3段落 素材を木から鉄に変更したことで乗客により多くのスリルと興奮を与えられるようになった。

① One major improvement came (with a change 〈in material〉).
              _S   _V

主な改善点の1つは (〈素材の〉変更) でした。

② Most companies built coasters (primarily out of wood) (until, (in 1959),
       _{S①}   _{V①}   _{O①}

Disney built the first steel roller coaster (at Disneyland Park 〈in California〉)).
  _{S②}   _{V②}   _{O②} 注6

大半の会社は (主に木材で) コースターを建設していました，((1959年に)，ディズニーが (〈カリフォ
ルニアの〉ディズニーランド・パークで) 最初の鉄製のジェットコースターを建設するまでは)。

③ The use ⟨of steel⟩ had many benefits ⟨for roller coaster designers⟩.
　　S　　　　　　　V　　O

⟨鉄の⟩使用は⟨ジェットコースターの設計者にとって⟩多くの利点がありました。

④ (Because steel is not as rigid (as wood)), it can be bent (easily) (to form
　　　　　S'　　V'　　　C'　　　　　　　S　　　V

loops, curves, and so on).

(鉄は (木材のように) 柔軟性のないものではないため), (ループやカーブなどを作るために) (簡単に)
曲げることができます。

⑤ (Using steel), modern roller coasters are able to take riders (on many more
　　　　　　　　　　　　S　　　　　　　V　　　　　O

twists and turns) (through the air) (than wooden coasters).

(鉄を使っているので), 現代のジェットコースターは (木製のコースターよりも) (空中で) (より多く
のひねりや回転を) 乗客に体験してもらうことができます。

⑥ The carriages can hang beneath the steel track (instead of [simply sitting on
　　　S　　　　　　V

top of it]), (allowing riders to coast (with no "floor" ⟨to block their view ⟨of the

ground⟩⟩)).

車体は ([鉄製の軌道上に単に載っている] のではなく) その下にぶら下がることができ, ((それによっ
て) 乗客は (⟨⟨地面への⟩視界をさえぎる⟩「床」なしで) 滑走することができます)。

⑦ Steel also offers a smoother ride ⟨for passengers⟩ (than wood).
　　S　　　　V　　O

鉄はまた (木材よりも) ⟨乗客に⟩ より滑らかな乗り心地をもたらしてくれます。

⑧ Thrill-seeking people welcomed this additional excitement, and most ⟨of the
　　　　　S①　　　　V①　　　　O①　　　　　　　S②

newest coasters⟩ (today) continue to be made (from steel).
　　　　　　　　　　　　　V②

スリルを求める人たちは, このさらなる興奮を歓迎し, (今日) ⟨最新型のジェットコースターの⟩大半
は (鉄から) 作り続けられています。

① (Today) there are incredible roller coasters (in amusement parks ⟨all over
the world⟩), and there is strong international competition ⟨to build the
longest, fastest, and tallest coasters⟩.

(今日)，(《世界中の》遊園地には) 途方もないジェットコースターが存在し，《最長，最速，そして最
も高さのあるジェットコースターを建設する》激しい国際競争があります。

② (According to the Guinness World Records group), the tallest roller coaster
is (currently) the 139-meter Kingda Ka coaster ⟨located (at an amusement
park ⟨in the U.S.⟩)⟩

(ギネスワールドレコーズ・グループによると)，最も高さのあるジェットコースターは (現在) 《(《米
国の》遊園地に) ある》139 メートルのキンダカ・コースターです。

③ (A few years ago), a different American amusement park announced plans
⟨to build an even taller coaster⟩, but was met with resistance ⟨from the
local government⟩.

(数年前)，別のアメリカの遊園地が《さらに高いジェットコースターを建設する》計画を発表しました
が，《地方政府の》反対に遭いました。

④ The proposed roller coaster designs violated local laws ⟨regarding height
limits ⟨for structures ⟨in that neighborhood⟩⟩⟩.

提案されたジェットコースターの設計が 《《《その近隣の》構造物の》高さ制限に関する》現地法に違反
していたのです。

⑤ A controversy occurred, but (in the end), the amusement park won the legal
battle.

論争が巻き起こりましたが，(結局)，遊園地側は法廷闘争に勝ちました。

⑥ The world's new tallest roller coaster, the Skyscraper, is expected to begin

<u>S</u> <u>V</u>

exciting thrillseekers (in 2021).

新たに世界で最も高さのあるジェットコースターとなるスカイスクレイパーは，（2021 年に）スリル
を求める人たちを興奮させ始めることになっています。

注1　the 最上級＋名詞＋ ever ＋ Vpp は「これまでに V された中で，最も…な～」という意味。

注2　in fact というつなぎ表現は「実際」という意味で，直前の内容をより詳しく述べる場合に使わ
れる。

注3　この文での would は過去の習慣を表すもので，「…したものだった」という意味で使われている。

注4　by はある時点までの完了を表す場合に用いられる前置詞。この文での過去完了形は，過去の時
点までの完了を表している。

注5　from which to release the carriages の部分は，from which they release the carriages
とも言い換えることができ，直前の名詞を修飾している。

注6　until は「～まで」という意味で，その時点まで継続的に行為を続ける場合に使われる。この文
のように until 以下の節が長い場合は，「そして，ついに…」のように前から読んでいくとよい。

注7　regarding ～は「～に関する」という意味の前置詞のはたらきをする語。concerning や
about とも言い換えることができる。

注8　カンマは直前の名詞を同格的に言い換えるはたらきをすることができる。この文では，The
world's new tallest roller coaster を，カンマを挟んで the Skyscraper に言い換えている。

サイトトランスレーション

⇒別冊 p.38 ～ 40

1 The roller coaster /	ジェットコースターは
is one of the most popular amusement park rides /	最も人気のある遊園地の乗り物の1つです
ever invented. //	これまでに発明された。
Some eager thrill-seekers even travel /	スリルを求めることに情熱を持つ人の中には旅する人さえいます
all over the world /	世界中を
seeking the adrenaline rush /	興奮の極致を求めて
provided by the tallest and fastest coasters. //	最も高さがあって最もスピードの速いコースターによってもたらされる。
While thousands of people /	数千人もの人が（…が）
in the U.S. alone /	米国だけで
are injured /	けがをしています
each year /	毎年
and some of them /	そして彼らの中の何人かは
are seriously injured, /	重傷を負っています,
roller coasters remain /	ジェットコースターは…のままです
a remarkably safe and exciting ride /	非常に安全で胸躍る乗り物
for children and adults alike. //	子供にとっても大人にとっても等しく。
In fact, /	実際に,
millions of people ride them /	数百万人もの人たちがそれらに乗っています
each year /	毎年
without any incidents, /	何の事故もなく,

and thanks to new computerized controls, /	そして新しいコンピューター制御のおかげで,
they are safer /	それらはより安全です
than ever before. //	かつてないほど。
But /	しかし
while the modern idea /	現代の概念は (…が)
of a "roller coaster" /	「ジェットコースター」についての
is familiar to many, /	多くの人にとってなじみ深いものです,
this ride has changed /	この乗り物は変化してきました
significantly /	大きく
during the course of its 400-year-long history. //	その400年の歴史の中で。
2 The structures /	構造物は
that we recognize /	私たちが認識している
today /	今日
as "roller coasters" /	「ジェットコースター」として
began /	始まりました
as ice slides /	氷の滑り台として
in Russia. //	ロシアで。
During the 17th century, /	17世紀の間,
residents of St. Petersburg /	サンクトペテルブルクの住民たちは
would climb /	よく登っていました
to the top of special structures /	特別な構造物の頂上に
and slide down /	そして滑り降りました
wooden ramps /	木製のスロープを

that were covered /	覆われた
with thick sheets of ice. //	氷の厚い板で。
Over time, /	時が経つにつれて,
these slides became popular /	このような滑り台は人気が高まりました
among European upper-class people /	ヨーロッパの上流階級の人々の間で
and were recreated /	そして同様のものが作られました
outside of Russia. //	ロシア以外でも。
By the 18th century, /	18世紀までには,
both the Russians and the French had engineered /	ロシア人もフランス人も設計しました
a ride /	乗り物を
that was similar to the original ice slides /	元の氷の滑り台と似ている
that did not require any ice. //	氷をまったく必要としない。
The new ride, /	その新しい乗り物は,
called a "coaster," /	「コースター」と呼ばれ,
used wheeled carriages /	車輪付きの台車を使いました
attached to tracks /	軌道に取り付けられた
— similar to train tracks /	—— 列車の線路に似た
— that guided riders up and over /	—— それは乗り越えて乗客を運びました
a series of small hills. //	連続する小さな丘を。
It could be ridden /	それは乗ることができました
at any time of the year. //	一年中いつでも。
Soon, /	やがて,
people began to build /	人々は作り始めました

bigger coasters /	より大きなコースターを
that incorporated loops /	ループが組み込まれた
and higher platforms /	そしてより高さのある乗降場
from which to release the carriages. //	そこから車両を解き放つための。
Public demand /	一般市民からの要望は
for roller coasters /	ジェットコースターに対する
continued to grow /	増え続けました
throughout the years, /	年々,
and coaster designs continued /	そしてコースターの設計は続けました
to improve. //	改善を。
3 One major improvement /	1つの主な改善点は
came with a change /	変更を伴いました
in material. //	素材の。
Most companies built /	大半の会社は建設しました
coasters /	コースターを
primarily out of wood /	主に木材で
until, in 1959, Disney built /	1959年になって, 初めて, ディズニーが建設しました
the first steel roller coaster /	最初の鉄製のジェットコースターを
at Disneyland Park /	ディズニーランド・パークに
in California. //	カリフォルニアの。
The use of steel /	鉄の使用は
had many benefits /	多くの利点がありました
for roller coaster designers. //	ジェットコースターの設計者にとって。

Because steel is not as rigid as wood, /	鉄は木材のように柔軟性のないものではないため,
it can be bent /	それは曲げられます
easily /	簡単に
to form loops, /	ループを形作るために,
curves, /	カーブ,
and so on. //	など。
Using steel, /	鉄を使っているので,
modern roller coasters are able to take /	現代のジェットコースターは体験させることができます
riders /	乗客に
on many more twists and turns /	より多くのひねりや回転を
through the air /	空中で
than wooden coasters. //	木製のコースターよりも。
The carriages can hang /	車体はぶら下がることができます
beneath the steel track /	鉄製の軌道の下に
instead of simply sitting /	単に載っているのではなく
on top of it, /	その上に,
allowing riders to coast /	乗客は滑走することができます
with no "floor" /	「床」なしで
to block their view of the ground. //	地面への視界をさえぎる。
Steel also offers /	鉄はまたもたらします
a smoother ride /	より滑らかな乗り心地を
for passengers /	乗客に
than wood. //	木材よりも。
Thrill-seeking people welcomed /	スリルを求める人たちは歓迎しました

this additional excitement, /	このさらなる興奮を,
and most of the newest coasters /	そして最新型のジェットコースターの大半は
today /	今日
continue to be made /	作られ続けています
from steel. //	鉄から。
4 Today /	今日
there are incredible roller coasters /	途方もないジェットコースターが存在しています
in amusement parks /	遊園地には
all over the world, /	世界中の,
and there is strong international competition /	そして激しい国際競争があります
to build the longest, fastest, and tallest coasters. //	最長, 最速, そして最も高さのあるジェットコースターを建設する。
According to the Guinness World Records group, /	ギネスワールドレコーズ・グループによると,
the tallest roller coaster /	最も高さのあるジェットコースターは
is currently the 139-meter Kingda Ka coaster /	現在は139メートルのキンダカ・コースターです
located at an amusement park /	遊園地にある
in the U.S. //	米国の。
A few years ago, /	数年前,
a different American amusement park announced /	別のアメリカの遊園地が発表しました
plans to build /	建設する計画を
an even taller coaster, /	さらに高いジェットコースターを,
but was met with resistance /	しかし反対に遭いました

211

from the local government. //	地方政府からの。
The proposed roller coaster designs violated /	提案されたジェットコースターの設計が違反していました
local laws /	現地法に
regarding height limits /	高さ制限に関する
for structures in that neighborhood. //	その近隣の構造物の。
A controversy occurred, /	論争が巻き起こりました,
but in the end, /	しかし結局,
the amusement park won /	その遊園地は勝ちました
the legal battle. //	法廷闘争に。
The world's new tallest roller coaster, /	世界で新しく最も高さのあるジェットコースター,
the Skyscraper, /	スカイスクレイパーは,
is expected to begin exciting thrillseekers /	スリルを求める人たちを興奮させ始めることになっています
in 2021. //	2021 年に。

The Historical Ups and Downs of Roller Coasters

The roller coaster is one of the most popular amusement park rides ever invented. Some eager thrill-seekers even travel all over the world seeking the adrenaline rush provided by the tallest and fastest coasters. While thousands of people in the U.S. alone are injured each year and some of them are seriously injured, roller coasters remain a remarkably safe and exciting ride for children and adults alike. In fact, millions of people ride them each year without any incidents, and thanks to new computerized controls, they are safer than ever before. But while the modern idea of a "roller coaster" is familiar to many, this ride has changed significantly during the course of its 400-year-long history.

The structures that we recognize today as "roller coasters" began as ice slides in Russia. During the 17th century, residents of St. Petersburg would climb to the top of special structures and slide down wooden ramps that were covered with thick sheets of ice. Over time, these slides became popular among European upper-class people and were recreated outside of Russia. By the 18th century, both the Russians and the French had engineered a ride that was similar to the original ice slides that did not require any ice. The new ride, called a "coaster," used wheeled carriages attached to tracks — similar to train tracks — that guided riders up and over a series of small hills. It could be ridden at any time of the year. Soon, people began to build bigger coasters that incorporated loops and higher platforms from which to release the carriages. Public demand for roller coasters continued to grow throughout the years, and coaster designs continued to improve.

One major improvement came with a change in material. Most companies built coasters primarily out of wood until, in 1959, Disney built the first steel roller coaster at Disneyland Park in California. The use of steel had many benefits for roller coaster designers. Because steel is not as rigid as wood, it can be bent easily to form loops, curves, and so on. Using steel, modern roller coasters are able to take riders on many more twists and turns through the air than wooden coasters. The carriages can hang beneath the steel track instead of simply sitting on top of it, allowing riders to coast with no "floor" to block their view of the ground. Steel also offers a smoother ride for passengers than wood. Thrill-seeking people welcomed this additional excitement, and most of the newest coasters today continue to be made from steel.

Today there are incredible roller coasters in amusement parks all over the world, and there is strong international competition to build the longest, fastest, and tallest coasters. According to the Guinness World Records group, the tallest roller coaster is currently the 139-meter Kingda Ka coaster located at an amusement park in the U.S. A few years ago, a different American amusement park announced plans to build an even taller coaster, but was met with resistance from the local government. The proposed roller coaster designs violated local laws regarding height limits for structures in that neighborhood. A controversy occurred, but in the end, the amusement park won the legal battle. The world's new tallest roller coaster, the Skyscraper, is expected to begin exciting thrillseekers in 2021.

ジェットコースターの歴史上の浮き沈み

　ジェットコースターは，これまでに発明された最も人気のある遊園地の乗り物の1つです。スリルを求めることに情熱を持つ人の中には，最も高さがあって最もスピードの速いコースターがもたらす興奮の極致を求めて世界中を旅する人もいます。米国だけでも毎年数千人もの人がけがをし，その中には重傷を負う人もいますが，ジェットコースターは子供にとっても大人にとっても非常に安全で，胸躍る乗り物です。実際に毎年，数百万人もの人たちが何の事故もなく乗っており，新しいコンピューター制御のおかげで，かつてないほど安全になっています。しかし，「ジェットコースター」についての現代の概念は，多くの人にとってなじみ深いものですが，この乗り物はその400年の歴史の中で大きく変化してきました。

　今日「ジェットコースター」として私たちが認識している構造物は，ロシアにあった氷の滑り台に起源がありました。17世紀に，サンクトペテルブルクの住民たちは，特別な構造物の頂上

に登って厚い氷の板で覆われた木製のスロープを滑り降りていました。時が経つにつれて，このような滑り台はヨーロッパの上流階級の人々の間で人気が高まり，ロシア以外でも同様のものが作られました。18世紀までには，ロシア人とフランス人が，元の氷の滑り台と似ているものの，氷をまったく必要としない乗り物を設計しました。「コースター」と呼ばれたこの新しい乗り物では，軌道——列車の線路のような——に取り付けられた車輪付きの台車を使い，それが乗客を連続する小さな丘を乗り越えて運びました。これは一年中いつでも乗ることができました。やがて，人はループ軌道や，車両を解き放つためにより高さのある乗降場を取り入れた大規模なコースターを作り始めました。一般市民からのジェットコースターに対する要望は年々増え続け，コースターの設計は改善され続けました。

　主な改善点の1つが，素材の変更でした。ほとんどの会社は，主に木材でコースターを建設していましたが，1959年になってディズニーがカリフォルニアのディズニーランド・パークで最初の鉄製のジェットコースターを建設しました。鉄を使うことは，ジェットコースターの設計者にとって多くの利点がありました。鉄は木材よりも柔軟性があるため，簡単に曲げてループやカーブなどを作ることができます。鉄を使った現代のジェットコースターは，木製のコースターよりも空中でより多くのひねりや回転を乗客に体験してもらうことができます。車体は，鉄製の軌道上に単に載っているのではなく，その下にぶら下がることができ，それによって乗客は地面への視界をさえぎる「床」なしで滑走することができます。鉄はまた，木材よりも乗客に滑らかな乗り心地をもたらしてくれます。スリルを求める人たちは，このさらなる興奮を歓迎し，今ある最新型のジェットコースターの大半は，鉄を使って作り続けられています。

　今日，世界中の遊園地には途方もないジェットコースターが存在し，最長，最速，そして最も高さのあるジェットコースターを建設する激しい国際競争があります。ギネスワールドレコーズ・グループによると，最も高さのあるジェットコースターは，現在，米国の遊園地にある139メートルのキンダカ・コースターです。数年前，別のアメリカの遊園地がさらに高いジェットコースターを建設する計画を発表しましたが，地方政府の反対に遭いました。提案されたジェットコースターの設計が，その近隣の構造物の高さ制限に関する現地法に違反していたのです。論争が巻き起こりましたが，結局，遊園地側は法廷闘争に勝ちました。新たに世界で最も高さのあるジェットコースターとなるスカイスクレイパーは，2021年にはスリルを求める人たちを興奮させ始めることになっています。

⇒別冊 p.41 ～ 43

解答と解説

解答

(1) ②　　(2) ③　　(3) ③　　(4) ②

解説

(1) 第 1 段落の最後から 2 番目の文に「1973 年までに 30 州が議決を済ませ，ほぼ誰もが成功を確信していた」とあるので，2 が正解。ERA は今に至るまで憲法の一部となっていないから，1 は誤り。成功のためには国会と州政府の両方の承認が必要だから，4 は誤り。3 は本文に記述なし。

設問・選択肢の和訳

(1) 1973 年に，男女平等憲法修正条項は…

× 1 憲法の一部となっていたが，数年後には数州が修正を削除することを無理強いした。

○ 2 国会と多数の州政府で議決されたので，憲法の一部となるのは確実に思われた。

× 3 女性の権利が法律によって保護されていなかったため大衆の圧倒的な支持を得た。

× 4 米国の国会には承認されなかったが，州政府の 4 分の 3 が支持すれば成功の見込みがあった。

(2) 第 2 段落の第 3・4 文の内容に一致する 3 が正解。シュラフリーは，男女同権を追求しすぎると女性を守るための法律まで失ってしまうと主張した。ほかの選択肢は本文の内容に一致しない。

設問・選択肢の和訳

(2) フィリス・シュラフリーは，ERA について何を信じていたか。

× 1 夫と離婚する決心をする女性が増える可能性がある。

× 2 キリスト教徒の女性が自由に宗教を信仰することがずっと困難になるだろう。

○ 3 離婚した女性に金銭を提供するというこれまでの法律ほど経済的に効果はないだろう。

× 4 機会を求める女性がアメリカ軍で働くのが難しくなる可能性がある。

(3) 第 3 段落の第 2・3 文の内容に一致する 3 が正解。憲法改正のハードルは高いので，ERA が憲法に盛り込まれれば簡単には変更されないが，一般の法律では有権者の一時的な判断で撤廃されるおそれがあると説明されている。ほかの選択肢はその内容に合わない。

設問・選択肢の和訳

(3) ERA の支持者たちがその敗北に不満な 1 つの理由は何か。

× 1 その敗北によって有権者が女性の権利を保護するために制定された法律を支持しなくなるだろうと彼らは考えている。

× 2 その敗北によって将来憲法に重要な変更を行うのが難しくなるだろうと彼らは考えている。

○ 3 ERA なしでは女性が法的保護を簡単に失ってしまうだろうと彼らは考えている。

× 4 それが失敗して以来，女性の権利を保護する法律が非常に弱まっていると彼らは考えている。

(4) 最終段落の最後の文の内容から考えて，2が正解。本文によれば，ERAが成立しなかったのは，誰もが女性の権利を守るべきだと考えていたのに，その方法に関して意見の対立が生じたからである。ほかの選択肢はその趣旨をとらえていない。

設問・選択肢の和訳

(4) 憲法にERAを取り入れる試みの1つの長期的な影響は何か。

× 1 国会が女性の権利を保護するほかの法律を可決するのがより難しくなった。

○ 2 女性の権利を高める最善の方法について，フェミニストの間に意見の対立が生まれた。

× 3 最高裁判所が女性の権利を支持する決定を下す可能性が低くなった。

× 4 それが女性に多くの保護を与えすぎたので，行き過ぎだと苦情を言う人もいる。

語句

〈タイトル〉

☐ amendment　（名）改正

〈第1段落〉

☐ feminism　（名）フェミニズム，男女同権主義

☐ guarantee　（名）保証

☐ Constitution　（名）憲法

☐ Congress　（名）国会，連邦議会

☐ a flood of ～　大量の～

☐ overwhelming　（形）圧倒的な

☐ opinion poll　世論調査

☐ lawmaker　（名）立法者，（国会）議員

☐ extend　（動）～を延ばす，延期する

〈第2段落〉

☐ defeat　（動）～を挫折させる

☐ churchgoing　（形）教会に行く

☐ ex-wife　（名）元妻

☐ confirmation　（名）確立，承認

〈第3段落〉

☐ point to ～　～を指摘する

☐ voter　（名）有権者

〈第4段落〉

☐ defeat　（名）失敗，敗北

☐ the Supreme Court　最高裁判所

☐ reintroduce　（動）～を再提出する

☐ legacy　（名）遺産，遺物

〈設問・選択肢〉

☐ legal protection　法的保護

☐ feminist　（名）フェミニスト，男女同権論者

構造確認 ※誤読した部分の確認に使用してください。　　　　⇒別冊 p.41 ～ 43

第1段落 アメリカはフェミニズムの国として知られているが憲法に女性の平等を保証する文言はない。

① (While America has long been known (as a world leader 〈in feminism and
　　　　　　　S'　　　　V'
women's rights〉)), (surprisingly), there is no guarantee 〈of equality 〈for
　　　　　　　　　　　　　　　　　　V　　　　S
women〉〉 (in the United States Constitution). 注1

（アメリカは（《フェミニズムと女性の権利における》世界的リーダーとして）長く知られてきましたが），（驚くべきことに），（合衆国憲法の中には）《《女性への》平等の》保証はまったくありません。

② (During the 1960s), feminist leaders helped to create support 〈for [adding
　　　　　　　　　　　　　S　　　　　　　V　　　　　　O
a new section (to the Constitution)]〉.

（1960 年代），フェミニストの指導者たちは《[（憲法に）新しい条項を追加すること]への》支持を生み出すことに貢献しました。

③ The Equal Rights Amendment (ERA) would give women "Equality 〈of rights〉
　　　S　　　　　　　　　　　　　　　V　　　O　　　O
〈under the law〉". 注2

男女平等憲法修正条項 (ERA) は女性に「《法の下での》《権利の》平等」を与えることになるでしょう。

④ [Making amendments (to the Constitution)] is a complicated process,
　　　　　　　　S　　　　　　　　　　　　　V　　　C
(however).

（しかしながら），[（憲法に）修正を加えること]は複雑な作業です。

⑤ Both the national government, 〈known (as Congress)〉, and a three-quarter
　　　　S①　　　　　　　　　　　　　　　　　　　　　　　S②
majority 〈of the 50 states〉 must approve any change.
　　　　　　　　　　　　　　　V　　　O

《（連邦議会として）知られる》，中央政府と，《50 州の》4 分の 3 の多数がどのような変更でも承認しなければなりません。

⑥ Incidents 〈like nationwide women's protests, a flood of media articles, and
 S
overwhelming support 〈in opinion polls〉〉 convinced the nation's lawmakers
                                            V   O
to approve the ERA (in 1972).   注3

〈女性による全国規模の抗議集会，メディアにあふれる記事，〈世論調査での〉圧倒的な支持などの〉出
来事が (1972年に) 連邦議員に ERA を承認させました。

⑦ (Although a seven-year time limit was set (for 38 〈of the 50 states〉) (to
                        S① 　　　　　　 V①
pass the ERA)), 30 had already done so (by 1973), (convincing nearly
                 S V   O
everyone [that it would succeed]).
              S'②   V'②

((ERA を可決するために)(〈50州のうちの〉38州 (の承認) には) 7年という期限が設けられていま
したが)，(1973年までに) すでに 30州が承認しており，(誰もが [それが成功するであろうこと] を
ほぼ確信していました)。

⑧ (When the deadline came (in 1979)), (however), only 35 states had passed
        S'①   V'①   S①   V①
it, and (although the deadline was extended), the amendment died.
O①   S'②   V'②   S②   V②

(しかし)，((1979年に) 期限を迎えた時)，それを可決したのは 35州のみで，(期限は延長されたも
のの)，修正案は廃案となりました。

第2段落 法律家シュラフリーは ERA が女性を保護する従来の法律を否定する可能性が高いと主張した。

① One woman, a lawyer 〈named Phyllis Schlafly〉, is widely thought to have
                    S   V
been responsible (for [defeating the ERA]).   注4

1人の女性，(すなわち)〈フィリス・シュラフリーという〉法律家が，([ERA を廃案とすること] に)
貢献したと広く考えられています。

② Schlafly created a large group 〈of volunteers〉〈composed mainly of
    S   V   O
churchgoing Christians〉〈who helped to convince large numbers of citizens
                            V'   O'
and politicians [that the ERA would not have the effect 〈people
expected〉]〉.

シュラフリーは《多くの市民と政治家に [ERA は《人々の期待するような》効果を持たない] と説得するのを支援してくれる》《主に敬虔なキリスト教徒で構成される》《ボランティアの》大規模な団体を組織しました。

③ The group focused (on earlier laws 〈intended to protect women〉, 〈such as
    S   V
those 〈forcing men to provide financial support (to their ex-wives) (in the
event 〈of a divorce〉), or allowing women to avoid required service 〈in the
military〉〉〉).
注5

この団体は (《《(《離婚した》際に) 男性に (元の妻に) 金銭的支援をすることを強制したり, 女性に《軍務に》服することを免除することを認めたりする》ことのような》,《女性を保護することを目的とした》従来の法律を) 重要視しました。

④ Schlafly argued [that the ERA would likely kill these laws (because they
   S   V   O   S'   V'   O'
would mean [that men and women were not being treated "equally"])].

シュラフリーは [(こうした法律は [男性と女性が「平等」に扱われていないこと] を意味するので) ERA がこれらを否定する可能性が高くなる] と主張しました。

⑤ This shocked people 〈who had (previously) supported the ERA (as a
  S   V①   O①   V'   O'
symbolic confirmation 〈of women's equality〉)〉 and convinced politicians 〈in
                                          V②   O②
many states〉 to stop [supporting it].

このことは《(それまで)(《女性の平等の》確立を象徴するものとして) ERA を支持してきた》人々に衝撃を与え,《多くの州の》政治家に [それを支持すること] を思いとどまらせるよう促したのです。

第3段落 多くの女性がその権利には継続的な諸問題があり, ERA は憲法の一部になるべきと思っている。

① Many women feel [that the ERA should have become part 〈of the
     S   V   O   S'   V'   C'
Constitution〉], (pointing to continuing problems 〈like the fact 〈that women's
average salaries are still lower than men's〉〉).
注6

多くの女性は [ERA が《憲法の》一部になるべきだった] と思っており, (《女性の平均給与がいまだに男性のものよりも低い》事実などの》継続的な諸問題を指摘しています)。

② They argue [that (although (today) there are various laws ⟨that protect
   S   V   O

women's rights⟩), (if voters change their minds ⟨about a law ⟨that protects

women's rights⟩⟩), it can easily be removed (from the law books)].
                            S'   V'

彼女たちは [((今日) ⟨女性の権利を守る⟩ さまざまな法律があるものの), (有権者が ⟨⟨女性の権利を
保護する⟩法律についての⟩考えを変えたなら), それは (法律書から) 簡単に削除されてしまうかもし
れない] と主張しています。

③ [Having the ERA (in the Constitution)], (however), would make this
               S   V   O

extremely unlikely to happen.

(しかし), [(憲法に) ERA があれば], このようなことが起こる可能性は非常に低くなります。

第4段落 ERA が招いた分裂が女性の社会的地位を向上させる目標達成のための協力を難しくしている。

① (Despite the ERA's defeat), many of its supporters' goals have been
                                  S   V

achieved (in other ways, ⟨such as laws ⟨passed (by Congress)⟩ and

actions ⟨taken (by the Supreme Court)⟩⟩).

(ERA の敗北にもかかわらず), その支持者の多くが掲げている目標は (⟨⟨(連邦議会で) 可決された⟩
法律や⟨(最高裁判所によって) とられた⟩措置など), 別の形で) 達成されています。

② Laws ⟨such as Title IX⟩ forced universities to offer more educational
   S   V   O

opportunities ⟨to women⟩, (for example).

(例えば), ⟨「タイトル IX」などの⟩法律により, 大学は⟨女性に⟩より多くの教育の機会を提供するよ
うに強制されました。

③ The ERA is reintroduced (into Congress) (every year), but it generally
   S①   V①   S②

attracts little attention.
   V②   O②

ERA は (毎年) (議会に) 再提出されますが, 一般にはあまり注目を集めていません。

④ (Perhaps) the saddest legacy 〈of the ERA〉 is the break-up 〈of a once
　　　　　　S　　　　　　　　　　　　　V　　　 C
unified feminist movement〉.

（おそらく），〈ERA の〉最も残念な遺産は〈かつて団結していたフェミニスト運動の〉分裂です。

⑤ (Today), there is tremendous disagreement 〈about [whether to advance the
　　　　　　　　 V①　　　　 S①
rights 〈of women〉 (through the ERA) or (through other methods)]〉 and this
　　　　　　　　　　　　　　　　　　　　　　　　　　　　　　　　S②
has prevented them (from [working together (to achieve other goals 〈that
　 V②　　　　 O②
would improve women's status 〈in society〉〉)]).　　　　　　　　　📌注8

（今日），〈[〈女性の〉権利を (ERA を通して) 推進するべきか，それとも (ほかの方法で) 推進するべき
か] について〉大きな意見の相違があり，このことが ([(〈〈社会での〉女性の地位を向上させることに
なる〉ほかの目標を達成するために) 協力すること] を) 妨げているのです。

注1　while S V は「S は V するが」「S は V する一方で」という意味で，主節の前に置かれ，譲歩
　　　を表すことができる。
注2　ERA は現在施行されているものではないため，施行されている場合を仮定して，仮定法で用い
　　　られる would という助動詞が使われている。このように，仮定的な内容を述べる場合には
　　　would, could, might などの助動詞が用いられる。
注3　protests, articles, support という名詞を中心とする3つの名詞句が，前置詞の like の目的語
　　　となっている。この文全体の主語は Incidents，述語動詞は convinced である。
注4　to have Vpp という完了不定詞は，主文の動詞 is thought よりも前のことであるのを示すた
　　　めに用いられている。
注5　those は代名詞で，earlier laws という名詞の反復を避けるために用いられている。
注6　should have Vpp は「V すべきだった」という意味で，実際にはそうされなかったことに対
　　　する後悔の気持ちを含む。
注7　この文の主語は having という動名詞で，make が述語動詞となっている。
注8　whether to V は「…するかどうか」という意味の名詞句を作るが，A or B という表現ととも
　　　に使われることも多い。この文では，through the ERA と through other methods が A と
　　　B に当たる。

サイトトランスレーション

⇒別冊 p.41 ～ 43

1 While America has long been known /	アメリカは長く知られてきましたが
as a world leader /	世界的リーダーとして
in feminism and women's rights, /	フェミニズムと女性の権利における,
surprisingly, /	驚くべきことに,
there is no guarantee /	保証はまったくありません
of equality for women /	女性の平等の
in the United States Constitution. //	合衆国憲法の中に。
During the 1960s, /	1960 年代の間,
feminist leaders helped to create /	フェミニストの指導者たちは生み出すことに貢献しました
support for adding a new section /	新しい条項を追加することへの支持を
to the Constitution. //	憲法に。
The Equal Rights Amendment (ERA) /	男女平等憲法修正条項 (ERA) は
would give women /	女性に与えるものです
"Equality of rights under the law." //	「法の下での権利の平等」を。
Making amendments to the Constitution /	憲法に修正を加えることは
is a complicated process, /	複雑な作業です,
however. //	しかしながら。
Both the national government, /	中央政府と…の両方が,
known as Congress, /	連邦議会として知られる,
and a three-quarter majority /	そして 4 分の 3 の多数
of the 50 states /	50 州の

must approve /	承認しなければなりません
any change. //	どのような変更でも。
Incidents /	出来事が
like nationwide women's protests, /	女性による全国規模の抗議集会などの,
a flood of media articles, /	メディアにあふれる記事,
and overwhelming support in opinion polls /	そして世論調査での圧倒的な支持
convinced the nation's lawmakers /	連邦議員に納得させました
to approve the ERA /	ERA を承認することを
in 1972. //	1972 年に。
Although a seven-year time limit was set /	7 年という期限が設けられていましたが
for 38 of the 50 states /	50 州のうちの 38 州 (の承認) には
to pass the ERA, /	ERA を可決するための,
30 had already done so /	すでに 30 州が承認していました
by 1973, /	1973 年までに,
convincing nearly everyone /	誰もがほぼ確信していました
that it would succeed. //	それが成功するだろうと。
When the deadline came /	期限を迎えた時
in 1979, /	1979 年に,
however, /	しかし,
only 35 states had passed it, /	それを可決したのは 35 州のみでした,
and although the deadline was extended, /	そして期限は延長されましたが,
the amendment died. //	修正案は廃案となりました。
2 One woman, /	1 人の女性が,

a lawyer /	法律家
named Phyllis Schlafly, /	フィリス・シュラフリーという名の,
is widely thought /	広く考えられています
to have been responsible /	貢献したと
for defeating the ERA. //	ERA を廃案とすることに。
Schlafly created /	シュラフリーは作りました
a large group of volunteers /	大きなボランティア団体を
composed mainly of churchgoing Christians /	主に敬虔なキリスト教徒で構成された
who helped to convince /	説得するのを支援してくれる
large numbers of citizens and politicians /	多くの市民と政治家を
that the ERA would not have the effect /	ERA は効果をもたないであろうと
people expected. //	人々が期待する。
The group focused /	この団体は重要視しました
on earlier laws /	従来の法律を
intended to protect women, /	女性を保護することを目的とした,
such as those forcing men to provide /	男性に与えることを強制するなどの
financial support /	金銭的支援を
to their ex-wives /	元の妻に
in the event of a divorce, /	離婚した際に,
or allowing women to avoid /	あるいは女性に免れることを許可する
required service in the military. //	軍務に服することを。
Schlafly argued /	シュラフリーは主張しました
that the ERA would likely kill /	ERA が消す可能性が高いであろうということを

225

these laws /	これらの法律を
because they would mean /	なぜならそれらは意味するであろうから
that men and women were not being treated /	男性と女性が扱われていないということを
"equally." //	「平等」に。
This shocked people /	これは人々に衝撃を与えました
who had previously supported the ERA /	それまで ERA を支持してきた
as a symbolic confirmation /	確立を象徴するものとして
of women's equality /	女性の平等の
and convinced politicians in many states /	そして多くの州の政治家に納得させました
to stop supporting it. //	その支持を思いとどまるように。
3 Many women feel /	多くの女性は感じています
that the ERA should have become /	ERA はなるべきだったと
part of the Constitution, /	憲法の一部に,
pointing to continuing problems /	継続的な諸問題を指摘しています
like the fact /	事実のような
that women's average salaries are still lower /	女性の平均給与がいまだに低いという
than men's. //	男性のものよりも。
They argue /	彼女たちは主張しています
that although today there are various laws /	今はさまざまな法律がありますが
that protect women's rights, /	女性の権利を守る,
if voters change their minds /	有権者が考えを変えたなら
about a law /	法律についての

that protects women's rights, /	女性の権利を保護する,
it can easily be removed /	それは簡単に削除されてしまうかもしれません
from the law books. //	法律書から。
Having the ERA in the Constitution, /	憲法に ERA があれば,
however, /	しかし,
would make this extremely unlikely to happen. //	こうしたことが起こる可能性は非常に低くなります。
4 Despite the ERA's defeat, /	ERA の敗北にもかかわらず,
many of its supporters' goals /	その支持者の目標の多くは
have been achieved /	達成されています
in other ways, /	別の形で,
such as laws /	法律など
passed by Congress /	連邦議会で可決された
and actions taken by the Supreme Court. //	そして最高裁判所によってとられた措置。
Laws /	法律が
such as Title IX /	「タイトル IX」などの
forced universities to offer /	提供することを大学に義務づけました
more educational opportunities /	より多くの教育の機会を
to women, /	女性に,
for example. //	例えば。
The ERA is reintroduced /	ERA は再提出されています
into Congress /	議会に
every year, /	毎年,
but it generally attracts little attention. //	しかしそれは一般にはほとんど注目を集めていません。

227

Perhaps /	おそらく
the saddest legacy /	最も残念な遺産は
of the ERA /	ERA の
is the break-up /	分裂です
of a once unified feminist movement. //	かつて団結していたフェミニスト運動の。
Today, /	今日,
there is tremendous disagreement /	大きな意見の相違があります
about whether to advance the rights of women /	女性の権利を推進するべきかについて
through the ERA /	ERA を通して
or through other methods /	それともほかの方法で
and this has prevented them from working together /	そしてこれが協力を妨げています
to achieve other goals /	ほかの目標を達成するための
that would improve women's status /	女性の地位を向上させるであろう
in society. //	社会での。

The Equal Rights Amendment

While America has long been known as a world leader in feminism and women's rights, surprisingly, there is no guarantee of equality for women in the United States Constitution. During the 1960s, feminist leaders helped to create support for adding a new section to the Constitution. The Equal Rights Amendment (ERA) would give women "Equality of rights under the law." Making amendments to the Constitution is a complicated process, however. Both the national government, known as Congress, and a three-quarter majority of the 50 states must approve any change. Incidents like nationwide women's protests, a flood of media articles, and overwhelming support in opinion polls convinced the nation's lawmakers to approve the ERA in 1972. Although a seven-year time limit was set for 38 of the 50 states to pass the ERA, 30 had already done so by 1973, convincing nearly everyone that it would succeed. When the deadline came in 1979, however, only 35 states had passed it, and although the deadline was extended, the amendment died.

One woman, a lawyer named Phyllis Schlafly, is widely thought to have been responsible for defeating the ERA. Schlafly created a large group of volunteers composed mainly of churchgoing Christians who helped to convince large numbers of citizens and politicians that the ERA would not have the effect people expected. The group focused on earlier laws intended to protect women, such as those forcing men to provide financial support to their ex-wives in the event of a divorce, or allowing women to avoid required service in the military. Schlafly argued that the ERA would likely kill these laws because they would mean that men and women were not being treated "equally." This shocked people who had previously supported the ERA as a symbolic confirmation of women's equality and convinced politicians in many states to stop supporting it.

Many women feel that the ERA should have become part of the Constitution, pointing to continuing problems like the fact that women's average salaries are still lower than men's. They argue that although today there are various laws that protect women's rights, if voters change their minds about a law that protects women's rights, it can easily be removed from the law books. Having the ERA in the Constitution, however, would make this extremely unlikely to happen.

Despite the ERA's defeat, many of its supporters' goals have been achieved in other ways, such as laws passed by Congress and actions taken by the Supreme Court. Laws such as Title IX forced universities to offer more educational opportunities to women, for example. The ERA is reintroduced into Congress every year, but it generally attracts little attention. Perhaps the saddest legacy of the ERA is the break-up of a once unified feminist movement. Today, there is tremendous disagreement about whether to advance the rights of women through the ERA or through other methods and this has prevented them from working together to achieve other goals that would improve women's status in society.

男女平等憲法修正条項

アメリカはフェミニズムと女性の権利における世界的リーダーとして長く知られてきましたが，驚くべきことに，合衆国憲法の中には女性の平等を保証する文言はまったくありません。1960年代，フェミニストの指導者たちは，憲法に新しい条項を追加することへの支持を生み出すことに貢献しました。男女平等憲法修正条項（ERA）は女性に「法の下での権利の平等」を与えるものです。しかしながら，憲法に修正を加えることは複雑な作業です。どのような変更でも，連邦議会として知られる中央政府と，50州の4分の3の多数が承認しなければなりません。女性による全国規模の抗議集会，メディアにあふれる記事，世論調査での圧倒的な支持などの出来事によって，1972年に連邦議員はERAを承認しました。ERAを可決するために必要な50州のうちの38州の承認には7年という期限が設けられていましたが，すでに1973年までに30州が承認しており，誰もがほぼ成功すると確信していました。しかし，1979年に期限を迎えた時，それを可決したのは35州のみで，期限は延長されたものの修正案は廃案となりました。

1人の女性，すなわちフィリス・シュラフリーという法律家が，ERAを廃案とすることに貢献したと広く考えられています。シュラフリーは，主に敬虔なキリスト教徒で構成される大規模なボランティア団体を組織し，その支援もあって，多くの市民と政治家にERAは人々の期待するような効果をもたらさないと説得したのです。この団体は，離婚した際に男性に元の妻に金銭的支援をすることを強制する法律や，女性が軍務に服することを免除することを認める法律など，女性を保護することを目的とした従来の法律を重要視しました。シュラフリーの主張によると，そうした法律は，男性と女性が「平等」に扱われていないことになるため，ERAがそれを否定する可能性が高くなるというのです。このことは，それまで女性の平等の確立を象徴するものとしてERAを支持してきた人々に衝撃を与え，多くの州の政治家にその支持を思いとどまらせるよう促したのです。

多くの女性は，ERAが憲法の一部になるべきだったと思っており，女性の平均給与がいまだに男性のものよりも低いことなど，継続的な諸問題があることを指摘しています。彼女たちの主張によると，今は女性の権利を守るさまざまな法律があるものの，有権者が女性の権利を保護する法律についての考えを変えたなら，それは法律書から簡単に削除されてしまうかもしれません。しかし，憲法にERAがあれば，そのようなことが起こる可能性は非常に低くなります。

ERAの敗北にもかかわらず，その支持者が掲げている目標の多くは，連邦議会で可決された法律や最高裁判所によってとられた措置など，別の形で達成されています。例えば，「タイトルIX」などの法律により，大学は女性により多くの教育の機会を提供することを義務化させられました。ERAは毎年議会に再提出されますが，一般にはあまり注目を集めていません。おそらく，ERAの最も残念な遺産は，かつて団結していたフェミニスト運動の分裂です。今日，女性の権利を，ERAを通して推進するべきか，それともほかの方法で推進するべきかについて大きな意見の相違があり，このことが，女性の社会的地位を向上させることになるほかの目標を達成するための協力を難しくしたのです。

●英文校閲　Karl Matsumoto

英語4技能　ハイパートレーニング
長文読解　(5)上級編

2020 年 7 月 1 日　初　版第 1 刷発行

監修者	安河内 哲也
	アンドリュー・ロビンス
発行人	門間 正哉
発行所	株式会社 桐原書店
	〒 160-0023 東京都新宿区西新宿 4-15-3
	住友不動産西新宿ビル 3 号館
	TEL：03-5302-7010 （販売）
	www.kirihara.co.jp
装丁・本文レイアウト	戸塚 みゆき （ISSHIKI）
DTP	有限会社マーリンクレイン
印刷・製本	図書印刷株式会社

ISBN978-4-342-20584-2
Printed in Japan

桐原書店のアプリ